THE HOUSE OF
WHISPERS

William Le Queux

1st WORLD
LIBRARY
Literary Society

The House Of Whispers

William Le Queux

© 1st World Library, 2006
PO Box 2211
Fairfield, IA 52556
www.1stworldlibrary.com
First Edition

LCCN: 2006907735

Softcover ISBN: 1-4218-2463-9
Hardcover ISBN: 1-4218-2363-2
eBook ISBN: 1-4218-2563-5

Purchase *"The House Of Whispers"*
as a traditional bound book at:
www.1stWorldLibrary.com/purchase.asp?ISBN=1-4218-2463-9

1st World Library is a literary, educational organization
dedicated to:

- Creating a free internet library of downloadable ebooks

- Hosting writing competitions and offering book
  publishing scholarships.

Interested in more 1st World Library books?
contact: literacy@1stworldlibrary.com
Check us out at: www.1stworldlibrary.com

1st World Library Literary Society

Giving Back to the World

"If you want to work on the core problem, it's early school literacy."

- James Barksdale, former CEO of Netscape

"No skill is more crucial to the future of a child, or to a democratic and prosperous society, than literacy."

- Los Angeles Times

Literacy... means far more than learning how to read and write... The aim is to transmit... knowledge and promote social participation."

- UNESCO

"Literacy is not a luxury, it is a right and a responsibility. If our world is to meet the challenges of the twenty-first century we must harness the energy and creativity of all our citizens."

- President Bill Clinton

"Parents should be encouraged to read to their children, and teachers should be equipped with all available techniques for teaching literacy, so the varying needs and capacities of individual kids can be taken into account."

- Hugh Mackay

CONTENTS

CHAPTER I

THE LAIRD OF GLENCARDINE

"Why, what's the matter, child? Tell me."

"Nothing, dad - really nothing."

"But you are breathing hard; your hand trembles; your pulse beats quickly. There's something amiss - I'm sure there is. Now, what is it? Come, no secrets."

The girl, quickly snatching away her hand, answered with a forced laugh, "How absurd you really are, dear old dad! You're always fancying something or other."

"Because my senses of hearing and feeling are sharper and more developed than those of other folk perhaps," replied the grey-bearded old gentleman, as he turned his sharp-cut, grey, but expressionless countenance to the tall, sweet-faced girl standing beside his chair.

No second glance was needed to realise the pitiful truth. The man seated there in his fine library, with the summer sunset slanting across the red carpet from the open French windows, was blind.

Since his daughter Gabrielle had been a pretty, prattling child of nine, nursing her dolly, he had never looked upon her fair face. But he was ever as devoted to her as she to him.

Surely his was a sad and lonely life. Within the last fifteen years or so great wealth had come to him; but, alas! he was unable to enjoy it. Until eleven years ago he had been a prominent figure in politics and in society in London. He had sat in the House for one of the divisions of Hampshire, was a member of the Carlton, and one year he found his name among the Birthday Honours with a K.C.M.G. For him everybody predicted a brilliant future. The Press gave prominence to his speeches, and to his house in Park Street came Cabinet Ministers and most of the well-known men of his party. Indeed, it was an open secret in a certain circle that he had been promised a seat in the Cabinet in the near future.

Then, at the very moment of his popularity, a terrible tragedy had occurred. He was on the platform of the Albert Hall addressing a great meeting at which the Prime Minister was the principal speaker. His speech was a brilliant one, and the applause had been vociferous. Full of satisfaction, he drove home that night to Park Street; but next morning the report spread that his brilliant political career had ended. He had suddenly been stricken by blindness.

In political circles and in the clubs the greatest consternation was caused, and some strange gossip became rife.

It was whispered in certain quarters that the affliction was not produced by natural causes. In fact, it was a mystery, and one that had never been solved. The first oculists of Europe had peered into and tested his eyes, but all to no purpose. The sight had gone for ever.

Therefore, full of bitter regrets at being thus compelled to renounce the stress and storm of political life which he loved so well, Sir Henry Heyburn had gone into strict retirement at Glencardine, his beautiful old Perthshire home, visiting London but very seldom.

He was essentially a man of mystery. Even in the days of his universal popularity the source of his vast wealth was unknown. His father, the tenth Baronet, had been sadly impoverished by the depreciation of agricultural property in Lincolnshire, and had ended his days in the genteel quietude of the Albany. But Sir Henry, without betraying to the world his methods, had in fifteen years amassed a fortune which people guessed must be considerably over a million sterling.

From a life of strenuous activity he had, in one single hour, been doomed to one of loneliness and inactivity. His friends sympathised, as indeed the whole British public had done; but in a month the tragic affair and its attendant mysterious gossip had been forgotten, as in truth had the very name of Sir Henry Heyburn, whom the Prime Minister, though his political opponent, had one night designated in the House as "one of the most brilliant and talented young men who has ever sat upon the Opposition benches."

In his declining years the life of this man was a pitiful tragedy, his filmy eyes sightless, his thin white fingers ever eager and nervous, his hours full of deep thought and silent immobility. To him, what was the benefit of that beautiful Perthshire castle which he had purchased from Lord Strathavon a year before his compulsory retirement? What was the use of the old ancestral manor near Caistor in Lincolnshire, or the town-house in Park Street, the snug hunting-box at Melton, or the beautiful palm-shaded, flower-embowered villa overlooking the blue southern sea at San Remo? He remembered them all. He had misty visions of their splendour and their luxury; but since his blindness he had seldom, if ever, entered them. That big library up in Scotland in which he now sat was the room he preferred; and with his daughter Gabrielle to bear him company, to smooth his brow with her soft hand, to chatter and to gossip, he wished for no other companion. His life was of the past, a meteor that had flashed and had vanished for ever.

"Tell me, child, what is troubling you?" he was asking in a calm, kind voice, as he still held the girl's hand in his. The sweet scent of the roses from the garden beyond filled the room.

A smart footman in livery opened the door at that moment, asking, "Stokes has just returned with the car from Perth, Sir Henry, and asks if you want him further at present."

"No," replied his blind master. "Has he brought back her ladyship?"

"Yes, Sir Henry," replied the man. "I believe he is taking her to the ball over at Connachan to-night."

"Oh, yes, of course. How foolish I am! I quite forgot," said the Baronet with a slight sigh. "Very well, Hill."

And the clean-shaven young man, with his bright buttons bearing the chevron *gules* betwixt three boars' heads erased *sable*, of the Heyburns, bowed and withdrew.

"I had quite forgotten the ball at Connachan, dear," exclaimed her father, stretching out his thin white hand in search of hers again. "Of course you are going?"

"No, dad; I'm staying at home with you."

"Staying at home!" echoed Sir Henry. "Why, my dear Gabrielle, the first year you're out, and missing the best ball in the county! Certainly not. I'm all right. I shan't be lonely. A little box came this morning from the Professor, didn't it?"

"Yes, dad."

"Then I shall be able to spend the evening very well alone. The Professor has sent me what he promised the other day."

"I've decided not to go," was the girl's firm reply.

"I fear, dear, your mother will be very annoyed if you refuse," he remarked.

"I shall risk that, dear old dad, and stay with you to-night. Please allow me," she added persuasively, taking his hand in hers and bending till her red lips touched his white brow. "You have quite a lot to do, remember. A big packet of papers came from Paris this morning. I must read them over to you."

"But your mother, my dear! Your absence will be commented upon. People will gossip, you know."

"There is but one person I care for, dad - yourself," laughed the girl lightly.

"Perhaps you're disappointed over a new frock or something, eh?"

"Not at all. My frock came from town the day before yesterday. Elise declares it suits me admirably, and she's very hard to please, you know. It's white, trimmed with tiny roses."

"A perfect dream, I expect," remarked the blind man, smiling. "I wish I could see you in it, dear. I often wonder what you are like, now that you've grown to be a woman."

"I'm like what I always have been, dad, I suppose," she laughed.

"Yes, yes," he sighed, in pretence of being troubled. "Wilful as always. And - and," he faltered a moment later, "I often hear your dear dead mother's voice in yours." Then he was silent, and by the deep lines in his brow she knew that he was thinking.

Outside, in the high elms beyond the level, well-kept lawn, with its grey old sundial, the homecoming rooks were cawing prior to settling down for the night. No other sound broke the stillness of that quiet sunset hour save the solemn ticking of the long, old-fashioned clock at the farther end of the big, book-lined room, with its wide fireplace, great overmantel of carved stone with emblazoned arms, and its three long windows of old stained glass which gave it a somewhat ecclesiastical aspect.

"Tell me, child," repeated Sir Henry at length, "what was it that upset you just now?"

"Nothing, dad - unless - well, perhaps it's the heat. I felt rather unwell when I went out for my ride this morning," she answered with a frantic attempt at excuse.

The blind man was well aware that her reply was but a subterfuge. Little, however, did he dream the cause. Little did he know that a dark shadow had fallen upon the young girl's life - a shadow of evil.

"Gabrielle," he said in a low, intense voice, "why aren't you open and frank with me as you once used to be? Remember that you, my daughter, are my only friend!"

Slim, dainty, and small-waisted, with a sweet, dimpled face, and blue eyes large and clear like a child's, a white throat, a well-poised head, and light-chestnut hair dressed low with a large black bow, she presented the picture of happy, careless youth, her features soft and refined, her half-bare arms well moulded, and hands delicate and white. She wore only one ornament - upon her left hand was a small signet-ring with her monogram engraved, a gift from one of her governesses when a child, and now worn upon the little finger.

That face was strikingly beautiful, it had been remarked more than once in London; but any admiration only called forth the covert sneers of Lady Heyburn.

"Why don't you tell me?" urged the blind man. "Why don't you tell me the truth?" he protested.

Her countenance changed when she heard his words. In her blue eyes was a look of abject fear. Her left hand was tightly clenched and her mouth set hard, as though in resolution.

"I really don't know what you mean, dad," she responded with a hollow laugh. "You have such strange fancies nowadays."

"Strange fancies, child!" echoed the afflicted man, lifting his grey, expressionless face to hers. "A blind man has always vague, suspicious, and black forebodings engendered by the darkness and loneliness of his life. I am no exception," he sighed. "I think ever of the might-have-beens."

"No, dear," exclaimed the girl, bending until her lips touched his white brow softly. "Forget it all, dear old dad. Surely your days here, with me, quiet and healthful in this beautiful Perthshire, are better, better by far, than if you had been a politician up in London, ever struggling, ever speaking, and ever bearing the long hours at the House and the eternal stress of Parliamentary life?"

"Yes, yes," he said, just a trifle impatiently. "It is not that. I don't regret that I had to retire, except - well, except for your sake perhaps, dear."

"For my sake! How?"

"Because, had I been a member of this Cabinet - which some of my friends predicted - you would have had the chance of a good marriage. But buried as you are down here instead, what chances have you?"

"I want no chance, dad," replied the girl. "I shall never marry."

A painful thought crossed the old man's mind, being mirrored upon his brow by the deep lines which puckered there for a few brief moments. "Well," he exclaimed, smiling, "that's surely no reason why you should not go to the ball at Connachan to-night."

"I have my duty to perform, dad; my duty is to remain with you," she said decisively. "You know you have quite a lot to do, and when your mother has gone we'll spend an hour or two here at work."

"I hear that Walter Murie is at home again at Connachan. Hill told me this morning," remarked her father.

"So I heard also," answered the girl.

"And yet you are not going to the ball, Gabrielle, eh?" laughed the old man mischievously.

"Now come, dad," the girl exclaimed, colouring slightly, "you're really too bad! I thought you had promised me not to mention him again."

"So I did, dear; I - I quite forgot," replied Sir Henry apologetically. "Forgive me. You are now your own mistress. If you prefer to stay away from Connachan, then do so by all means. Only, make a proper excuse to your mother; otherwise she will be annoyed."

"I think not, dear," his daughter replied in a meaning tone. "If I remain at home she'll be rather glad than otherwise."

"Why?" inquired the old man quickly.

The girl hesitated. She saw instantly that her remark was an unfortunate one. "Well," she said rather lamely, "because my absence will relieve her of the responsibility of acting as chaperon."

What else could she say? How could she tell her father - the kindly but afflicted man to whom she was devoted - the bitter truth? His lonely, dismal life was surely sufficiently hard to bear without the extra burden of suspicion, of enforced inactivity, of fierce hatred, and of bitter regret. So she slowly disengaged her hand, kissed him again, and with an excuse that she had the menus to write for the dinner-table, went out, leaving him alone.

When the door had closed a great sigh sounded through the long, book-lined room, a sigh that ended in a sob.

The old man had leaned his chin upon his hands, and his sightless eyes were filled with tears. "Is it the truth?" he murmured to himself. "Is it really the truth?"

CHAPTER II

FROM OUT THE NIGHT

There are few of the Perthshire castles that more plainly declare their feudal origin and exhibit traces of obsolete power than does the great gaunt pile of ruins known as Glencardine. Its situation is both picturesque and imposing, and the stern aspect of the two square baronial towers which face the south, perched on a sheer precipice that descends to the Ruthven Water deep below, shows that the castle was once the residence of a predatory chief in the days before its association with the great Montrose.

Two miles from the long, straggling village of Auchterarder, in the centre of a fine, well-wooded, well-kept estate, the great ruined castle stands a silent monument of warlike days long since forgotten. There, within those walls, now overgrown with ivy and weeds, and where big trees grow in the centre of what was once the great paved courtyard, Montrose schemed and plotted, and, according to tradition, kept certain of his enemies in the dungeons below.

In the twelfth century the aspect of the deep glen was very different from what it is to-day. In those days the Ruthven was a broad river, flowing swiftly down to the Earn, and forming, by reason of a moat, an effective barrier against attack. To-day, however, the river has diminished into a mere burn meandering through a beautiful wooded glen three hundred feet below, a glen the charms of which are well known

William Le Queux

throughout the whole of Scotland, and where in summer tourists from England endeavour to explore, but are warned back by Stewart, Sir Henry's Highland keeper.

A quarter of a mile from the great historic ruin is the modern castle, built mainly of stone from the ancient structure early in the eighteenth century, with oak-panelled rooms, many quaint gables, stained glass, and long, echoing corridors - a residence well adapted for entertaining on a lavish scale, the front overlooking the beautiful glen, and the back with level lawns and stretch of undulating park, well wooded and full of picturesque beauty.

The family traditions and history of the old place and its owners had induced Sir Henry Heyburn, himself a Fellow of the Society of Antiquaries, to purchase it from Lord Strathavon, into whose possession it had passed some forty years previously.

History showed that William de Graeme or Graham, who settled in Scotland in the twelfth century, became Lord of Glencardine, and the great castle was built by his son. They were indeed a noble race, as their biographer has explained. Ever fearless in their country's cause, they sneered at the mandates from impregnable Stirling, and were loyal in every generation.

Glencardine was a stronghold feared by all the surrounding nobles, and its men were full of valour and bravery. One story of them is perhaps worth the telling. In the year 1490 the all-powerful Abbot of Inchaffray issued an order for the collection of the teinds of the Killearns' lands possessed by the Grahams of Glencardine in the parish of Monzievaird, of which he was titular. The order was rigorously executed, the teinds being exacted by force.

Lord Killearn of Dunning Castle was from home at the time; but in his absence his eldest son, William, Master of Dunning, called out a number of his clansmen, and marched towards

Glencardine for the purpose of putting a stop to the abbot's proceedings. The Grahams of Glencardine, having been apprised of their neighbour's intention, mustered in strong force, and marched to meet him. The opposing forces encountered each other at the north side of Knock Mary, about two miles to the south-west of Crieff, while a number of the clan M'Robbie, who lived beside the Loch of Balloch, marched up the south side of the hill, halting at the top to watch the progress of the combat. The fight began with great fury on both sides. The Glencardine men, however, began to get the upper hand and drive their opponents back, when the M'Robbies rushed down the hill to the succour of the Killearns. The tables were now turned. The Grahams were unable to maintain their ground against the combined forces which they had now to face, and fled towards Glencardine, taking refuge in the Kirk of Monzievaird. The Killearns had no desire to follow up their success any farther, but at this stage they were joined by Duncan Campbell of Dunstaffnage, who had come across from Argyllshire to avenge the death of his father-in-law, Robert of Monzie, who, along with his two sons, had a short time before been killed by the Lord of Glencardine.

An arrow shot from the church fatally wounded one of Campbell's men, and so enraged were the besiegers at this that they set fire to the heather-thatched building. Of the one hundred and sixty human beings who are supposed to have been in the church, only one young lad escaped, and this was effected by the help of one of the Killearns, who caught the boy in his arms as he leaped out of the flames. The Killearns did not go unpunished for their barbarous deed. Their leader, with several of his chief retainers, was afterwards beheaded at Stirling, and an assessment was imposed on the Killearns for behoof of the wives and children of the Grahams who had perished by their hands.

The Killearn by whose aid the young Graham had been saved was forced to flee to Ireland, but he afterwards returned to Scotland, where he and his attendants were known by the name of "Killearn Eirinich" (or Ernoch), meaning Killearn of Ireland. The estate which he held, and which is situated near Comrie, still bears that name. The site of the Kirk of Monzievaird is now occupied by the mausoleum of the family of Murray of Ochtertyre, which was erected in 1809. When the foundations were being excavated a large quantity of charred bones and wood was found.

The history of Scotland is full of references to the doings at Glencardine, the fine home of the great Lord Glencardine, and of events, both in the original stronghold and in the present mansion, which have had important bearings upon the welfare of the country.

In the autumn of 1825 the celebrated poetess Baroness Nairne, who had been born at Gask, a few miles away, visited Glencardine and spent several weeks in the pleasantest manner. Within those gaunt ruins of the old castle she first became inspired to write her celebrated "Castell Gloom," near Dollar:

Oh Castell Gloom! thy strength is gone,
The green grass o'er thee growin';
On Hill of Care thou art alone,
The Sorrow round thee flowin'.

Oh Castell Gloom! on thy fair wa's
Nae banners now are streamin';
The howlit flits amang thy ha's,
And wild birds there are screamin'.

Oh, mourn the woe! oh, mourn the crime
Frae civil war that flows!
Oh, mourn, Argyll, thy fallen line,
And mourn the great Montrose!
The lofty Ochils bright did glow,
Though sleepin' was the sun;
But mornin's light did sadly show
What ragin' flames had done!
Oh, mirk, mirk was the misty cloud

That hung o'er thy wild wood!
Thou wert like beauty in a shroud,
And all was solitude.

A volume, indeed, could be written upon the history, traditions, and superstitions of Glencardine Castle, a subject in which its blind owner took the keenest possible interest. But, tragedy of it all, he had never seen the lovely old domain he had acquired! Only by Gabrielle's descriptions of it, as she led him so often across the woods, down by the babbling burn, or over the great ivy-covered ruins, did he know and love it.

Every shepherd of the Ochils knows of the Lady of Glencardine who, on rare occasions, had been seen dressed in green flitting before the modern mansion, and who was said to be the spectre of the young Lady Jane Glencardine, who in 1710 was foully drowned in the Earn by her jealous lover, the Lord of Glamis, and whose body was never recovered. Her appearance always boded ill-fortune to the family in residence.

Glencardine was scarcely ever without guests. Lady Heyburn, a shallow and vain woman many years younger than her husband, was always surrounded by her own friends. She hated the country, and more especially what she declared to be the "deadly dullness" of her Perthshire home. That moment was no exception. There were half-a-dozen guests staying in the house, but neither Gabrielle nor her father took the slightest interest in any of them. They had been, of course, invited to the ball at Connachan, and at dinner had expressed surprise when their host's pretty daughter, the belle of the county, had declared that she was not going.

"Oh, Gabrielle is really such a wayward child!" declared her ladyship to old Colonel Burton at her side. "If she has decided not to go, no power on earth will persuade her."

"I'm not feeling at all well, mother," the girl responded from the farther end of the table. "You'll make nice excuses for me, won't you?"

"I think it's simply ridiculous!" declared the Baronet's wife. "Your first season, too!"

Gabrielle glanced round the table, coloured slightly, but said nothing. The guests knew too well that in the Glencardine household there had always been, and always would be, slightly strained relations between her ladyship and her stepdaughter.

For an hour after dinner all was bustle and excitement; then, in the covered wagonette, the gay party drove away, while Gabrielle, standing at the door, shouted after them a merry adieu.

It was a bright, clear, moonlit night, so beautiful indeed that, twisting a shawl about her shoulders, she went to her father's den, where he usually smoked alone, and, taking his arm, led him out for a walk into the park over that gravelled drive where, upon such nights as that, 'twas said that the unfortunate Lady Jane could be seen.

When alone, the sightless man could find his way quite well with the aid of his stick. He knew every inch of his domain. Indeed, he could descend from the castle by the winding path that led deep into the glen, and across the narrow foot-bridges of the rushing Ruthven Water, or he could traverse the most intricate paths through the woods by means of certain landmarks which only he himself knew. He was ever fond of wandering about the estate alone, and often took solitary walks on bright nights with his stout stick tapping before him. On rare occasions, however, when, in the absence of her ladyship, he enjoyed the company of pretty Gabrielle, they would wander in the park arm-in-arm, chatting and exchanging confidences.

The departure of their house-party had lifted a heavy weight from both their hearts. It would be dawn before they returned. She loved her father, and was never happier than when describing to him things - the smallest objects sometimes - which he himself could not see.

As they strolled on beneath the shadows of the tall elms, the stillness of the night was broken only by the quick scurry of a rabbit into the tall bracken or the harsh cry of some night-bird startled by their approach.

Before them, standing black against the night-sky, rose the quaint, ponderous, but broken walls of the ancient stronghold, where an owl hooted weirdly in the ivy, and where the whispering of the waters rose from the deep below.

"It's a pity, dear, that you didn't go to the dance," the old man was saying, her arm held within his own. "You've annoyed your mother, I fear."

"Mother is quite happy with her guests, dad; while I am quite happy with you," she replied softly. "Therefore, why discuss it?"

"But surely it is not very entertaining for you to remain here with a man who is blind. Remember, you are young, and these golden days of youth will very soon pass."

"Why, you always entertain and instruct me, dad," she declared; "from you I've learnt so much archaeology and so much about mediaeval seals that I believe I am qualified to become a Fellow of the Society of Antiquaries, if women were admitted to fellowship."

"They will be one day, my dear, if the Suffragettes are allowed their own way," he laughed.

And then, during the full hour they strolled together, their conversation mostly consisted of questions asked by her father concerning some improvements being made in one of the farms which she had visited on the previous day, and her description of what had been done.

The stable-clock had struck half-past ten on its musical chimes before they re-entered the big hall, and, being relieved by Hill of the wraps, passed together into the library, where, from a locked cabinet in a corner, Gabrielle took a number of business papers and placed them upon the writing-table before her father.

"No," he said, running his thin white hands over them, "not business to-night, dear, but pleasure. Where is that box from the Professor?"

"It's here, dad. Shall I open it?"

"Yes," he replied. "That dear old fellow never forgets his old friend. Never a seal finds its way into the collection at Cambridge but he first sends it to me for examination before it is catalogued. He knows what pleasure it is to me to decipher them and make out their history - almost, alas! the only pleasure left to me, except you, my darling."

"Professor Moyes adopts your opinion always, dad. He knows, as every other antiquary knows, that you are the greatest living authority on the subject which you have made a lifetime study - that of the bronze seals of the Middle Ages."

"Ah!" sighed the old man, "if I could only write my great book! It is the pleasure debarred me. Years ago I started to collect material; but my affliction came, and now I can only feel the matrices and picture them in my mind. I see through your eyes, dear Gabrielle. To me, the world I loved so much is only a blank darkness, with your dear voice sounding out of it - the only voice, my child, that is music to my ears."

The girl said nothing. She only glanced at the sad, expressionless face, and, cutting the string of the small packet, displayed three bronze seals - two oval, about two inches long, and the third round, about one inch in diameter, and each with a small kind of handle on the reverse. With them were sulphur-casts or impressions taken from them, ready to be placed in the museum at Cambridge.

The old man's nervous fingers travelled over the surfaces quickly, an expression of complete satisfaction in his face.

"Have you the magnifying-glass, dear? Tell me what you make of the inscriptions," he said, at the same time carefully feeling the curious mediaeval lettering of one of the casts.

At the same instant she started, rose quickly from her chair, and held her breath.

A man, tall, dark-faced, and wearing a thin black overcoat, had entered noiselessly from the lawn by the open window, and stood there, with his finger upon his lips, indicating silence. Then he pointed outside, with a commanding gesture that she should follow.

Her eyes met his in a glance of fierce resentment, and instinctively she placed her hand upon her breast, as though to stay the beating of her heart.

Again he pointed in silent authority, and she as though held in some mysterious thraldom, made excuse to the blind man, and, rising, followed in his noiseless footsteps.

CHAPTER III

SEALS OF DESTINY

Ten minutes later she returned, panting, her face pale and haggard, her mouth hard-set. For a moment she stood in silence upon the threshold of the open doors leading to the grounds, her hand pressed to her breast in a strenuous endeavour to calm herself. She feared that her father might detect her agitation, for he was so quick in discovering in her the slightest unusual emotion. She glanced behind her with an expression full of fear, as though dreading the reappearance of that man who had compelled her to follow him out into the night. Then she looked at her father, who, still seated motionless with his back to her, was busy with his fingers upon something on the blotting-pad before him.

In that brief absence her countenance had entirely changed. She was pale to the lips, with drawn brows, while about her mouth played a hard, bitter expression, as though her mind were bent upon some desperate resolve.

That the man who had come there by stealth was no stranger was evident; yet that between them was some deep-rooted enmity was equally apparent. Nevertheless, he held her irresistibly within his toils. His clean-shaven face was a distinctly evil one. His eyes were set too close together, and in his physiognomy was something unscrupulous and relentless. He was not the man for a woman to trust.

She stepped back from the threshold, and for a few seconds halted outside, her ears strained to catch any sound. Then, as though reassured, she pushed the chestnut hair from her hot, fevered brow, held her breath with strenuous effort, and, re-entering the library, advanced to her father's side.

"I wondered where you had gone, dear," he said in his low, calm voice, as he detected her presence. "I hoped you would not leave me for long, for it is not very often we enjoy an evening so entirely alone as to-night."

"Leave you, dear old dad! Why, of course not!" She laughed gaily, as though nothing had occurred to disturb her peace of mind. "We were just about to look at those seals Professor Moyes sent you to-day, weren't we? Here they are;" and she placed them before the helpless and afflicted man, endeavouring to remain undisturbed, and taking a chair at his side, as was her habit when they sat together.

"Yes," he said cheerfully. "Let us see what they are."

The first of the yellow sulphur-casts which he examined bore the full-length figure of an abbot, with mitre and crosier, in the act of giving his blessing. Behind him were three circular towers with pointed roofs surmounted by crosses, while around, in bold early Gothic letters, ran the inscription

+ S. BENEDITI . ABBATIS . SANTI . AMBROSII . D'RANCIA +

Slowly and with great care his fingers travelled over the raised letters and design of the oval cast. Then, having also examined the battered old bronze matrix, he said, "A most excellent specimen, and in first-class preservation, too! I wonder where it has been found? In Italy, without doubt."

"What do you make it out to be, dad?" asked the girl, seated in the chair at his side and as interested in the little antiquity as he was himself.

"Thirteenth century, my dear - early thirteenth century," he declared without hesitation. "Genuine, quite genuine, no doubt. The matrix shows signs of considerable wear. Is there much patina upon it?" he asked.

She turned it over, displaying that thick green corrosion which bronze acquires only by great age.

"Yes, quite a lot, dad. The raised portion at the back is pierced by a hole very much worn."

"Worn by the thong by which it was attached to the girdle of successive abbots through centuries," he declared. "From its inscription, it is the seal of the Abbot Benedict of the Monastery of St. Ambrose, of Rancia, in Lombardy. Let me think, now. We should find the history of that house probably in Sassolini's *Memorials*. Will you get it down, dear? - top shelf of the fifth case, on the left."

Though blind, he knew just where he could put his hand upon all his most cherished volumes, and woe betide any one who put a volume back in its wrong place!

Gabrielle rose, and, obtaining the steps, reached down the great leather-bound quarto book, which she carried to a reading-desk and at once searched the index.

The work was in Italian, a language which she knew fairly well; and after ten minutes or so, during which time the blind man continued slowly to trace the inscription with his finger-tips, she said, "Here it is, dad. 'Rancia, near Cremona. The religious brotherhood was founded there in 1132, and the Abbot Benedict was third abbot, from 1218 to 1231. The church still exists. The magnificent pulpit in marble, embellished with mosaics, presented in 1272, rests on six columns supported by lions, with an inscription: "*Nicolaus de Montava marmorarius hoc opus fecit.*" Opposite it is the ambo (1272), in a simple style, with a representation of Jonah being swallowed by a whale. In the choir is the throne adorned by mosaics, and the

Cappella di San Pantaleone contains the blood of the saint, together with some relics of the Abbot Benedict. The cloisters still exist, though, of course, the monastery is now suppressed.'"

"And this," remarked Sir Henry, turning over the old bronze seal in his hand, "belonged to the Abbot Ambrose six hundred and fifty years ago!"

"Yes, dad," declared the girl, returning to his side and taking the matrix herself to examine it under the green-shaded reading-lamp. "The study of seals is most interesting. It carries one back into the dim ages. I hope the Professor will allow you to keep these casts for your collection."

"Yes, I know he will," responded the old Baronet. "He is well aware what a deep interest I take in my hobby."

"And also that you are one of the first authorities in the world upon the subject," added his daughter.

The old man sighed. Would that he could see with his eyes once again; for, after all, the sense of touch was but a poor substitute for that of sight!

He drew towards him the impression of the second of the oval seals. The centre was divided into two portions. Above was the half-length figure of a saint holding a closed book in his hand, and below was a youth with long hands in the act of adoration. Between them was a scroll upon which was written: "Sc. Martine O.P.N.," while around the seal were the words in Gothic characters:

+ SIGIL . HEINRICHI . PLEBANI . D' DOELSC'H +

"This is fourteenth century," pronounced the Baronet, "and is from Dulcigno, on the Adriatic - the seal of Henry, the vicar of the church of that place. From the engraving and style," he said, still fingering it with great care, now and then turning to the matrix in order to satisfy himself, "I should place it as having been executed about 1350. But it is really a very beautiful specimen, done at a time when the art of seal-engraving was at its height. No engraver could to-day turn out a more ornate and at the same time bold design. Moyes is really very fortunate in securing this. You must write, my dear, and ask him how these latest treasures came into his hands."

At his request she got down another of the ponderous volumes of Sassolini from the high shelf, and read to him, translating from the Italian the brief notice of the ancient church of Dulcigno, which, it appeared, had been built in the Lombard-Norman style of the eleventh century, while the campanile, with columns from Paestum, dated from 1276.

The third seal, the circular one, was larger than the rest, being quite two inches across. In the centre of the top half was the Madonna with Child, seated, a male and female figure on either side. Below were three female figures on either side, the two scenes being divided by a festoon of flowers, while around the edge ran in somewhat more modern characters - those of the early sixteenth century - the following:

+ SIGILLVM . VICARIS . GENERALIS . ORDINIS . BEATA . MARIA . D' MON . CARMEL +

"This," declared Sir Henry, after a long and most minute examination, "is a treasure probably unequalled in the collection at Cambridge, being the actual seal of the Vicar-General of the Carmelite order. Its date I should place at about 1150. Look well, dear, at those flower garlands; how beautifully they are engraved! Seal-making is, alas! to-day a lost art. We have only crude and heavy attempts. The company seal seems to-day the only thing the engraver can turn out - those machines which emboss upon a big red wafer." And his busy fingers were continuously feeling the great circular bronze matrix, and a moment afterwards its sulphur-cast.

He was an enthusiastic antiquary, and long ago, in the days

when the world was light, had read papers before the Society of Antiquaries at Burlington House upon mediaeval seals and upon the early Latin codices. Nowadays, however, Gabrielle acted as his eyes; and so devoted was she to her father that she took a keen interest in his dry-as-dust hobbies, so that after his long tuition she could decipher and read a twelfth-century Latin manuscript, on its scrap of yellow, crinkled parchment, and with all its puzzling abbreviations, almost as well as any professor of palaeography at the universities, while inscriptions upon Gothic seals were to her as plain as a paragraph in a newspaper. More than once, white-haired, spectacled professors who came to Glencardine as her father's guests were amazed at her intelligent conversation upon points which were quite abstruse. Indeed, she had no idea of the remarkable extent of her own antiquarian knowledge, all of it gathered from the talented man whose affliction had kept her so close at his side.

For quite an hour her father fingered the three seal-impressions, discussing them with her in the language of a savant. She herself examined them minutely and expressed opinions. Now and then she glanced apprehensively to that open window. He pointed out to her where she was wrong in her estimate of the design of the circular one, explaining a technical and little-known detail concerning the seals of the Carmelite order.

From the window a cool breath of the night-wind came in, fanning the curtains and carrying with it the sweet scent of the flowers without.

"How refreshing!" exclaimed the old man, drawing in a deep breath. "The night is very close, Gabrielle, dear. I fear we shall have thunder."

"There was lightning only a moment ago," explained the girl. "Shall I put the casts into your collection, dad?"

"Yes, dear. Moyes no doubt intends that I should keep them."

Gabrielle rose, and, passing across to a large cabinet with many shallow drawers, she opened one, displaying a tray full of casts of seals, each neatly arranged, with its inscription and translation placed beneath, all in her own clear handwriting.

Some of the drawers contained the matrices as well as the casts; but as matrices of mediaeval seals are rarities, and seldom found anywhere save in the chief public museums, it is no wonder that the bulk of private collections consist of impressions.

Presently, at the Baronet's suggestion, she closed and locked the cabinet, and then took up a bundle of business documents, which she commenced to sort out and arrange.

She acted as her father's private secretary, and therefore knew much of his affairs. But many things were to her a complete mystery, be it said. Though devoted to her father, she nevertheless sometimes became filled with a vague suspicion that the source of his great income was not altogether an open and honest one. The papers and letters she read to him often contained veiled information which sorely puzzled her, and which caused her many hours of wonder and reflection. Her father lived alone, with only her as companion. Her stepmother, a young, good-looking, and giddy woman, never dreamed the truth.

What would she do, how would she act, Gabrielle wondered, if ever she gained sight of some of those private papers kept locked in the cavity beyond the black steel door concealed by the false bookcase at the farther end of the fine old restful room?

The papers she handled had been taken from the safe by Sir Henry himself. And they contained a man's secret.

CHAPTER IV

SOMETHING CONCERNING JAMES FLOCKART

In the spreading dawn the house party had returned from
Connachan and had ascended to their rooms, weary with the
night's revelry, the men with shirt-fronts crumpled and ties
awry, the women with hair disordered, and in some cases with
flimsy skirts torn in the mazes of the dance. Yet all were merry
and full of satisfaction at what one young man from town had
declared to be "an awfully ripping evening." All retired at once
- all save the hostess and one of her male guests, the man who
had entered the library by stealth earlier in the evening and had
called Gabrielle outside.

Lady Heyburn and her visitor, James Flockart, had managed to
slip away from the others, and now stood together in the
library, into which the grey light of dawn was at that moment
slowly creeping.

He drew up one of the blinds to admit the light; and there,
away over the hills beyond, the glen showed the red flush that
heralded the sun's coming. Then, returning to where stood the
young and attractive woman in pale pink chiffon, with
diamonds on her neck and a star in her fair hair, he looked her
straight in the face and asked, "Well, and what have you
decided?"

She raised her eyes to his, but made no reply. She was
hesitating.

William Le Queux

The gems upon her were heirlooms of the Heyburn family, and in that grey light looked cold and glassy. The powder and the slight touch of carmine upon her cheeks, which at night had served to heighten her beauty, now gave her an appearance of painted artificiality. She was undeniably a pretty woman, and surely required no artificial aids to beauty. About thirty-three, yet she looked five years younger; while her husband was twenty years senior to herself. She still retained a figure so girlish that most people took her for Gabrielle's elder sister, while in the matter of dress she was admitted in society to be one of the leaders of fashion. Her hair was of that rare copper-gold tint, her features regular, with a slightly protruding chin, soft eyes, and cheeks perfect in their contour. Society knew her as a gay, reckless, giddy woman, who, regardless of the terrible affliction which had fallen upon the brilliant man who was her husband, surrounded herself with a circle of friends of the same type as herself, and who thoroughly enjoyed her life regardless of any gossip or of the malignant statements by women who envied her.

Men were fond of "Winnie Heyburn," as they called her, and always voted her "good fun." They pitied poor Sir Henry; but, after all, he was blind, and preferred his hobbies of collecting old seals and dusty parchment manuscripts to dances, bridge-parties, theatres, aero shows at Ranelagh, and suppers at the Carlton or Savoy.

Like most wealthy women of her type, she had a wide circle of male friends. Younger men declared her to be "a real pal," and with some of the older beaux she would flirt and be amused by their flattering speeches.

Gabrielle's mother, the second daughter of Lord Buckhurst, had been dead several years when the brilliant politician met his second wife at a garden-party at Dollis Hill. She was daughter of a man named Lambert, a paper manufacturer, who acted as political agent in the town of Bedford; and she was, therefore, essentially a country cousin. Her beauty was, however, remarked everywhere. The Baronet was struck by her, and within three months they were married at St. George's, Hanover Square, the world congratulating her upon a very excellent match. From the very first, however, the difference in the ages of husband and wife proved a barrier. Ere the honeymoon was over she found that her husband, tied by his political engagements and by his eternal duties at the House, was unable to accompany her out of an evening; hence from the very first they had drifted apart, until, eight months later, the terrible affliction of blindness fell upon him.

For a time this drew her back to him. She was his constant and dutiful companion everywhere, leading him hither and thither, and attending to his wants; but very soon the tie bored her, and the attractions of society once again proved too great. Hence for the past nine years - Gabrielle being at school, first at Eastbourne and afterwards at Amiens - she had amused herself and left her husband to his dry-as-dust hobbies and the loneliness of his black and sunless world.

The man who had just put that curious question to her was perhaps her closest friend. To her he owed everything, though the world was in ignorance of the fact. That they were friends everybody knew. Indeed, they had been friends years ago in Bedford, before her marriage, for James was the only son of the Reverend Henry Flockart, vicar of one of the parishes in the town. People living in Bedford recollected that the parson's son had turned out rather badly, and had gone to America. But a year or two after that the quiet-mannered old clergyman had died, the living had been given to a successor, and Bedford knew the name of Flockart no more. After Winifred's marriage, however, London society - or rather a gay section of it - became acquainted with James Flockart, who lived at ease in his pretty bachelor-rooms in Half-Moon Street, and who soon gathered about him a large circle of male acquaintances. Sir Henry knew him, and raised no objection to his wife's friendship towards him. They had been boy and girl together; therefore what more natural than that they should be friends in later life?

In her schooldays Gabrielle knew practically nothing of this man; but now she had returned to be her father's companion she had met him, and had bitter cause to hate both him and Lady Heyburn. It was her own secret. She kept it to herself. She hid the truth from her father - from every one. She watched closely and in patience. One day she would speak and tell the truth. Until then, she resolved to keep to herself all that she knew.

"Well?" asked the man with the soft-pleated shirt-front and white waistcoat smeared with cigarette-ash. "What have you decided?" he asked again.

"I've decided nothing," was her blank answer.

"But you must. Don't be a silly fool," he urged. "You've surely had time to think over it?"

"No, I haven't."

"The girl knows nothing. So what have you to fear?" he endeavoured to assure her.

Lady Heyburn shrugged her shoulders. "How can you prove that she knows nothing?"

"Oh, she has eyes for nobody but the old man," he laughed. "To-night is an example. Why, she wouldn't come to Connachan, even though she knew that Walter was there. She preferred to spend the evening here with her father."

"She's a little fool, of course, Jimmy," replied the woman in pink; "but perhaps it was as well that she didn't come. I hate to have to chaperon the chit. It makes me look so horribly old."

"I wish to goodness the girl was out of the way!" he declared. "She's sharper than we think, and, by Jove! if ever she did know what was in progress it would be all up for both of us - wouldn't it? Phew! think of it!"

"If I thought she had the slightest suspicion," declared her ladyship with a sudden hardness of her lips, "I'd - I'd close her mouth very quickly."

"And for ever, eh?" he asked meaningly.

"Yes, for ever."

"Bah!" he laughed. "You'd be afraid to do that, my dear Winnie," added the man, lowering his voice. "Your husband is blind, it's true; but there are other people in the world who are not. Recollect, Gabrielle is now nineteen, and she has her eyes open. She's the eyes and ears of Sir Henry. Not the slightest thing occurs in this household but it is told to him at once. His indifference to all is only a clever pretence."

"What!" she gasped quickly; "do you think he suspects?"

"Pray, what can he suspect?" asked the man very calmly, both hands in his trouser-pockets, as he leaned back against the table in front of her.

"He can only suspect things which his daughter knows," she said.

"But what does she know? What can she know?" he asked.

"How can we tell? I have watched, but can detect nothing. I am, however, suspicious, because she did not come to Connachan with us to-night."

"Why?"

"Walter Murie may know something, and may have told her."

"If so, then to close her lips would be useless. It would only bring a heavier responsibility upon us - and -" But he hesitated, without finishing his sentence. His meaning was apparent from the wry face she pulled at his remark. He did

William Le Queux

not tell her how he had, while she had been dancing and flirting that night, made his way back to the castle, or how he had compelled Gabrielle to go forth and speak with him. His action had been a bold one, yet its result had confirmed certain vague suspicions he had held.

Well he knew that the girl hated him heartily, and that she was in possession of a certain secret of his - one which might easily result in his downfall. He feared to tell the truth to this woman before him, for if he did so she would certainly withdraw from all association with him in order to save herself.

The key to the whole situation was held by that slim, sweet-faced girl, so devoted to her afflicted father. He was not quite certain as to the actual extent of her knowledge, and was as yet undecided as to what attitude he should adopt towards her. He stood between the Baronet's wife and his daughter, and hesitated in which direction to follow.

What did she really know, he wondered. Had she overheard any of that serious conversation between Lady Heyburn and himself while they walked together in the glen on the previous evening? Such a *contretemps* was surely impossible, for he remembered they had taken every precaution lest even Stewart, the head gamekeeper, might be about in order to stop trespassers, who, attracted by the beauties of Glencardine, tried to penetrate and explore them, and by so doing disturbed the game.

"And if the girl really knows?" he asked of the woman who stood there motionless, gazing out across the lawn fixedly towards the dawn.

"If she knows, James," she said in a hard, decisive tone, "then we mustact together, quickly and fearlessly. We must carry out that - that plan you proposed a year ago!"

"You are quite fearless, then," he asked, looking straight into her fine eyes.

"Fearless? Of course I am," she answered unflinchingly. "We must get rid of her."

"Providing we can do so without any suspicion falling upon us."

"You seem to have become quite white-livered," she exclaimed to him with a harsh, derisive laugh. "You were not so a year ago - in the other affair."

His brows contracted as he reflected upon all it meant to him. The girl knew something; therefore, to seal her lips was imperative for their own safety. She was their enemy.

"You are mistaken," he answered in a low calm voice. "I am just as determined - just as fearless - as I was then."

"And you will do it?" she asked.

"If it is your wish," he replied simply.

"Good! Give me your hand. We are agreed. It shall be done."

And the man took the slim white hand the woman held out to him, and a moment later they ascended the great oak staircase to their respective rooms.

The pair were in accord. The future contained for Gabrielle Heyburn - asleep and all unconscious of the dastardly conspiracy - only that which must be hideous, tragic, fatal.

CHAPTER V

THE MURIES OF CONNACHAN

Elise, Lady Heyburn's French maid, discovered next morning that an antique snake-bracelet was missing, a loss which occasioned great consternation in the household.

Breakfast was late, and at table, when the loss was mentioned, Gabrielle offered to drive over to Connachan in the car and make inquiry and search. The general opinion was that it had been dropped in one of the rooms, and was probably still lying there undiscovered.

The girl's offer was accepted, and half an hour later the smaller of the two Glencardine cars - the "sixteen" Fiat - was brought round to the door by Stokes, the smart chauffeur. Young Gellatly, fresh down from Oxford, begged to be allowed to go with her, and his escort was accepted.

Then, in motor-cap and champagne-coloured dust-veil, Gabrielle mounted at the wheel, with the young fellow at her side and Stokes in the back, and drove away down the long avenue to the high-road.

The car was her delight. Never so happy was she as when, wrapped in her leather-lined motor-coat, she drove the "sixteen." The six-cylinder "sixty" was too powerful for her, but with the "sixteen" she ran half-over Scotland, and was quite a common object on the Perth to Stirling road. Possessed of nerve and full of self-confidence, she could negotiate traffic in Edinburgh or Glasgow, and on one occasion had driven her father the whole way from Glencardine up to London, a distance of four hundred and fifty miles. Her fingers pressed the button of the electric horn as they descended the sharp incline to the lodge-gates; and, turning into the open road, she was soon speeding along through Auchterarder village, skirted Tullibardine Wood, down through Braco, and along by the Knaik Water and St. Patrick's Well into Glen Artney, passing under the dark shadow of Dundurn, until there came into view the broad waters of Loch Earn.

The morning was bright and cloudless, and at such a pace they went that a perfect wall of dust stood behind them.

From the margin of the loch the ground rose for a couple of miles until it reached a plateau upon which stood the fine, imposing Priory, the ancestral seat of the Muries of Connachan. The aspect as they drove up was very imposing. The winding road was closely planted with trees for a large portion of its course, and the stately front of the western entrance, with its massive stone portico and crenulated cornice, burst unexpectedly upon them.

From that point of view one seemed to have reached the gable-end of a princely edifice, crowned with Gothic belfries; yet on looking round it was seen that the approach by which the doorway had been reached was lined on one side with buildings hidden behind the clustering foliage; and through the archway on the left one caught a glimpse of the ivy-covered clock-tower and spacious stable-yard and garage extending northwards for a considerable distance.

Gabrielle ran the car round to the south side of the house, where in the foreground were the well-kept parks of Connachan, the smooth-shaven lawn fringed with symmetrically planted trees, and the fertile fields extending away to the very brink of the loch.

The original fortalice of the Muries, half a mile distant, was, like Glencardine, a ruin. The present Priory, notwithstanding its old-fashioned towers and lancet windows, was a comparatively modern structure, and the ivy which partially covered some of the windows could claim no great antiquity; yet the general effect of the architectural grouping was most pleasing, and might well deceive the visitor or tourist into the supposition that it belonged to a very remote period. It was, as a matter of fact, the work of Atkinson, who in the first years of the nineteenth century built Scone, Abbotsford, and Taymouth Castle.

With loud warning blasts upon the horn, Gabrielle Heyburn pulled up; but ere she could descend, Walter Murie, a good-looking, dark-haired young man in grey flannels, and hatless, was outside, hailing her with delight.

"Hallo, Gabrielle!" he cried cheerily, taking her hand, "what brings you over this morning, especially when we were told last night that you were so very ill?"

"The illness has passed," exclaimed young Gellatly, shaking his friend's hand. "And we're now in search of a lost bracelet - one of Lady Heyburn's."

"Why, my mother was just going to wire! One of the maids found it in the boudoir this morning, but we didn't know to whom it belonged. Come inside. There are a lot of people staying over from last night." Then, turning to Gabrielle, he added, "By Jove! what dust there must be on the road! You're absolutely covered."

"Well," she laughed lightly, "it won't hurt me, I suppose. I'm not afraid of it."

Stokes took charge of the car and shut off the petrol, while the three went inside, passing into a long, cool cloister, down which was arranged the splendid collection of antiques discovered or acquired by Malcolm Murie, the well-known antiquary, who had spent many years in Italy, and died in 1794. In cases ranged down each side of the long cloister, with its antique carved chairs, armour, and statuary, were rare Etruscan and Roman terra-cottas, one containing relics from the tomb of a warrior, which included a sword-hilt adorned with gold and a portion of a golden crown formed of lilies *in relievo* of pure gold laid upon a mould of bronze; another case was full of bronze ornaments unearthed near Albano, and still another contained rare Abyssinian curios. The collection was renowned among antiquaries, and was often visited by Sir Henry, who would be brought there in the car by Gabrielle, and spend hours alone fingering the objects in the various cases.

Sir George Murie and Sir Henry Heyburn were close friends; therefore it was but natural that Walter, the heir to the Connachan estate, and Gabrielle should often be thrown into each other's company, or perhaps that the young man - who for the past twelve months had been absent on a tour round the world - should have loved her ever since the days when she wore short skirts and her hair down her back. He had been sorely puzzled why she had not at the last moment come to the ball. She had promised that she would be with them, and yet she had made the rather lame excuse of a headache.

Truth to tell, Walter Murie had during the past week been greatly puzzled at her demeanour of indifference. Seven days ago he had arrived in London from New York, but found no letter from her awaiting him at the club, as he had expected. The last he had received in Detroit a month before, and it was strangely cold, and quite unusual. Two days ago he had arrived home, and in secret she had met him down at the end of the glen at Glencardine. At her wish, their first meeting had been clandestine. Why?

Both their families knew of their mutual affection. Therefore, why should she now make a secret of their meeting after twelve months' separation? He was puzzled at her note, and he was further puzzled at her attitude towards him. She was cold and unresponsive. When he held her in his arms and kissed her soft lips, she only once returned his passionate caress, and then as though it were a duty forced upon her. She had, however, promised to come to the ball. That promise she had deliberately broken.

Though he could not understand her, he made pretence of unconcern. He regretted that she had not felt well last night - that was all.

At the end of the cloister young Gellatly found one of Lady Murie's guests, a girl named Violet Priest, with whom he had danced a good deal on the previous night, and at once attached himself to her, leaving Walter with the sweet-faced, slim-waisted object of his affections.

The moment they were alone in the long cloister he asked her quickly, "Tell me, Gabrielle, the real reason why you did not come last night. I had looked forward very much to seeing you. But I was disappointed - sadly disappointed."

"I am very sorry," she laughed, with assumed nonchalance; "but I had to assist my father with some business papers."

"Your mother told everyone that you do not care for dancing," he said.

"That is untrue, Walter. I love dancing."

"I knew it was untrue, dearest," he said, standing before her. "But why does Lady Heyburn go out of her way to throw cold water upon you and all your works?"

"How should I know?" asked the girl, with a slight shrug. "Perhaps it is because my father places more confidence in me than in her."

"And his confidence is surely not misplaced," he said. "I tell you frankly that I don't like Lady Heyburn."

"She pretends to like you."

"Pretends!" he echoed. "Yes, it's all pretence. But," he added, "do tell me the real reason of your absence last night, Gabrielle. It has worried me."

"Why worry, my dear Walter? Is it really worth troubling over? I'm only a girl, and, as such, am allowed vagaries of nerves - and all that. I simply didn't want to come, that's all."

"Why?"

"Well, to tell you the truth, I hate the crowd we have staying in our house. They are all mother's friends; and mother's friends are never mine, you know."

He looked at her slim figure, so charming in its daintiness. "What a dear little philosopher you've grown to be in a single year!" he declared. "We shall have you quoting Friedrich Nietzsche next."

"Well," she laughed, "if you would like me to quote him I can do so. I read *Zarathustra* secretly at school. One of the girls got a copy from Germany. Do you remember what Zarathustra says: 'Verily, ye could wear no better masks, ye present-day men, than your own faces,' Who could recognise you?"

"I hope that's not meant to be personal," he laughed, gazing at the girl's beautiful countenance and great, luminous eyes.

"You may take it as you like," she declared with a delightfully mischievous smile. "I only quoted it to show you that I have read Nietzsche, and recollect his many truths."

"You certainly do seem to have a gay house-party at Glencardine," he remarked, changing the subject. "I noticed Jimmy Flockart there as usual." .

"Yes. He's one of mother's greatest friends. She makes good

use of him in every way. Up in town they are inseparable, it seems. They knew each other, I believe, when they were boy and girl."

"So I've heard," replied the young man thoughtfully, leaning against a big glass case containing a collection of *lares* and *penates* - images of Jupiter, Hercules, Mercury, &c., used as household gods. "I expected that he would be dancing attendance upon her during the whole of the evening; but, curiously enough, soon after his arrival he suddenly disappeared, and was not seen again until nearly two o'clock." Then, looking straight in the girl's fathomless eye, he added, "Do you know, Gabrielle, I don't like that fellow. Beware of him."

"Neither do I. But your warning is quite unnecessary, I assure you. He doesn't interest me in the least."

Walter Murie was silent for a moment, silent as though in doubt. A shadow crossed his well-cut features, but only for a single second. Then he smiled again upon the fair-faced, soft-spoken girl whom he loved so honestly and so well, the woman who was all in all to him. How could he doubt her - she who only a year ago had, out yonder in the park, given him her pledge of affection, and sealed it with her hot, passionate kisses? Remembrance of those sweet caresses still lingered with him. But he doubted her. Yes, he could not conceal from himself certain very ugly facts - facts within his own knowledge. Yet was not his own poignant jealousy misleading him? Was not her refusal to attend the ball perhaps due to some sudden pique or unpleasantness with her giddy stepmother? Was it? He only longed to be able to believe that it might be so. Alas! however, he had discovered the shadow of a strange and disagreeable truth.

CHAPTER VI

CONCERNS GABRIELLE'S SECRET

Along the cloister they went to the great hall, where Walter's mother advanced to greet her. Full of regrets at the girl's inability to attend the dance, she handed her the missing bracelet, saying, "It is such a curious and unusual one, dear, that we wondered to whom it belonged. Brown found it when she was sweeping my boudoir this morning. Take it home to your mother, and suggest that she has a stronger clasp put on it."

The girl held the golden snake in her open hand. This was the first time she had ever seen it. A fine example of old Italian workmanship, it was made flexible, with its flat head covered with diamonds, and two bright emeralds for the eyes. The mouth could be opened, and within was a small cavity where a photo or any tiny object could be concealed. Where her mother had picked it up she could not tell. But Lady Heyburn was always purchasing quaint odds and ends, and, like most giddy women of her class, was extraordinarily fond of fantastic jewellery and ornaments such as other women did not possess.

Several members of the house-party at Connachan entered and chatted, all being full of the success of the previous night's entertainment. Lady Murie's husband had, it appeared, left that morning for Edinburgh to attend a political committee.

A little later Walter succeeded in getting Gabrielle alone again

William Le Queux

in a small, well-furnished room leading off the library - a room in which she had passed many happy hours with him before he had gone abroad. He had been in London reading for the Bar, but had spent a good deal of his time up in Perthshire, or at least all he possibly could. At such times they were inseparable; but after he had been "called" - there being no necessity for him to practise, he being heir to the estates - he had gone to India and Japan "to broaden his mind," as his father had explained.

"I wonder, Gabrielle," he said hesitatingly, holding her hand as they stood at the open window - "I wonder if you will forgive me if I put a question to you. I - I know I ought not to ask it," he stammered; "but it is only because I love you so well, dearest, that I ask you to tell me the truth."

"The truth!" echoed the girl, looking at him with some surprise, though turning just a trifle paler, he thought. "The truth about what?"

"About that man James Flockart," was his low, distinct reply.

"About him! Why, my dear Walter," she laughed, "whatever do you want to know about him? You know all that I know. We were agreed long ago that he is not a gentleman, weren't we?"

"Yes," he said. "Don't you recollect our talk at your house in London two years ago, soon after you came back from school? Do you remember what you then told me?"

She flushed slightly at the recollection. "I - I ought not to have said that," she exclaimed hurriedly. "I was only a girl then, and I - well, I didn't know."

"What you said has never passed my lips, dearest. Only, I ask you again to-day to tell me honestly and frankly whether your opinion of him has in any way changed. I mean whether you still believe what you then said."

She was silent for a few moments. Her lips twitched nervously, and her eyes stared blankly out of the window. "No, I repeat what - I - said - then," she answered in a strange hoarse voice.

"And only you yourself suspect the truth?"

"You are the only person to whom I have mentioned it, and I have been filled with regret ever since. I had no right to make the allegation, Walter. I should have kept my secret to myself."

"There was surely no harm in telling me, dearest," he exclaimed, still holding her hand, and looking fixedly into those clear-blue, fathomless eyes so very dear to him. "You know too well that I would never betray you."

"But if he knew - if that man ever knew," she cried, "he would avenge himself upon me! I know he would."

"But what have you to fear, little one?" he asked, surprised at the sudden change in her.

"You know how my mother hates me, how they all detest me - all except dear old dad, who is so terribly helpless, misled, defrauded, and tricked - as he daily is - by those about him."

"I know, darling," said the young man. "I know it all only too well. Trust in me;" and, bending, he kissed her softly upon the lips.

What was the real, the actual truth, he wondered. Was she still his, as she had ever been, or was she playing him false?

Little did the girl dream of the extent of her lover's knowledge of certain facts which she was hiding from the world, vainly believing them to be her own secret. Little did she dream how very near she was to disaster.

Walter Murie had, after a frivolous youth, developed at the age of six-and-twenty into as sound, honest, and upright a young

William Le Queux

man as could be found beyond the Border. As full of high spirits as of high principles, he was in every way worthy the name of the gallant family whose name he bore, a Murie of Connachan, both for physical strength and scrupulous honesty; while his affection for Gabrielle Heyburn was that deep, all-absorbing devotion which makes men sacrifice themselves for the women they love. He was not very demonstrative. He never wore his heart upon his sleeve, but deep within him was that true affection which caused him to worship her as his idol. To him she was peerless among women, and her beauty was unequalled. Her piquant mischievousness amused him. As a girl, she had always been fond of tantalising him, and did so now. Yet he knew her fine character; how deeply devoted she was to her afflicted father, and how full of discomfort was her dull life, now that she had exchanged her school for the same roof which covered Sir Henry's second wife. Indeed, this latter event was the common talk of all who knew the family. They sighed and pitied poor Sir Henry. It was all very sad, they said; but there their sympathy ended. During Walter's absence abroad something had occurred. What that something was he had not yet determined. Gabrielle was not exactly the same towards him as she used to be. His keen sensitiveness told him this instinctively, and, indeed, he had made a discovery that, though he did not admit it now, had staggered him.

He stood there at the open window chatting with her, but what he said he had no idea. His one thought - the one question which now possessed him - was whether she still loved him, or whether the discovery he had made was the actual and painful truth. Tall and good-looking, clean-shaven, and essentially easy-going, he stood before her with his dark eyes fixed upon her - eyes full of devotion, for was she not his idol?

She was telling him of a garden-party which her mother had arranged for the following Thursday, and pressing him to attend it.

"I'm afraid I may have to be in London that day, dearest," he responded. "But if I may I'll come over to-morrow and play tennis. Will you be at home in the afternoon?"

"No," she declared promptly, with a mischievous laugh, "I shan't. I shall be in the glen by the first bridge at four o'clock, and shall wait for you there."

"Very well, I'll be there," he laughed. "But why should we meet in secret like this, when everybody knows of our engagement?"

"Well, because I have a reason," she replied in a strained voice - "a strong reason."

"You've grown suddenly shy, afraid of chaff, it seems."

"My mother is, I fear, not altogether well disposed towards you, Walter," was her quick response. "Dad is very fond of you, as you well know; but Lady Heyburn has other views for me, I think."

"And is that the only reason you wish to meet me in secret?" he asked.

She hesitated, became slightly confused, and quickly turned the conversation into a different channel, a fact which caused him increased doubt and reflection.

Yes, something certainly had occurred. That was vividly apparent. A gulf lay between them.

Again he looked straight into her beautiful face, and fell to wondering. What could it all mean? So true had she been to him, so sweet her temperament, so high all her ideals, that he could not bring himself to believe ill of her. He tried to fight down those increasing doubts. He tried to put aside the naked truth which had arisen before him since his return to England. He loved her. Yes, he loved her, and would think no ill of her until he had proof, actual and indisputable.

As far as the eligibility of Walter Murie was concerned there was no question. Even Lady Heyburn could not deny it when she discussed the matter over the tea-cups with her intimate friends.

The family of the Muries of Connachan claimed a respectable antiquity. The original surname of the family was De Balinhard, assumed from an estate of that name in the county of Forfar. Sir Jocelynus de Baldendard, or Balinhard, who witnessed several charters between 1204 and 1225, is the first recorded of the name, but there is no documentary proof of descent before that time; and, indeed, most of the family papers having been burned in 1452, little remains of the early history beyond the names and succession of the possessors of Balinhard from about 1250 till 1350, which are stated in a charter of David II. Now preserved in the British Museum. This charter records the grant made by William de Maule to John de Balinhard, *filio et heredi quondam Joannis filii Christini filii Joannis de Balinhard*, of the lands of Murie, in the county of Perthshire, and from that period, about 1350, the family has borne the name of De Murie instead of De Balinhard. In 1409 Duthac de Murie obtained a charter of the Castle of Connachan, possession of which has been held by the family uninterruptedly ever since, except for about thirty years, when the lands were under forfeiture on account of the Rebellion of 1715.

Near Crieff Junction station the lands of Glencardine and Connachan march together; therefore both Sir Henry Heyburn and his friend, Sir George Murie, had looked upon an alliance between the two houses as quite within the bounds of probability.

If the truth were told, Gabrielle had never looked upon any other man save Walter with the slightest thought of affection. She loved him with the whole strength of her being. During that twelve long months of absence he had been daily in her thoughts, and his constant letters she had read and re-read dozens of times. She had, since she left school, met many eligible young men at houses to which her mother had grudgingly taken her - young men who had been nice to her, flattered her, and flirted with her. But she had treated them all with coquettish disdain, for in the world there was but one man who was her lover and her hero - her old friend Walter Murie.

At this moment, as they were together in that cosy, well-furnished room, she became seized by a twinge of conscience. She knew quite well that she was not treating him as she ought. She had not been at all enthusiastic at his return, and she had inquired but little about his wanderings. Indeed, she had treated him with a studied indifference, as though his life concerned her but little. And yet if he only knew the truth, she thought; if he could only see that that cool, unresponsive attitude was forced upon her by circumstances; if he could only know how quickly her heart throbbed when he was present, and how dull and lonely all became when he was absent!

She loved him. Ah, yes! as truly and devotedly as he loved her. But between them there had fallen a dark, grim shadow - one which, at all hazards and by every subterfuge, she must endeavour to hide. She loved him, and could, therefore, never bear to hear his bitter reproaches or to witness his grief. He worshipped her. Would that he did not, she thought. She must hide her secret from him as she was hiding it from all the world.

He was speaking. She answered him calmly yet mechanically. He wondered what strange thoughts were concealed beneath those clear, wide-open, child-like eyes which he was trying in vain to fathom. What would he have thought had he known the terrible truth: that she had calmly, and after long reflection, resolved to court death - death by her own hand - rather than face the exposure with which she had that previous night been threatened.

CHAPTER VII

CONTAINS CURIOUS CONFIDENCES

A week had gone by. Stewart, the lean, thin-faced head-keeper, who spoke with such a strong accent that guests from the South often failed to understand him, and who never seemed to sleep, so vigilant was he over the Glencardine shootings, had reported the purchase of a couple of new pointers.

Therefore, one morning Lady Heyburn and her constant cavalier, Flockart, had walked across to the kennels close to the castle to inspect them.

At the end of the big, old-fashioned stable-yard, with grey stone outbuildings ranged down either side, and the ancient mounting-block a conspicuous object, were ranged the modern iron kennels full of pointers and spaniels. In that big, old, paved quadrangle, the cobbles of which were nowadays stained by the oil of noisy motor-cars, many a Graham of Glencardine had mounted to ride into Stirling or Edinburgh, or to drive in his coach to far-off London. The stables were now empty, but the garage adjoining, whence came the odour of petrol, contained the two Glencardine cars, besides three others belonging to members of that merry, irresponsible house-party.

The inspection of the pointers was a mere excuse on her ladyship's part to be alone with Flockart.

She wished to speak with him, and with that object suggested that they should take the by-road which, crossing one of the main roads through the estate, led through a leafy wood away to a railway level-crossing half a mile off. The road was unfrequented, and they were not likely to meet any of the guests, for some were away fishing, others had motored into Stirling, and at least three had walked down into Auchterarder to take a telegram for their blind host.

"Well, my dear Jimmy," asked the well-preserved, fair-haired woman in short brown skirt and fresh white cotton blouse and sun-hat, "what have you discovered?"

"Very little," replied the easy-going man, who wore a suit of rough heather-tweed and a round cloth fishing-hat. "My information is unfortunately very meagre. You have watched carefully. Well, what have you found out?"

"That she's just as much in love with him as before - the little fool!"

"And I suppose he's just as devoted to her as ever - eh?"

"Of course. Since you've been away these last few days he's been over here from Connachan, on one pretext or another, every day. Of course I've been compelled to ask him to lunch, for I can't afford to quarrel with his people, although I hate the whole lot of them. His mother gives herself such airs, and his father is the most terrible old bore in the whole country."

"But the match would be an advantageous one - wouldn't it?" suggested the man strolling at her side, and he stopped to light a cigarette which he took from a golden case.

"Advantageous! Of course it would! But we can't afford to allow it, my dear Jimmy. Think what such an alliance would mean to us!"

"To you, you mean."

"To you also. An ugly revelation might result, remember. Therefore it must not be allowed. While Walter was abroad all was pretty plain sailing. Lots of the letters she wrote him I secured from the post-box, read them, and afterwards burned them. But now he's back there is a distinct peril. He's a cute young fellow, remember."

Flockart smiled. "We must discover a means by which to part them," he said slowly but decisively. "I quite agree with you that to allow the matter to go any further would be to court disaster. We have a good many enemies, you and I, Winnie - many who would only be too pleased and eager to rake up that unfortunate episode. And I, for one, have no desire to figure in a criminal dock."

"Nor have I," she declared quickly.

"But if I went there you would certainly accompany me," he said, looking straight at her.

"What!" she gasped in quick dismay. "You would tell the truth and - and denounce me?"

"I would not; but no doubt there are others who would," was his answer.

For a few moments her arched brows were knit, and she remained silent. Her reflections were uneasy ones. She and the man at her side, who for years had been her confidant and friend, were both in imminent peril of exposure. Their relations had always been purely platonic; therefore she was not afraid of any allegation against her honour. What her enemies had said were lies - all of them. Her fear lay in quite a different direction.

Her poor, blind, helpless husband was in ignorance of that terrible chapter of her own life - a chapter which she had believed to be closed for ever, and yet which was, by means of a chain of unexpected circumstances, in imminent danger of being reopened.

"Well," she inquired at last in a blank voice, "and who are those others who, you believe, would be prepared to denounce me?"

"Certain persons who envy you your position, and who, perhaps, think that you do not treat poor old Sir Henry quite properly."

"But I do treat him properly!" she declared vehemently. "If he prefers the society of that chit of a girl of his to mine, how can I possibly help it? Besides, people surely must know that, to me, the society of a blind old man is not exactly conducive to gaiety. I would only like to put those women who malign me into my place for a single year. Perhaps they would become even more reckless of the *convenances* than I am!"

"My dear Winnie," he said, "what's the use of discussing such an old and threadbare theme? Things are not always what they seem, as the man with a squint said when he thought he saw two sovereigns where there was but one. The point before us is the girl's future."

"It lies in your hands," was her sharp reply.

"No; in yours. I have promised to look after Walter Murie."

"But how can I act?" she asked. "The little hussy cares nothing for me - only sees me at table, and spends the whole of her day with her father."

"Act as I suggested last week," was his rejoinder. "If you did that the old man would turn her out of the place, and the rest would be easy enough."

"But -"

"Ah!" he laughed derisively, "I see you've some sympathy with

William Le Queux

the girl after all. Very well, take the consequences. It is she who will be your deadliest enemy, remember; she who, if the disaster falls, will give evidence against you. Therefore, you'd best act now, ere it's too late. Unless, of course, you are in fear of her."

"I don't fear her!" cried the woman, her eyes flashing defiance. "Why do you taunt me like this? You haven't told me yet what took place on the night of the ball."

"Nothing. The mystery is just as complete as ever."

"She defied you - eh?"

Her companion nodded.

"Then how do you now intend to act?"

"That's just the question I was about to put to you," he said. "There is a distinct peril - one which becomes graver every moment that the girl and young Murie are together. How are we to avert it?"

"By parting them."

"Then act as I suggested the other day. It's the only way, Winnie, depend upon it - the only way to secure our own safety."

"And what would the world say of me, her stepmother, if it were known that I had done such a thing?"

"You've never yet cared for what the world said. Why should you care now? Besides, it never will be known. I should be the only person in the secret, and for my own sake it isn't likely that I'd give you away. Is it? You've trusted me before," he added; "why not again?"

"It would break my husband's heart," she declared in a low,

intense voice. "Remember, he is devoted to her. He would never recover from the shock."

"And yet the other night after the ball you said you were prepared to carry out the suggestion, in order to save yourself," he remarked with a covert sneer.

"Perhaps I was piqued that she should defy my suggestion that she should go to the ball."

"No, you were not. You never intended her to go. That you know."

When he spoke to her this man never minced matters. The woman was held by him in a strange thraldom which surprised many people; yet to all it was a mystery. The world knew nothing of the fact that James Flockart was without a penny, and that he lived - and lived well, too - upon the charity of Lady Heyburn. Two thousand pounds were placed, in secret, every year to his credit from her ladyship's private account at Coutts's, besides which he received odd cheques from her whenever his needs required. To his friends he posed as an easy-going man-about-town, in possession of an income not large, but sufficient to supply him with both comforts and luxuries. He usually spent the London season in his cosy chambers in Half-Moon Street; the winter at Monte Carlo or at Cairo; the summer at Aix, Vichy, or Marienbad; and the autumn in a series of visits to houses in Scotland.

He was not exactly a ladies' man. Courtly, refined, and a splendid linguist, as he was, the girls always voted him great fun; but from the elder ones, and from married women especially, he somehow held himself aloof. His one woman-friend, as everybody knew, was the flighty, go-ahead Lady Heyburn.

Of the country-house party he was usually the life and soul. No man could invent so many practical jokes or carry them on with such refinement of humour as he. Therefore, if the hostess wished to impart merriment among her guests, she sought out and sent a pressing invitation to "Jimmy" Flockart. A first-class shot, an excellent tennis-player, a good golfer, and quite a good hand at putting a stone in curling, he was an all-round sportsman who was sure to be highly popular with his fellow-guests. Hence up in the north his advent was always welcomed with loud approbation.

To those who knew him, and knew him well, this confidential conversation with the woman whose platonic friendship he had enjoyed through so many years would certainly have caused greatest surprise. That he was a schemer was entirely undreamed of. That he was attracted by "Winnie Heyburn" was declared to be only natural, in view of the age and affliction of her own husband. Cases such as hers are often regarded with a very lenient eye.

They had reached the level-crossing where, beside the line of the Caledonian Railway, stands the mail-apparatus by which the down-mail for Euston picks up the local bag without stopping, while the up-mail drops its letters and parcels into the big, strong net. For a few moments they halted to watch the dining-car express for Euston pass with a roar and a crash as she dashed down the incline towards Crieff Junction.

Then, as they turned again towards the house, he suddenly exclaimed, "Look here, Winnie. We've got to face the music now. Every day increases our peril. If you are actually afraid to act as I suggest, then tell me frankly and I'll know what to do. I tell you quite openly that I have neither desire nor intention to be put into a hole by this confounded girl. She has defied me; therefore she must take the consequences."

"How do you know that your action the other night has not aroused her suspicions?"

"Ah! there you are quite right. It may have done so. If it has, then our peril has very considerably increased. That's just my argument."

"But we'll have Walter to reckon with in any case. He loves her."

"Bah! Leave the boy to me. I'll soon show him that the girl's not worth a second thought," replied Flockart with nonchalant air. "All you have to do is to act as I suggested the other night. Then leave the rest to me."

"And suppose it were discovered?" asked the woman, whose face had grown considerably paler.

"Well, suppose the worst happened, and it were discovered?" he asked, raising his brows slightly. "Should we be any worse off than would be the case if this girl took it into her head to expose us - if the facts which she could prove placed us side by side in an assize-court?"

The woman - clever, scheming, ambitious - was silent. The question admitted of no reply. She recognised her own peril. The picture of herself arraigned before a judge, with that man beside her, rose before her imagination, and she became terrified. That slim, pale-faced girl, her husband's child, stood between her and her own honour, her own safety. Once the girl was removed, she would have no further fear, no apprehension, no hideous forebodings concerning the imminent future. She saw it all as she walked along that moss-grown forest-road, her eyes fixed straight before her. The tempter at her side had urged her to commit a dastardly, an unpardonable crime. In that man's hands she was, alas! as wax. He poured into her ear a vivid picture of what must inevitably result should Gabrielle reveal the ugly truth, at the same time calmly watching the effect of his words upon her. Upon her decision depended his whole future as well as hers. What was Gabrielle's life to hers, asked the man point-blank. That was the question which decided her - decided her, after long and futile resistance, to promise to commit the act which he had suggested. She gave the man her hand in pledge.

Then a slight smile of triumph played about his cruel nether lip, and the pair retraced their steps towards the castle in silence.

CHAPTER VIII

CASTING THE BAIT

Loving and perishing: these have tallied from eternity. Love and death walk hand-in-hand. The will to love means also to be ready for death.

Gabrielle Heyburn recognised this truth. She had the will to love, and she had the resolve to perish - perish by her own hand - rather than allow her secret to be exposed. Those who knew her - a young, athletic, merry-faced, open-air girl on the verge of budding womanhood, so true-hearted, frank, and free - little dreamed of the terrible nature of that secret within her young heart.

She held aloof from her lover as much as she dared. True, Walter came to Glencardine nearly every day, but she managed to avoid him whenever possible. Why? Because she knew her own weakness; she feared being compelled by his stronger nature, and by the true affection in which she held him, to confess. They walked together in the cool, shady glen beside the rippling burn, climbed the neighbouring hills, played tennis, or else she lay in the hammock at the edge of the lawn while he lounged at her side smoking cigarettes. She did all this because she was compelled.

Her most enjoyable hours were the quiet ones spent at Her father's side. Alone in the library, she read to him, in French, those curious business documents which came so often by registered post. They were so strangely worded that, not knowing their true import, she failed to understand them. All were neatly typed, without any heading to the paper. Sometimes a printed address in the Boulevard des Capucines, Paris, would appear on letters accompanying the enclosures. But all were very formal, and to Gabrielle extremely puzzling.

Sir Henry always took the greatest precaution that no one should obtain sight of these confidential reports or overhear them read by his daughter. Before she sat down to read, she always shot the small brass bolt on the door to prevent Hill or any other intruder from entering. More than once the Baronet's wife had wanted to come in while the reading was in progress, whereupon Sir Henry always excused himself, saying that he locked his door against his guests when he wished to be alone, an explanation which her ladyship accepted.

These strangely worded reports in French always puzzled the Baronet's daughter. Sometimes she became seized by a vague suspicion that her father was carrying on some business which was not altogether honourable. Why should he enjoin such secrecy? Why should he cause her to write and despatch with her own hand such curiously worded telegrams, addressed always to the registered address: "METEFOROS, PARIS"?

Those neatly typed pages which she read could be always construed in two or three senses. But only her father knew the actual meaning which the writer intended to convey. For hours she would often be engaged in reading them. Sometimes, too, telegrams in cipher arrived, and she would then obtain the little, dark-blue covered book from the safe, and by its aid decipher the messages from the French capital.

Questions, curious questions, were frequently asked by the anonymous sender of the reports; and to these her father replied by means of his private code. She had become during the past year quite an expert typist, and therefore to her the Baronet entrusted the replies, always impressing upon her the need of absolute secrecy, even from her mother.

"My affairs," he often declared, "concern nobody but myself. I trust in you, Gabrielle dear, to guard my secrets from prying eyes. I know that you yourself must often be puzzled, but that is only natural."

Unfamiliar as the girl was with business in any form, she had during the past year arrived at the conclusion, after much debate within herself, that this source of her father's income was a distinctly mysterious one. The estates were, of course, large, and he employed agents to manage them; but they could not produce that huge income which she knew he possessed, for had she not more than once seen the amount of his balance at his banker's as well as the large sum he had on deposit? The source of his colossal wealth was a mystery, but was no doubt connected with his curious and constant communications with Paris.

At rare intervals a grey-faced, grey-bearded, and rather stout Frenchman - a certain Monsieur Goslin - called, and on such occasions was closeted for a long time alone with Sir Henry, evidently discussing some important affair in secret. To her ladyship, as well as to Gabrielle, the Frenchman was most courteous, but refused the pressing invitations to remain the night. He always arrived by the morning train from Perth, and left for the south the same night, the express being stopped for him by signal at Auchterarder station. The mysterious visitor puzzled Gabrielle considerably. Her father entrusted him with secrets which he withheld from her, and this often caused her both surprise and annoyance. Like every other girl, she was of course full of curiosity.

Towards her Flockart became daily more friendly. On two occasions, after breakfast, he had invited her to spend an hour or two fishing for trout in the burn, which was unexpectedly in spate, and they had thus been some time in each other's company.

She, however, regarded him with distinct distrust. He was undeniably good-looking, nonchalant, and a thorough-going man of the world. But his intimate friendship with Lady Heyburn prevented her from regarding him as a true friend. Towards her he was ever most courteous, and paid her many little compliments. He tied her flies, he fitted her rod, and if her line became entangled in the trees he always put matters right. Not, however, that she could not do it all herself. In her strong, high fishing-boots, her short skirts hemmed with leather, her burberry, and her dark-blue tam-o'-shanter set jauntily on her chestnut hair, she very often fished alone, and made quite respectable baskets. To wade into the burn and disentangle her line from beneath a stone was to her quite a small occurrence, for she would never let either Stewart or any of the under-keepers accompany her.

Why Flockart had so suddenly sought her society she failed to discern. Hitherto, though always extremely polite, he had treated her as a child, which she naturally resented. At length, however, he seemed to have realised that she now possessed the average intelligence of a young woman.

He had never repeated those strange words he had uttered when, on the night of the ball at Connachan, he returned in secret to the castle and beckoned her out upon the lawn. He had, indeed, never referred to his curious action. Sometimes she wondered, so changed was his manner, whether he had actually forgotten the incident altogether. He had showed himself in his true colours that night. Whatever suspicions she had previously held were corroborated in that stroll across the lawn in the dark shadow. His tactics had altered, it seemed, and their objective puzzled her.

"It must be very dull for you here, Miss Heyburn," he remarked to her one bright morning as they were casting up-stream near one another. They were standing not far from a rustic bridge in a deep, leafy glen, where the sunshine penetrated here and there through the canopy of leaves, beneath which the burn pursued its sinuous course towards the Earn. The music of the rippling waters over the brown, moss-grown boulders mingled with the rustle of the leaves above, as now and then the soft wind swept up the narrow valley. They were treading a carpet of wild-flowers, and the air was full of the delicious perfume of the summer day. "You must be very dull, living here so much, and going up to town so very seldom," he said.

"Oh dear no!" she laughed. "You are quite mistaken. I really enjoy a country life. It's so jolly after the confinement and rigorous rules of school. One is free up here. I can wear my old clothes, and go cycling, fishing, shooting, curling; in fact, I'm my own mistress. That I shouldn't be if I lived in London, and had to make calls, walk in the Park, go shopping, sit out concerts, and all that sort of thing."

"But though you're out, you never go anywhere. Surely that's unusual for one so active and - well" - he hesitated - "I wonder whether I might be permitted to say so - so good-looking as you are, Gabrielle."

"Ah!" replied the girl, protesting, but blushing at the same time, "you're poking fun at me, Mr. Flockart. All I can reply is, first, that I'm not good-looking; and, secondly, I'm not in the least dull - perhaps I should be if I hadn't my father's affairs to attend to."

"They seem to take up a lot of your time," he said with pretended indifference, but, to his annoyance, landed a salmon parr at the same moment.

"We work together most evenings," was her reply.

The question which he then put as he threw the parr back into the burn struck her as curious. It was evident that he was endeavouring to learn from her the nature of her father's correspondence. But she was shrewd enough to parry all his ingenious cross-questioning. Her father's secrets were her own.

"Some ill-natured people gossip about Sir Henry," he remarked presently, as he made another long cast up-stream and allowed the flies to be carried down to within a few yards from where he stood. "They say that his source of income is mysterious, and that it is not altogether open and above-board."

"What!" she exclaimed, looking at him quickly. "And who, pray, Mr. Flockart, makes this allegation against my father?"

"Oh, I really don't know who started the gossip. The source of such tales is always difficult to discover. Some enemy, no doubt. Every man in this world of ours has enemies."

"What do you mean by the source of dad's income not being an honourable one?"

The man shrugged his shoulders. "I really don't know," he declared. "I only repeat what I've heard once or twice up in London."

"Tell me exactly what they say," demanded the girl, with quick interest.

Her companion hesitated for a few seconds. "Well, whatever has been said, I've always denied; for, as you know, I am a friend of both Lady Heyburn and of your father."

The girl's nostrils dilated slightly. Friend! Why, was not this man her father's false friend? Was he not behind every sinister action of Lady Heyburn's, and had not she herself, with her own ears, one day at Park Street, four years ago, overheard her ladyship express a dastardly desire in the words, "Oh, Henry is such a dreadful old bore, and so utterly useless, that it's a shame a woman like myself should be tied up to him. Fortunately for me, he already has one foot in the grave. Otherwise I couldn't tolerate this life at all!" Those cruel words of her stepmother's, spoken to this man who was at that moment her companion, recurred to her. She recollected, too, Flockart's reply.

This hollow pretence of friendship angered her. She knew that the man was her father's enemy, and that he had united with the clever, scheming woman in some ingenious conspiracy against the poor, helpless man.

Therefore she turned, and, facing him boldly, said, "I wish, Mr. Flockart, that you would please understand that I have no intention to discuss my father or his affairs. The latter concern himself alone. He does not even speak of them to his wife; therefore why should strangers evince any interest in them?"

"Because there are rumours - rumours of a mystery; and mysteries are always interesting and attractive," was his answer.

"True," she said meaningly. "Just as rumours concerning certain of my father's guests possess an unusual interest for him, Mr. Flockart. Though my father may be blind, his hearing is still excellent. And he is aware of much more than you think."

The man glanced at her for an instant, and his face darkened. The girl's ominous words filled him with vague apprehension. Was it possible that the blind man had any suspicion of what was intended? He held his breath, and made another vicious cast far up the rippling stream.

CHAPTER IX

REVEALS A MYSTERIOUS BUSINESS

In the few days which followed, Lady Heyburn's attitude towards Gabrielle became one of marked affection. She even kissed her in the breakfast-room each morning, called her "dear," and consulted her upon the day's arrangements.

Poor Sir Henry was but a cipher in the household. He usually took all his meals alone, except dinner, and was very seldom seen, save perhaps when he would come out for an hour or so to walk in the park, led by his daughter, or else, alone, tapping before him with his stout stick. On such occasions he would wear a pair of big blue spectacles to hide the unsightliness of his gray, filmy eyes. Sometimes he would sit on one of the garden seats on the south side of the house, enjoying the sunshine, and listening to the songs of the birds, the hum of the insects, and the soft ripples of the burn far below. And on such occasions one of his wife's guests would join him to chat and cheer him, for everyone felt pity for the lonely man living his life of darkness.

No one was more full of words of sympathy than James Flockart. Gabrielle longed to warn her father of that man, but dared not do so. There was a reason - a strong reason - for her silence. Sir Henry had declared that he was interested in the man's intellectual conversation, and that he rather liked him, though he had never looked upon his face. In some things the old gentleman was ever ready to adopt his daughter's advice and rely upon her judgment; but in others he was quite obstinate and treated her pointed remarks with calm indifference.

One day, at Lady Heyburn's suggestion, Gabrielle, accompanied by Flockart and another of the guests, a retired colonel, had driven over in the big car to Perth to make a call; and on their return she spent some hours in the library with her father, attending to his correspondence.

That morning a big packet of those typed reports in French had arrived in the usual registered, orange-coloured envelope, and after she had read them over to the Baronet, he had given her the key, and she had got out the code-book. Then, at his instructions, she had written upon a yellow telegraph-form a cipher message addressed to the mysterious "Meteforos, Paris." It read, when decoded: -

> "Arrange with amethyst. I agree the price of pearls. Have no fear of Smithson, but watch Peters. If London refuses, then Mayfair. Expect report of Bedford."

It was not signed by the Baronet's name, but by the signature he always used on such telegraphic replies: "Senrab."

From such a despatch she could gather nothing. At his request she took away the little blue-covered book and relocked it in the safe. Then she rang for Hill, and told him to send the despatch by messenger down to Auchterarder village.

"Very well, miss," replied the man, bowing.

"The car is going down to take Mr. Seymour to the station in about a quarter of an hour, so Stokes will take it."

"And look here," exclaimed the blind man, who was standing before the window with his back to the crimson sunset, "you can tell her ladyship, Hill, that I'm very busy, and I shan't come in to dinner to-night. Just serve a snack here for me, will you?"

"Very well, Sir Henry," responded the smart footman; and, bowing again, he closed the door.

"May I dine with you, dad?" asked the girl. "There are two or three people invited to-night, and they don't interest me in the least."

"My dear child, what do you mean? Why, aren't Walter Murie and his mother dining here to-night? I know your mother invited them ten days ago."

"Oh, why, yes," replied the girl rather lamely; "I did not recollect. Then, I suppose, I must put in an appearance," she sighed.

"Suppose!" he echoed. "What would Walter think if you elected to dine with me instead of meeting him at table?"

"Now, dad, it is really unkind of you!" she said reprovingly. "Walter and I thoroughly understand each other. He's not surprised at anything I do."

"Ah!" laughed the sightless man, "he's already beginning to understand the feminine perverseness, eh? Well, my child, dine here with me if you wish, by all means. Tell Hill to lay the table for two. We have lots of work to do afterwards."

So the bell was rung again and Hill was informed that Miss Gabrielle would dine with her father in the library.

Then they turned again to the Baronet's mysterious private affairs; and when she had seated herself at the typewriter and re-read the reports - confidential reports they were, but framed in a manner which only the old man himself could understand - he dictated to her cryptic replies, the true nature of which were to her a mystery.

The last of the reports, brief and unsigned, read as follows: -

"Mon petit garcon est tres gravement malade, et je supplie Dieu a genoux de ne pas me punir si severement, de ne pas me prendre mon enfant.

"D'apres le dernier bulletin du Professeur Knieberger, il a la fievre scarlatine, et l'issue de la maladie est incertaine. Je ne quitte plus son chevet. Et sans cesse je me dis, 'C'est une punition du Ciel.'"

Gabrielle saw that, to the outside world, it was a statement by a frantic mother that her child had caught scarlet-fever. "What could it really mean?" she wondered.

Slowly she read it, and as she did so noticed the curious effect it had upon her father, seated as he was in the deep saddle-bag chair. His face grew very grave, his thin white hands clenched themselves, and there was an unusually bitter expression about his mouth.

"Eh?" he asked, as though not quite certain of the words. "Read it again, child, slower. I - I have to think."

She obeyed, wondering if the key to the cryptic message were contained in some conjunction of letters or words. It seemed as though, in imagination, he was setting it down before him as she pronounced the words. This was often so. At times he would have reports repeated to him over and over again.

"Ah!" he gasped at last, drawing a long breath, his hands still tightly clenched, his countenance haggard and drawn. "I - I expected that. And so it has come - at last!"

"What, dad?" asked the girl in surprise, staring at the crisp typewritten sheet before her.

"Oh, well, nothing child - nothing," he answered, bestirring himself.

"But the lady whoever she is, seems terribly concerned about her little boy. The judgment of Heaven, she calls it."

"And well she may, Gabrielle," he answered in a hoarse strained voice. "Well she may, my dear. It is a punishment sent upon the wicked."

"Is the mother wicked, then?" asked the girl in curiosity.

"No, dear," he urged. "Don't try to understand, for you can never do that. These reports convey to me alone the truth. They are intended to mislead you, as they mislead other people."

"Then there is no little boy suffering from scarlet-fever?"

"Yes. Because it is written there," was his smiling reply. "But it only refers to an imaginary child, and, by so doing, places a surprising and alarming truth before me."

"Is the matter so very serious, dad?" she asked, noticing the curious effect the words had had upon him.

"Serious!" he echoed, leaning forward in his chair. "Yes," he answered in a low voice, "it is very serious, child, both to me and to you."

"I don't understand you, dad," she exclaimed, walking to his chair throwing herself upon her knees, and placing her arms around his neck. "Won't you be more explicit? Won't you tell me the truth? Surely you can rely upon my secrecy?"

"Yes, child," he said, groping until his hand fell upon her hair, and then stroking it tenderly; "I trust you. You keep my affairs from those people who seek to obtain knowledge of them. Without you, I would be compelled to employ a secretary; but he could be bought, without a doubt. Most secretaries can."

"Ford was very trustworthy, was he not?"

"Yes, poor Ford," he sighed. "When he died I lost my right hand. But fortunately you were old enough to take his place."

"But in a case like this, when you are worried and excited, as you are at this moment, why not confide in me and allow me to help you?" she suggested. "You see that, although I act as your secretary, dad, I know nothing of the nature of your business."

"And forgive me for speaking very plainly, child, I do not intend that you should," the old man said.

"Because you cannot trust me!" she pouted. "You think that because I'm a woman I cannot keep a secret."

"Not at all," he said. "I place every confidence in you, dear. You are the only real friend left to me in the whole world. I know that you would never willingly betray me to my enemies; but -"

"Well, but what?"

"But you might do so unknowingly. You might by one single chance-word place me within the power of those who seek my downfall."

"Who seeks your downfall, dad?" she asked very seriously.

"That's a matter which I desire to keep to myself. Unfortunately, I do not know the identity of my enemies; hence I am compelled to keep from you certain matters which, in other circumstances, you might know. But," he added, "this is not the first time we've discussed this question, Gabrielle dear. You are my daughter, and I trust you. Do not, child, misjudge me by suspecting that I doubt your loyalty."

"I don't, dad; only sometimes I -"

"Sometimes you think," he said, still stroking her hair - "you think that I ought to tell you the reason I receive all these reports from Paris, and their real significance. Well, to tell the truth, dear, it is best that you should not know. If you reflect for a moment," went on the old man, tears welling slowly in his filmy, sightless eyes, "you will realise my unhappy situation - how I am compelled to hide my affairs even from Lady Heyburn herself. Does she ever question you regarding them?"

"She used to at one time; but she refrains nowadays, for I would tell her nothing."

"Has anyone else ever tried to glean information from you?" he inquired, after a long breath.

"Mr. Flockart has done so on several occasions of late. But I pleaded absolute ignorance."

"Oh, Flockart has been asking you, has he?" remarked her father with surprise. "Well, I suppose it is only natural. A blind man's doings are always more or less a mystery to the world."

"I don't like Mr. Flockart, dad," she said.

"So you've remarked before, my dear," her father replied. "Of course you are right in withholding any information upon a subject which is my own affair; yet, on the other hand, you should always remember that he is your mother's very good friend - and yours also."

"Mine!" gasped the girl, starting up. Would that she were free to tell the poor, blind, helpless man the ghastly truth! "My friend, dad! What makes you think that?"

"Because he is always singing your praises, both to me and your mother."

"Then I tell you that his expressions of opinion are false, dear dad."

"How?"

She was silent. She dared not tell her father the reason; therefore, in order to turn the subject, she replied, with a forced laugh, "Oh, well, of course, I may be mistaken; but that's my opinion."

"A mere prejudice, child; I'm sure it is. As far as I know, Flockart is quite an excellent fellow, and is most kind both to your mother and to myself."

Gabrielle's brow contracted. Disengaging herself, she rose to her feet, and, after a pause, asked, "What reply shall I send to the report, dad?"

"Ah, that report!" gasped the man, huddled up in his chair in serious reflection. "That report!" he repeated, rising to straighten himself. "Reply in these words: 'No effort is to be made to save the child's life. On the contrary, it is to be so neglected as to produce a fatal termination.'"

The girl had seated herself at the typewriter and rapidly clicked out the words in French - words that seemed ominous enough, and yet the true meaning of which she never dreamed. She was thinking only of her father's misplaced friendship in James Flockart. If she dared to tell him the naked truth! Oh, if her poor, blind, afflicted father could only see!

William Le Queux

CHAPTER X

DECLARES A WOMAN'S LOVE

At nine o'clock that night Gabrielle left her father, and ascended to her own pretty room, with its light chintz-covered furniture, its well-filled bamboo bookcases, its little writing-table, and its narrow bed in the alcove. It was a nest of rest and cosy comfort.

Exchanging her tweed dress, she put on an easy dressing-gown of pale blue cashmere, drew up an armchair, and, arranging her electric reading-lamp, sat down to a new novel she intended to finish.

Presently Elise came to her; but, looking up, she said she did not wish to be disturbed, and again coiled herself up in the chair, endeavouring to concentrate her thoughts upon her book. But all to no purpose. Ever and anon she would lift her big eyes from the printed page, sigh, and stare fixedly at the rose-coloured trellis pattern of the wall-paper opposite. Upon her there had fallen a feeling of vague apprehension such as she had never before experienced, a feeling that something was about to happen.

Lady Heyburn was, she knew, greatly annoyed that she had not made her appearance at dinner or in the drawing-room afterwards. Generally, when there were guests from the neighbourhood, she was compelled to sing one or other of her Italian songs. Her refusal to come to dinner would, she knew, cause her ladyship much chagrin, for it showed plainly to the guests that her authority over her step-daughter was entirely at an end.

Just as the stable-clock chimed half-past ten there came a light tap at the door. It was Hill, who, on receiving permission to enter, said, "If you please, miss, Mr. Murie has just asked me to give you this"; and he handed her an envelope.

Tearing it open eagerly, she found a visiting-card, upon which some words were scribbled in pencil. For a moment after reading them she paused. Then she said, "Tell Mr. Murie it will be all right."

"Very well, miss," the man replied, and, bowing, closed the door.

For a few moments she stood motionless in the centre of the room, her lover's card still in her hand. Then she walked to the open window, and looked out into the hot, oppressive night. The moon was hidden behind dark clouds, and the stillness was precursory of the thunderstorm which for the past hour or so had threatened. Across the room she paced slowly several times, a deep, anxious expression upon her pale countenance; then slowly she slipped off her gown and put on a dark stuff dress.

Until the clock had struck eleven she waited. Then, assuming her tam-o'-shanter and twisting a silk scarf about her neck, she crept along the corridor and down the wide oak stairs. Lights were still burning; but without detection she slipped out by the main door, and, crossing the broad drive, took the winding path into the woods.

The guests had all left, and the servants were closing the house for the night. Scarce had she gone a hundred yards when a dark figure in overcoat and a golf-cap loomed up before her, and she found Walter at her side.

William Le Queux

"Why, dearest!" he exclaimed, taking her hand and bending till he pressed it to his lips, "I began to fear you wouldn't come. Why haven't I seen you to-night?"

"Because - well, because I had a bad headache," was her lame reply. "I knew that if I went in to dinner mother would want me to sing, and I really didn't feel up to it. I hope, however, you haven't been bored too much."

"You know I have!" he said quickly in a low, earnest voice. "I came here purposely to see you, and you were invisible. I've run the car down the farm-road on the other side of the park, and left it there. The mater went home in the carriage nearly an hour ago. She's afraid to go in the car when I drive."

Slowly they strolled together along the dark path, he with her arm held tenderly under his own.

"Think, darling," he said, "I haven't seen you for four whole days! Why is it? Yesterday I went to the usual spot at the end of the glen, and waited nearly two hours; but you did not come, although you promised me, you know. Why are you so indifferent, dearest?" he asked in a plaintive tone. "I can't really make you out of late."

"I'm not indifferent at all, Walter," she declared. "My father has very much to attend to just now, and I'm compelled to assist him, as you are well aware. He's so utterly helpless."

"Oh, but you might spare me just half-an-hour sometimes," he said in a slight tone of reproach.

"I do. Why, we surely see each other very often!"

"Not often enough for me, Gabrielle," he declared, halting in the darkness and raising her soft little hand to his eager lips. "You know well enough how fondly I love you, how -"

"I know," she said in a sad, blank tone. Her own heart beat fast at his passionate words.

"Then why do you treat me like this?" he asked. "Is it because I have annoyed you, that you perhaps think I am not keeping faith with you? I know I was absent a long time, but it was really not my own fault. My people made me go round the world. I didn't want to, I assure you. I'd far rather have been up here at Connachan all the time, and near you, my own well-beloved."

"I believe you would, Walter," she answered, turning towards him with her hand upon his shoulder. "But I do wish you wouldn't reproach me for my undemonstrativeness each time we meet. It saddens me."

"I know I ought not to reproach you," he hastened to assure her. "I have no right to do so; but somehow you have of late grown so sphinx-like that you are not the Gabrielle I used to know."

"Why not?" And she laughed, a strange, hollow laugh. "Explain yourself."

"In the days gone by, before I went abroad, you were not so particular about our meetings being clandestine. You did not care who saw us or what people might say."

"I was a girl then. I have now learnt wisdom, and the truth of the modern religion which holds that the only sin is that of being found out."

"But why are you so secret in all your actions?" he demanded. "Whom do you fear?"

"Fear!" she echoed, starting and staring in his direction. "Why, I fear nobody! What - what makes you think that?"

"Because it has lately struck me that you meet me in secret because - well, because you are afraid of someone, or do not wish us to be seen."

"Why, how very foolish!" she laughed. "Don't my father and mother both know that we love each other? Besides, I am surely my own mistress. I would never marry a man I don't love," she added in a tone of quiet defiance.

"And am I to take it that you really do love me, after all?" he inquired very earnestly.

"Why, of course," she replied without hesitation, again placing her arm about his neck and kissing him. "How foolish of you to ask such a question, Walter! When will you be convinced that the answer I gave you long ago was the actual truth?"

"Men who love as fervently as I do are apt to be somewhat foolish," he declared.

"Then don't be foolish any longer," she urged in a matter-of-fact voice, lifting her lips to his and kissing him. "You know I love you, Walter; therefore you should also know that it I avoid you in public I have some good reason for doing so."

"A reason!" he cried. "What reason? Tell me."

She shook her head. "That is my own affair," she responded. "I repeat again that my affection for you is undiminished, if such repetition really pleases you, as it seems to do."

"Of course it pleases me, dearest," he declared. "No words are sweeter to my ears than the declaration of your love. My only regret is that, now I am at home again, I do not see so much of you, sweetheart, as I had anticipated."

"Walter," she exclaimed in a slow, changed voice, after a brief silence, "there is a reason. Please do not ask me to tell you - because - well, because I can't." And, drawing a long breath, she added, "All I beg of you is to remain patient and trust in me. I love you; and I love no other man. Surely that should be, for you, all-sufficient. I am yours, and yours only."

In an instant he had folded her slight, dainty form in his arms. The young man was satisfied, perfectly satisfied.

They strolled on together through the wood, and out across the open corn-fields. The moon had come forth again, the storm-clouds had passed, and the night was perfect. Though she was trying against her will to hold aloof from Walter Murie, yet she loved him with all her heart and soul. Many letters she had addressed to him in his travels had remained unanswered. This had, in a measure, piqued her. But she was in ignorance that much of his correspondence and hers had fallen into the hands of her ladyship and been destroyed.

As they walked on, talking as lovers will, she was thinking deeply, and full of regret that she dared not tell the truth to this man who, loving her so fondly, would, she knew, be prepared to make any sacrifice for her sake. Suppose he knew the truth! Whatever sacrifice he made would, alas! not alter facts. If she confessed, he would only hate her. Ah, the tragedy of it all! Therefore she held her silence; she dared not speak lest she might lose his love. She had no friend in whom she could confide. From her own father, even, she was compelled to hide the actual facts. They were too terrible. What would he think if the bitter truth were exposed?

The man at her side, tall, brave, strong - a lover whom she knew many girls coveted - believed that he was to marry her. But, she told herself within her grief-stricken heart, such a thing could never be. A barrier stood between them, invisible, yet nevertheless one that might for ever debar their mutual happiness.

An involuntary sigh escaped her, and he inquired the reason. She excused herself by saying that it was owing to the exertion of walking over the rough path. Therefore they halted, and, with the bright summer moonbeams falling upon her beautiful countenance, he kissed her passionately upon the lips again and yet again.

They remained together for over an hour, moving along slowly, heedless of where their footsteps led them; heedless, too, of being seen by any of the keepers who, at night, usually patrolled the estate. Their walk, however, lay at the farther end of the glen, in the coverts remote from the house and nearer the high-road; therefore there was but little danger of being observed.

Many were the pledges of affection they exchanged before parting. On Walter's part they were fervent and passionate, but on the part of his idol they were, alas! only the pretence of a happiness which she feared could never be permanent.

Presently they retraced their steps to the edge of the wood beyond which lay the house. They found the path, and there, at her request, he left her. It was not wise that he should approach the house at that hour, she urged.

So, after a long and fervent leave-taking, he held her in a last embrace, and then, raising his cap, and saying, "Good-night, my darling, my own well-beloved!" he turned away and went at a swinging pace down the farm-road where he had left his car with lights extinguished.

She watched him disappear. Then, sighing, she turned into the dark, winding path beneath the trees, the end of which came out upon the drive close to the house.

Half-way down, however, with sudden resolve, she took a narrower path to the left, and was soon on the outskirts of the wood and out again in the bright moonlight.

The night was so glorious that she had resolved to stroll alone, to think and devise some plan for the future. Before her, silhouetted high against the steely sky, rose the two great, black, ivy-clad towers of the ancient castle. The grim, crumbling walls stood dark and frowning amid the fairy-like scene, while from far below came up the faint rippling of the Ruthven Water. A great owl flapped lazily from the ivy as she approached those historic old walls which in bygone days had held within them some of Scotland's greatest men. She had explored and knew every nook and cranny in those extensive ruins. With Walter's assistance, she had once made a perilous ascent to the top of the highest of the two square towers, and had often clambered along the broken walls of the keep or descended into those strange little subterranean chambers, now half-choked with earth and rubbish, which tradition declared were the dungeons in which prisoners in the old days had been put to the rack, seared with red-hot irons, or submitted to other horrible tortures.

Her feet falling noiselessly, she entered the grass-grown courtyard, where stood the ancient spreading yew, the "dule-tree," under which the Glencardine charters had been signed and justice administered. Other big trees had sprung from seedlings since the place had fallen into ruin; and, having entered, she paused amidst its weird, impressive silence. Those high, ponderous walls about her spoke mutely of strength and impregnability. Those grass-grown mounds hid ruined walls and broken foundations. What tales of wild lawlessness and reckless bloodshed they all could tell!

Many of the strange stories she had heard concerning the old place - stories told by the people in the neighbourhood - were recalled as she stood there gazing wonderingly about her. Many romantic legends had, indeed, been handed down in Perthshire from generation to generation concerning old Glencardine and its lawless masters, and for her they had always possessed a strange fascination, for had she not inherited the antiquarian tastes of her father, and had she not read many works upon folklore and such-like subjects.

Suddenly, while standing in the deep shadow, gazing thoughtfully up at those high towers which, though ruined, still guarded the end of the glen, a strange thing occurred - something which startled her, causing her to halt breathless,

William Le Queux

petrified, rooted to the spot. She stared straight before her. Something uncanny was happening there, something that was, indeed, beyond human credence, and quite inexplicable.

CHAPTER XI

CONCERNS THE WHISPERS

What had startled Gabrielle was certainly extraordinary and decidedly uncanny. She was standing near the southern wall, when, of a sudden, she heard low but distinct whispers. Again she listened. Yes. The sounds were not due to her excited imagination at the recollection of those romantic traditions of love and hatred, or of those gruesome stories of how the Wolf of Badenoch had been kept prisoner there for five years and put to frightful tortures, or how the Laird of Weem was deliberately poisoned in that old banqueting-hall, the huge open fireplace of which still existed near where she stood.

There was the distinct sound of low, whispered words! She held her breath to listen. She tried to distinguish what the words were, but in vain. Then she endeavoured to determine whence they emanated, but was unable to do so. Again they sounded - again - and yet again. Then there was another voice, still low, still whispering, but not quite so deep as the first. It sounded like a woman's.

Local tradition had it that the place held the ghosts of those who had died in agony within its noisome dungeons; but she had always been far too matter-of-fact to accept stories of the supernatural. Yet at that moment her ears did not deceive her. That pile of grim, gaunt ruins was a House of Whispers!

Again she listened, never moving a muscle. An owl hooted

William Le Queux

weirdly in the ivy far above her, while near, at her feet, a rabbit scuttled away through the grass. Such noises she was used to. She knew every night-sound of the country-side; for when she had finished her work in the library she often went, unknown to the household, with Stewart upon his nocturnal rounds, and walked miles through the woods in the night. The grey-eyed, thin-nosed head-keeper was her particular favourite. He knew so much of natural history, and he taught her all he knew. She could distinguish the cries of birds in the night, and could tell by certain sounds made by them, as they were disturbed, that no other intruders were in the vicinity. But that weird whispering, coming as it did from an undiscovered source, was inhuman and utterly uncanny.

Was it possible that her ears had deceived her? Was it one of the omens believed in by the superstitious? The wall whence the voices appeared to emanate was, she knew, about seven feet thick - an outer wall of the old keep. She was aware of this because in one of the folio tomes in the library was a picture of the castle as it appeared in 1510, taken from some manuscript of that period preserved in the British Museum. She, who had explored the ruins dozens of times, knew well that at the point where she was standing there could be no place of concealment. Beyond that wall, the hill, covered with bushes and brushwood, descended sheer for three hundred feet or so to the bottom of the glen. Had the voices sounded from one or other of the half-choked chambers which remained more or less intact she would not have been so puzzled; but, as it was, the weird whisperings seemed to come forth from space. Sometimes they sounded so low that she could scarcely hear them; at others they were so loud that she could almost distinguish the words uttered by the unseen. Was it merely a phenomenon caused by the wind blowing through some crack in the ponderous lichen-covered wall?

She looked beyond at the great dark yew, the justice-tree of the Grahams. The night was perfectly calm. Not a leaf stirred either upon that or upon the other trees. The ivy, high above and exposed to the slightest breath of a breeze, was motionless;

only the going and coming of the night-birds moved it. No. She decided once and for all that the noise was that of voices, spectral voices though they might be.

Again she strained her eyes, when still again those soft, sibilant whisperings sounded weird and quite inexplicable.

Slowly, and with greatest caution, she moved along beneath the wall, but as she did so she seemed to recede from the sound. So back she went to the spot where she had previously stood, and there again remained listening.

There were two distinct voices; at least that was the conclusion at which she arrived after nearly a quarter of an hour of most minute investigation.

Once she fancied, in her excitement, that away in the farther corner of the ruined courtyard she saw a slowly moving form like a thin column of mist. Was it the Lady of Glencardine - the apparition of the hapless Lady Jane Glencardine? But on closer inspection she decided that it was merely due to her own distorted imagination, and dismissed it from her mind.

Those low, curious whisperings alone puzzled her. They were certainly not sounds that could be made by any rodents within the walls, because they were voices, distinctly and indisputably *voices*, which at some moments were raised in argument, and then fell away into sounds of indistinct murmuring. Whence did they come? She again moved noiselessly from place to place, at length deciding that only at one point - the point where she had first stood - could the sounds be heard distinctly. So to that spot once more the girl returned, standing there like a statue, her ears strained for every sound, waiting and wondering. But the Whispers had now ceased. In the distance the stable-clock chimed two. Yet she remained at her post, determined to solve the mystery, and not in the least afraid of those weird stories which the country-folk in the Highlands so entirely believed. No ghost, of whatever form, could frighten her, she told herself. She had never believed in omens or superstitions, and she steeled herself not to believe in them now. So she remained there in patience, seeking some natural solution of the extraordinary enigma.

But though she waited until the chimes rang out three o'clock and the moon was going down, she heard no other sound. The Whispers had suddenly ended, and the silence of those gaunt, frowning old walls was undisturbed. A slight wind had now sprung up, sweeping across the hills, and causing her to feel chill. Therefore, at last she was reluctantly compelled to quit her post of observation, and retrace her steps by the rough byroad to the house, entering by one of the windows of the morning-room, of which the burglar-alarm was broken, and which on many occasions she had unfastened after her nocturnal rambles with Stewart. Indeed, concealed under the walls she kept an old rusted table-knife, and by its aid it was her habit to push back the catch and so gain entrance, after reconcealing the knife for use on a future occasion.

On reaching her own room she stood for a few moments reflecting deeply upon her remarkable and inexplicable discovery. Had the story of those whisperings been told to her she would certainly have scouted them; but she had heard them with her own ears, and was certain that she had not been deceived. It was a mystery, absolute and complete; and, regarding it as such, she retired to bed.

But her thoughts were very naturally full of the weird story told of the dead and gone owners of Glencardine. She recollected that horrible story of the Ghaist of Manse and of the spectre of Bridgend. In the library she had, a year ago, discovered a strange old book - one which sixty years before had been in universal circulation - entitled *Satan's Invisible World Discovered*, and she had read it from beginning to end. This book had, perhaps, more influence upon the simple-minded country people in Scotland than any other work. It consisted entirely of relations of ghosts of murdered persons, witches, warlocks, and fairies; and as it was read as an indoor amusement in the presence of children, and followed up by unfounded tales of the same description, the youngsters were afraid to turn round in case they might be grasped by the "Old One." So strong, indeed, became this impression that even grown-up people would not venture, through fear, into another room or down a stair after nightfall.

Her experience in the old castle had, to say the least, been remarkable. Those weird whisperings were extraordinary. For hours she lay reflecting upon the many traditions of the old place, some recorded in the historic notices of the House of the Montrose, and others which had gathered from local sources - the farmers of the neighbourhood, the keepers, and servants. Those noises in the night were mysterious and puzzling.

Next morning she went alone to the kennels to find Stewart and to question him. He had told her many weird stories and traditions of the old place, and it struck her that he might be able to furnish her with some information regarding her strange discovery. Had anyone else heard those Whispers besides herself, she wondered.

She met several of the guests, but assiduously avoided them, until at last she saw the thin, long-legged keeper going towards his cottage with Dash, the faithful old spaniel, at his heels.

When she hailed him he touched his cap respectfully, changed his gun to the other arm, and wished her "Guid-mornin', Miss Gabrielle," in his strong Scotch accent.

She bade him put down his gun and walk with her up the hill towards the ruins.

"Look here, Stewart," she commanded in a confidential tone, "I'm going to take you into my confidence. I know I can trust you with a secret."

"Ye may, miss," replied the keen-eyed Scot. "I houp Sir Henry trusts me as a faithfu' servant. I've been on Glencardine estate noo, miss, thae forty year."

"Stewart, we all know you are faithful, and that you can keep your tongue still. What I'm about to tell you is in strictest confidence. Not even my father knows it."

"Ah! then it's a secret e'en frae the laird, eh?"

"Yes," she replied. "I want you to come up to the old castle with me," pointing to the great ruined pile standing boldly in the summer sunlight, "and I want you to tell me all you know. I've had a very uncanny experience there."

"What, miss!" exclaimed the man, halting and looking her seriously in the face; "ha'e ye seen the ghaist?"

"No, I haven't seen any ghost," replied the girl; "but last night I heard most extraordinary sounds, as though people were within the old walls."

"Guid sake, miss! an' ha'e ye actually h'ard the Whispers?" he gasped.

"Then other people have heard them, eh?" inquired the girl quickly. "Tell me all you know about the matter, Stewart."

"A'?" he said, slowly shaking his head. "I ken but a wee bittie aboot the noises."

"Who has heard them besides myself?"

"Maxwell o'Tullichuil's girl. She said she h'ard the Whispers ae nicht aboot a year syne. They're a bad omen, miss, for the lassie deed sudden a fortnicht later."

"Did anyone else hear them?"

"Auld Willie Buchan, wha lived doon in Auchterarder village, declared that ae nicht, while poachin' for rabbits, he h'ard the voices. He telt the doctor sae when he lay in bed a-deein' aboot three weeks aifterwards. Ay, miss, I'm sair sorry ye've h'ard the Whispers."

"Then they're regarded as a bad omen to those who overhear them?" she remarked.

"That's sae. There's bin ithers wha acted as eavesdroppers, an' they a' deed very sune aifterwards. There was Jean Kirkwood an' Geordie Menteith. The latter was a young keeper I had here aboot a year syne. He cam' tae me ae mornin' an' said that while lyin' up for poachers the nicht afore, he distinc'ly h'ard the Whispers. Kennin' what folk say aboot the owerhearin' o' them bein' fatal, I lauched at 'im an' told 'im no' to tak' ony tent o' auld wives' gossip. But, miss, sure enough, within a week he got blood-pizinin', an', though they took 'im to the hospital in Perth, he deed."

"Then popular superstition points to the fact that anyone who accidentally acts as eavesdropper is doomed to death, eh? A very nice outlook for me!" she remarked.

"Oh, Miss Gabrielle!" exclaimed the man, greatly concerned, "dinna treat the maitter lichtly, I beg o' ye. I did, wi' puir Menteith, an' he deed juist like the ithers."

"But what does it all mean?" asked the daughter of the house in a calm, matter-of-fact voice. She knew well that Stewart was just as superstitious as any of his class, for some of the stories he had told her had been most fearful and wonderful elaborations of historical fact.

"It means, I'm fear'd, miss," he replied, "that the Whispers which come frae naewhere are fore-warnin's o' daith."

CHAPTER XII

EXPLAINS SOME CURIOUS FACTS

Gabrielle was silent for a moment. No doubt Stewart meant what he said; he was not endeavouring to alarm her unduly, but thoroughly believed in supernatural agencies. "I suppose you've already examined the ruins thoroughly, eh?" she asked at last.

"Examined them?" echoed the gray-bearded man. "I should think sae, aifter forty-odd years here. Why, as a laddie I used to play there ilka day, an' ha'e been in ilka neuk an' cranny."

"Nevertheless, come up now with me," she said. "I want to explain to you exactly where and how I heard the voices."

"The Whispers are an uncanny thing," said the keeper, with his broad accent. "I dinna like them, miss; I dinna like tae hear what ye tell me ava."

"Oh, don't worry about me, Stewart," she laughed. "I'm not afraid of any omen. I only mean to fathom the mystery, and I want your assistance in doing so. But, of course, you'll say no word to a soul. Remember that."

"If it be yer wush, Miss Gabrielle, I'll say naething," he promised. And together they descended the steep grass-slope and overgrown foundations of the castle until they stood in the old courtyard, close to the ancient justice-tree, the exact spot where the girl had stood on the previous night.

"I could hear plainly as I stood just here," she said. "The sound of voices seemed to come from that wall there"; and she pointed to the gray flint wall, half-overgrown with ivy, about six yards away.

Stewart made no remark. It was not the first occasion on which he had examined that place in an attempt to solve the mystery of the nocturnal whisperings. He walked across to the wall, tapping it with his hand, while the faithful spaniel began sniffing in expectancy of something to bolt. "There's naething here, miss - absolutely naething," he declared, as they both examined the wall minutely. Its depth did not admit of any chamber, for it was an inner wall; and, according to the gamekeeper's statement, he had already tested it years ago, and found it solid masonry.

"If I went forward or backward, then the sounds were lost to me," Gabrielle explained, much puzzled.

"Ay. That's juist what they a' said," remarked the keeper, with an apprehensive look upon his face. "The Whispers are only h'ard at ae spot, whaur ye've juist stood. I've seen the lady a' in green masel', miss - aince when I was a laddie, an' again aboot ten year syne."

"You mean, Stewart, that you imagined that you saw an apparition. You were alone, I suppose?"

"Yes, miss, I was alane."

"Well, you thought you saw the Lady of Glencardine. Where was she?"

"On the drive, in front o' the hoose."

"Perhaps somebody played a practical joke on you. The Green Lady is Glencardine's favourite spectre, isn't she - perfectly harmless, I mean?"

"Ay, miss. Lots o' folk saw her ten year syne. But nooadays she seems to ha'e been laid. Somebody said they saw her last Glesca holidays, but I dinna believe 't."

"Neither do I, Stewart. But don't let's trouble about the unfortunate lady, who ought to have been at rest long ago. It's those weird whisperings I mean to investigate." And she looked blankly around her at the great, cyclopean walls and high, weather-beaten towers, gaunt yet picturesque in the morning sunshine.

The keeper shook his shaggy head. "I'm afear'd, Miss Gabrielle, that ye'll ne'er solve the mystery. There's somethin' sae fatal aboot the whisperin's," he said, speaking in his pleasant Highland tongue, "that naebody cares tae attempt the investigation. They div say that the Whispers are the voice o' the De'il himsel'."

The girl, in her short blue serge skirt, white cotton blouse, and blue tam-o'-shanter, laughed at the man's dread. There must be a distinct cause for this noise she had heard, she argued. Yet, though they both spent half-an-hour wandering among the ruins, standing in the roofless banqueting hall, and traversing stone corridors and lichen-covered, moss-grown, ruined chambers choked with weeds, their efforts to obtain any clue were all in vain.

To Gabrielle it was quite evident that the old keeper regarded the incident of the previous night as a fatal omen, for he was most solicitous of her welfare. He went so far as to crave permission to go to Sir Henry and put the whole of the mysterious facts before him.

But she would not hear of it. She meant to solve the mystery herself. If her father learnt of the affair, and of the ill-omen connected with it, the matter would surely cause him great uneasiness. Why should he be worried on her account? No, she would never allow it, and told Stewart plainly of her disapproval of such a course.

"But, tell me," she asked at last, as returning to the courtyard, they stood together at the spot where she had stood in that moonlit hour and heard with her own ears those weird, mysterious voices coming from nowhere - "tell me, Stewart, is there any legend connected with the Whispers? Have you ever heard any story concerning their origin?"

"Of coorse, miss. Through all Perthshire it's weel kent," replied the man slowly, not, it seemed, without considerable reluctance. "What is h'ard by those doomed tae daith is the conspiracy o' Charles Lord Glencardine an' the Earl o' Kintyre for the murder o' the infamous Cardinal Setoun o' St. Andrews, wha, as I dare say ye ken fra history, miss, was assassinated here, on this very spot whaur we stan'. The Earl o' Kintyre, thegither wi' Lord Glencardine, his dochter Mary, an' ane o' the M'Intyres o' Talnetry, an' Wemyss o' Strathblane, were a year later tried by a commission issued under the name o' Mary Queen o' Scots; but sae popular was the murder o' the Cardinal that the accused were acquitted."

"Yes," exclaimed the girl, "I remember reading something about it in Scottish history. And the Whispers are, I suppose, said to be the ghostly conspirators in conclave."

"That's what folk say, miss. They div say as weel that Auld Nick himsel' was present, an' gied the decision that the Cardinal, wha was to be askit ower frae Stirlin', should dee. It is his evil counsel that is h'ard by those whom death will quickly overtake."

"Really, Stewart," she laughed, "you make me feel quite uncomfortable."

"But, miss, Sir Henry already kens a' aboot the Whispers," said the man. "I h'ard him tellin' a young gentleman wha cam' doon last shootin' season a guid dale aboot it. They veesited the auld castle thegither, an' I happened tae be hereaboots."

This caused the girl to resolve to learn from her father what she could. He was an antiquary, and had the history of Glencardine at his finger-ends.

So presently she strolled back to Stewart's cottage, and after receiving from the faithful servant urgent injunctions to "have a care" of herself, she walked on to the tennis-lawn, where, shaded by the high trees, Lady Heyburn, in white serge, and three of her male guests were playing.

"Father," she said that same evening, when they had settled down to commence work upon those ever-arriving documents from Paris, "what was the cause of Glencardine becoming a ruin?"

"Well, the reason of its downfall was Lord Glencardine's change of front," he answered. "In 1638 he became a stalwart supporter of Episcopacy and Divine Right, a course which proved equally fatal to himself and to his ancient Castle of Glencardine. Reid, in his *Annals of Auchterarder*, relates how, after the Civil War, Lord Dundrennan, in company with his cousin, George Lochan of Ochiltree, and burgess of Auchterarder and the Laird of M'Nab, descended into Strathearn and occupied the castle with about fifty men. He hurriedly put it into a state of defence. General Overton besieged the place in person, with his army, consisting of eighteen hundred foot and eleven hundred horse, and battered the walls with cannon, having brought a number of great ordnance from Stirling Castle. For ten days the castle was held by the small but resolute garrison, and might have held out longer had not the well failed. With the prospect of death before them in the event of the place being taken, Dundrennan and Lochan contrived to break through the enemy, who surrounded the castle on all sides. A page of the name of John Hamilton, in attendance upon Lord Dundrennan, well acquainted with the localities of Glencardine, undertook to be their guide. When the moon was down, Dundrennan and Lochan issued from the castle by a small postern, where they found Hamilton waiting for them with three horses. They mounted, and, passing quietly through the enemy's force, they escaped, and reached Lord Glencardine in safety to the north. On the morning after their escape the castle was surrendered, and thirty-five of the garrison were sent to the Tolbooth of Edinburgh. General Overton ordered the remaining twelve of those who had surrendered to be shot at a post, and the castle to be burned, which was accordingly done."

"The country-folk in the neighbourhood are full of strange stories about ghostly whisperings being heard in the castle ruins," she remarked.

Her father started, and raising his expressionless face to hers, asked in almost a snappish tone, "Well, and who has heard them now, pray?"

"Several people, I believe."

"And they're gossiping as usual, eh?" he remarked in a hard, dry tone. "Up here in the Highlands they are ridiculously superstitious. Who's been telling you about the Whispers, child?"

"Oh, I've learnt of them from several people," she replied evasively. "Mysterious voices were heard, they say, last night, and for several nights previously. It's also a local tradition that all those who hear the whispered warning die within forty days."

"Bosh, my dear! utter rubbish!" the old man laughed. "Who's been trying to frighten you?"

"Nobody, dad. I merely tell you what the country people say."

"Yes," he remarked, "I know. The story is a gruesome one, and in the Highlands a story is not attractive unless it has some fatality in it. Up here the belief in demonology and witchcraft has died very hard. Get down Penny's *Traditions of Perth* - first

William Le Queux

shelf to the left beyond the second window, right-hand corner. It will explain to you how very superstitious the people have ever been."

"I know all that, dad," persisted the girl; "but I'm interested in this extraordinary story of the Whispers. You, as an antiquary, have, no doubt, investigated all the legendary lore connected with Glencardine. The people declare that the Whispers are heard, and, I am told, believe some extraordinary theory regarding them."

"A theory!" he exclaimed quickly. "What theory? What has been discovered?"

"Nothing, as far as I know."

"No, and nothing ever will be discovered," he said.

"Why not, dad?" she asked. "Do you deny that strange noises are heard there when there is so much evidence in the affirmative?"

"I really don't know, my dear. I've never had the pleasure of hearing them myself, though I've been told of them ever since I bought the place."

"But there is a legend which is supposed to account for them, is there not, dad? Do tell me what you know," she urged. "I'm so very much interested in the old place and its bygone history."

"The less you know concerning the Whispers the better, my dear," he replied abruptly.

Her father's ominous words surprised her. Did he, too, believe in the fatal omen, though he was trying to mislead her and poke fun at the local superstition?

"But why shouldn't I know?" she protested. "This is the first time, dad, that you've tried to withhold from me any antiquarian knowledge that you possess. Besides, the story of Glencardine and its lords is intensely fascinating to me."

"So might be the Whispers, if ever you had the misfortune to hear them."

"Misfortune!" she gasped, turning pale. "Why do you say misfortune?"

But he laughed a strange, hollow laugh, and, endeavouring to turn his seriousness into humour, said, "Well, they might give you a turn, perhaps. They would make me start, I feel sure. From what I've been told, they seem to come from nowhere. It is practically an unseen spectre who has the rather unusual gift of speech."

It was on the tip of her tongue to explain how, on the previous night, she had actually listened to the Whispers. But she refrained. She recognised that, though he would not admit it, he was nevertheless superstitious of ill results following the hearing of those weird whisperings. So she made eager pretence of wishing to know the historical facts of the incident referred to by the gamekeeper.

"No," exclaimed the blind man softly but firmly, taking her hand and stroking her arm tenderly, as was his habit when he wished to persuade her. "No, Gabrielle dear," he said; "we will change the subject now. Do not bother your head about absurd country legends of that sort. There are so many concerning Glencardine and its lords that a whole volume might be filled with them."

"But I want to know all about this particular one, dad," she said.

"From me you will never know, my dear," was his answer, as his gray, serious face was upturned to hers. "You have never heard the Whispers, and I sincerely hope that you never will."

CHAPTER XIII

WHAT FLOCKART FORESAW

The following afternoon was glaring and breathless. Gabrielle had taken Stokes, with May Spencer (a girl friend visiting her mother), and driven the "sixteen" over to Connachan with a message from her mother - an invitation to Lady Murie and her party to luncheon and tennis on the following day. It was three o'clock, the hour when silence is upon a summer house-party in the country. Beneath the blazing sun Glencardine lay amid its rose-gardens, its cut beech-hedges, and its bowers of greenery. The palpitating heat was terrible - the hottest day that summer.

At the end of the long, handsome drawing-room, with its pale blue carpet and silk-covered furniture, Lady Heyburn was lolling lazily in her chair near the wide, bright steel grate, with her inseparable friend, James Flockart, standing before her.

The striped blinds outside the three long, open windows subdued the sun-glare, yet the very odour of the cut flowers in the room seemed oppressive, while without could be heard the busy hum of insect life.

The Baronet's handsome wife looked cool and comfortable in her gown of white embroidered muslin, her head thrown back upon the silken cushion, and her eyes raised to those of the man, who was idly smoking a cigarette, at her side.

"The thing grows more and more inexplicable," he was saying to her in a low, strained voice. "All the inquiries I've caused to be made in London and in Paris have led to a negative result."

"We shall only know the truth when we get a peep of those papers in Henry's safe, my dear friend," was the woman's reply.

"And that's a pretty difficult job. You don't know where the old fellow keeps the key?"

"I only wish I did. Gabrielle knows, no doubt."

"Then you ought to compel her to divulge," he urged. "Once we get hold of that key for half-an-hour, we could learn a lot."

"A lot that would be useful to you, eh?" remarked the woman, with a meaning smile.

"And to you also," he said. "Couldn't we somehow watch and see where he hides the safe-key? He never has it upon him, you say."

"It isn't on his bunch."

"Then he must have a hiding-place for it, or it may be on his watch-chain," remarked the man decisively. "Get rid of all the guests as quickly as you can, Winnie. While they're about there's always a danger of eavesdroppers and of watchers."

"I've already announced that I'm going up to Inverness next week, so within the next day or two our friends will all leave."

"Good! Then the ground will be cleared for action," he remarked, blowing a cloud of smoke from his lips. "What's your decision regarding the girl?"

"The same as yours."

"But she hates me, you know," laughed the man in gray flannel.

"Yes; but she fears you at the same time, and with her you can do more by fear than by love."

"True. But she's got a spirit of her own, recollect."

"That must be broken."

"And what about Walter?"

"Oh, as soon as he finds out the truth he'll drop her, never fear. He's already rather fond of that tall, dark girl of Dundas's. You saw her at the ball. You recollect her?"

Flockart grunted. He was assisting this woman at his side to play a desperate game. This was not, however, the first occasion on which they had acted in conjunction in matters that were not altogether honourable. There had never been any question of affection between them. The pair regarded each other from a purely business standpoint. People might gossip as much as ever they liked; but the two always congratulated themselves that they had never committed the supreme folly of falling in love with each other. The woman had married Sir Henry merely in order to obtain money and position; and this man Flockart, who for years had been her most intimate associate, had ever remained behind her, to advise and to help her.

Perhaps had the Baronet not been afflicted he would have disapproved of this constant companionship, for he would, no doubt, have overheard in society certain tittle-tattle which, though utterly unfounded, would not have been exactly pleasant. But as he was blind and never went into society, he remained in blissful ignorance, wrapped up in his mysterious "business" and his hobbies.

Gabrielle, on her return from school, had at first accepted

Flockart as her friend. It was he who took her for walks, who taught her to cast a fly, to shoot rooks, and to play the national winter game of Scotland - curling. He had in the first few months of her return home done everything in his power to attract the young girl's friendship, while at the same time her ladyship showed herself extraordinarily well disposed towards her.

Within a year, however, by reason of various remarks made by people in her presence, and on account of the cold disdain with which Lady Heyburn treated her afflicted father, vague suspicions were aroused within her, suspicions which gradually grew to hatred, until she clung to her father, and, as his eyes and ears, took up a position of open defiance towards her mother and her adventurous friend.

The situation each day grew more and more strained. Lady Heyburn was, even though of humble origin, a woman of unusual intelligence. In various quarters she had been snubbed and ridiculed, but she gradually managed in every case to get the better of her enemies. Many a man and many a woman had had bitter cause to repent their enmity towards her. They marvelled how their secrets became known to her.

They did not know the power behind her - the sinister power of that ingenious and unscrupulous man, James Flockart - the man who made it his business to know other people's secrets. Though for years he had been seized with a desire to get at the bottom of Sir Henry's private affairs, he had never succeeded. The old Baronet was essentially a recluse; he kept himself so much to himself, and was so careful that no eyes save those of his daughter should see the mysterious documents which came to him so regularly by registered post, that all Flockart's efforts and those of Lady Heyburn had been futile.

"I had another good look at the safe this morning," the man went on presently. "It is one of the best makes, and would resist anything, except, of course, the electric current."

"To force it would be to put Henry on his guard," Lady Heyburn remarked, "If we are to know what secrets are there, and use our knowledge for our own benefit, we must open it with a key and relock it."

"Well, Winnie, we must do something. We must both have money - that's quite evident," he said. "That last five hundred you gave me will stave off ruin for a week or so. But after that we must certainly be well supplied, or else there may be revelations well - which will be as ugly for yourself as for me."

"I know," she exclaimed. "I fully realise the necessity of getting funds. The other affair, though we worked it so well, proved a miserable fiasco."

"And very nearly gave us away into the bargain," he declared. "I tell you frankly, Winnie, that if we can't pay a level five thousand in three weeks' time the truth will be out, and you know what that will mean."

He was watching her handsome face as he spoke, and he noticed how pale and drawn were her features as he referred to certain ugly truths that might leak out.

"Yes," she gasped, "I know, James. We'd both find ourselves under arrest. Such a *contretemps* is really too terrible to think of."

"But, my dear girl, it must be faced," he said, "if we don't get the money. Can't you work Sir Henry for a bit more, say another thousand. Make an excuse that you have bills to pay in London - dressmakers, jewellers, milliners - any good story will surely do. He gives you anything you ask for."

She shook her head and sighed. "I fear I've imposed upon his good-nature far too much already," she answered. "I know I'm extravagant; I'm sorry, but can't help it. Born in me, I suppose. A few months ago he found out that I'd been paying Mellish a hundred pounds each time to decorate Park Street with flowers for my Wednesday evenings, and he created an awful scene. He's getting horribly stingy of late."

"Yes; but the flowers were a bit expensive, weren't they?" he remarked.

"Not at all. Lady Fortrose, the wife of the soap-man, pays two hundred and fifty pounds for flowers for her house every Thursday in the season; and mine looked quite as good as hers. I think Mellish is much cheaper than anybody else. And, just because I went to a cheap man, Henry was horrible. He said all sorts of weird things about my reckless extravagance and the suffering poor - as though I had anything to do with them. The genuine poor are really people like you and me."

"I know," he said philosophically, lighting another cigarette. "But all this is beside the point. We want money, and money we must have in order to avoid exposure. You -"

"I was a fool to have had anything to do with that other little affair," she interrupted.

"It was not only myself who arranged it. Remember, it was you who suggested it, because it seemed so easy, and because you had an old score to pay off."

"The woman was sacrificed, and at the same time an enemy learnt our secret."

"I couldn't help it," he protested. "You let your woman's vindictiveness overstep your natural caution, my dear girl. If you'd taken my advice there would have been no suspicion."

Lady Heyburn was silent. She sat regarding the toe of her patent-leather shoe fixedly, in deep reflection. She was powerless to protest, she was so entirely in this man's hands. "Well," she asked at last, stirring uneasily in her chair, "and suppose we are not able to raise the money, what do you anticipate will be the result?"

"A rapid reprisal," was his answer. "People like them don't hesitate - they act."

"Yes, I see," she remarked in a blank voice. "They have nothing to lose, so they will bring pressure upon us."

"Just as we once tried to bring pressure upon them. It's all a matter of money. We pay the price arranged - a mere matter of business."

"But how are we to get money?"

"By getting a glance at what's in that safe," he replied. "Once we get to know this mysterious secret of Sir Henry's, I and my friends can get money easily enough. Leave it all to me."

"But how -"

"This matter you will please leave entirely to me, Winnie," he repeated with determination. "We are both in danger - great danger; and that being so, it is incumbent upon me to act boldly and fearlessly. I mean to get the key, and see what is within that safe."

"But the girl?" asked her ladyship.

"Within one week from to-day the girl will no longer trouble us," he said with an evil glance. "I do not intend that she shall remain a barrier against our good fortune any longer. Understand that, and remain perfectly calm, whatever may happen."

"But you surely don't intend - you surely will not -"

"I shall act as I think proper, and without any sentimental advice from you," he declared with a mock bow, but straightening himself instantly when at the door was heard a fumbling, and the gray-bearded man in blue spectacles, his thin white hand groping before him, slowly entered the room.

CHAPTER XIV

CONCERNS THE CURSE OF THE CARDINAL

Gabrielle and Walter were seated together under one of the big oaks at the edge of the tennis-lawn at Connachan. With May Spencer and Lady Murie they had been playing; but his mother and the young girl had gone into the house for tea, leaving the lovers alone.

"What's the matter with you to-day, darling?" he had asked as soon as they were out of hearing. "You don't seem yourself, somehow."

She started quickly, and, pulling herself up, tried to smile, assuring him that there was really nothing amiss.

"I do wish you'd tell me what it is that's troubling you so," he said. "Ever since I returned from abroad you've not been yourself. It's no use denying it, you know."

"I haven't felt well, perhaps. I think it must be the weather," she assured him.

But he, viewing the facts in the light of what he had noticed at their almost daily clandestine meetings, knew that she was concealing something from him.

Before his departure on that journey to Japan she had always been so very frank and open. Nowadays, however, she seemed

William Le Queux

to have entirely changed. Her love for him was just the same - that he knew; it was her unusual manner, so full of fear and vague apprehension, which caused him so many hours of grave reflection.

With her woman's cleverness, she succeeded in changing the topic of conversation, and presently they rose to join his mother at the tea-table in the drawing-room.

Half-an-hour later, while they were idling in the hall together, she suddenly exclaimed, "Walter, you're great on Scottish history, so I want some information from you. I'm studying the legends and traditions of our place, Glencardine. What do you happen to know about them?"

"Well," he laughed, "there are dozens of weird tales about the old castle. I remember reading quite a lot of extraordinary stories in some book or other about three years ago. I found it in the library here."

"Oh! do tell me all about it," she urged instantly. "Weird legends always fascinate me. Of course I know just the outlines of its history. It's the tales told by the country-folk in which I'm so deeply interested."

"You mean the apparition of the Lady in Green, and all that?"

"Yes; and the Whispers."

He started quickly at her words, and asked, "What do you know about them, dear? I hope you haven't heard them?"

She smiled, with a frantic effort at unconcern, saying, "And what harm, pray, would they have done me, even if I had?"

"Well," he said, "they are only heard by those whose days are numbered; at least, so say the folk about here."

"Of course, it's only a fable," she laughed. "The people of the

Ochils are so very superstitious."

"I believe the fatal result of listening to those mysterious Whispers has been proved in more than one instance," remarked the young man quite seriously. "For myself, I do not believe in any supernatural agency. I merely tell you what the people hereabouts believe. Nobody from this neighbourhood could ever be induced to visit your ruins on a moonlit night."

"That's just why I want to know the origin of the unexplained phenomenon."

"How can I tell you?"

"But you know - I mean you've heard the legend, haven't you?"

"Yes," was his reply. "The story of the Whispers of Glencardine is well known all through Perthshire. Hasn't your father ever told you?"

"He refuses."

"Because, no doubt, he fears that you might perhaps take it into your head to go there one night and try to listen for them," her lover said. "Do not court misfortune, dearest. Take my advice, and give the place a very wide berth. There is, without a doubt, some uncanny agency there."

The girl laughed outright. "I do declare, Walter, that you believe in these foolish traditions," she said.

"Well, I'm a Scot, you see, darling, and a little superstition is perhaps permissible, especially in connection with such a mystery as the strange disappearance of Cardinal Setoun."

"Then, tell me the real story as you know it," she urged. "I'm much interested. I only heard about the Whispers quite recently."

"The historical facts, so far as I can recollect reading them in the book in question," he said, "are to the effect that the Most Reverend James Cardinal Setoun, Archbishop of St. Andrews, Chancellor of the Kingdom, was in the middle of the sixteenth century directing all his energies towards consolidating the Romish power in Scotland, and not hesitating to resort to any crime which seemed likely to accomplish his purpose. Many were the foul assassinations and terrible tortures upon innocent persons performed at his orders. One person who fell into the hands of this infamous cleric was Margaret, the second daughter of Charles, Lord Glencardine, a beautiful girl of nineteen. Because she would not betray her lover, she was so cruelly tortured in the Cardinal's palace that she expired, after suffering fearful agony, and her body was sent back to Glencardine with an insulting message to her father, who at once swore to be avenged. The king had so far resigned the conduct of the kingdom into the hands of his Eminence that nothing save armed force could oppose him. Setoun knew that a union between Henry VIII. and James V. would be followed by the downfall of the papal power in Scotland, and therefore he laid a skilful plot. Whilst advising James to resist the dictation of his uncle, he privately accused those of the Scottish nobles who had joined the Reformers of meditated treason against His Majesty. This placed the king in a serious dilemma, for he could not proceed against Henry without the assistance of those very nobles accused as traitors. The wily Cardinal had hoped that James would, in self-defence, seek an alliance with France and Spain; but he was mistaken. You know, of course, how the forces of the kingdom were assembled and sent against the Duke of Norfolk. The invader was thus repelled, and the Cardinal then endeavoured to organise a new expedition under Romish leaders. This also failing, his Eminence endeavoured to dictate to the country through the Earl of Arran, the Governor of Scotland. By a clever ruse he pretended friendship with Erskine of Dun, and endeavoured to use him for his own ends. Curiously enough, over yonder" - and he pointed to a yellow parchment in a black ebony frame hanging upon the panelled wall of the hall - "over there is one of the Cardinal's letters to Erskine, which shows the infamous cleric's smooth, insinuating style when it suited his purpose. I'll go and get it for you to read."

The young man rose, and, taking it down, brought it to her. She saw that the parchment, about eight inches long by four wide, was covered with writing in brown ink, half-faded, while attached was a formidable oval red seal which bore a coat of arms surmounting the Cardinal's hat.

With difficulty they made out this interesting letter to read as follows:

"RYCHT HONOURABLE AND TRAIST COUSING, - I commend me hartlie to you, nocht doutting bot my lord governour hes written specialye to you at this tyme to keep the diet with his lordship in Edinburgh the first day of November nixt to cum, quhilk I dout nocht bot ye will kepe, and I know perfitlie your guid will and mynd euer inclinit to serue my lord governour, and how ye are nocht onnely determinit to serue his lordship, at this tyme be yourself bot als your gret wais and solistatioun maid with mony your gret freyndis to do the samin, quhilk I assuris you sall cum bayth to your hier honour and the vele of you and your houss and freyndis, quhilk ye salbe sure I sall procure and fortyfie euir at my power, as I have shewin in mair speciale my mynd heirintil to your cousin of Brechin, Knycht: Praing your effectuously to kepe trist, and to be heir in Sanct Androwis at me this nixt Wedinsday, that we may depairt all togydder by Thurisday nixt to cum, towart my lord governour, and bring your frendis and servandis with you accordantly, and as my lord governour hais speciale confidence in you at this tyme; and be sure the plesour I can do you salbe evir reddy at my power as knawis God, quha preserve you eternall.

"At Sanct Androwis, the 25th day of October (1544). J. CARDINALL OFF SANCT ANDROWIS.

"To the rycht honourable and our rycht traist cousing the lard of Dvn."

"Most interesting!" declared the young girl, holding the frame in her hands.

"It's doubly interesting, because it is believed that Erskine's brother Henry, finding himself befooled by the crafty Cardinal, united with Lord Glencardine to kill him and dispose of his body secretly, thus ridding Scotland of one of her worst enemies," Walter went on. "For the past five years stories had been continually leaking out of Setoun's inhuman cruelty, his unscrupulous, fiendish tortures inflicted upon all those who displeased him, and how certain persons who stood in his way had died mysteriously or disappeared, no one knew whither. Hence it was that, at Erskine's suggestion, Wemyss of Strathblane went over to Glencardine, and with Charles, Lord Glencardine, conspired to invite the Cardinal there, on pretence of taking counsel against the Protestants, but instead to take his life. The conspirators were, it is said, joined by the Earl of Kintyre and by Mary, the sixteen-year-old daughter of Lord Charles, and sister of the poor girl so brutally done to death by his Eminence. On several successive nights the best means of getting rid of Setoun were considered and discussed, and it is declared that the Whispers now heard sometimes at Glencardine are the secret deliberations of those sworn to kill the infamous Cardinal. Mary, the daughter of the house, was allowed to decide in what manner her sister's death should be avenged, and at her suggestion it was resolved that the inhuman head of the Roman Church should, before his life was taken, be put to the same fiendish tortures as those to which her sister had been subjected in his palace."

"It is curious that after his crime the Cardinal should dare to visit Glencardine," Gabrielle remarked.

"Not exactly. His lordship, pretending that he wished to be appointed Governor of Scotland in the place of the Earl of Arran, had purposely made his peace with Setoun, who on his part was only too anxious to again resume friendly relations with so powerful a noble. Therefore, early in May, 1546, he went on a private visit, and almost unattended, to Glencardine, within the walls of which fortress he disappeared for ever. What exactly occurred will never be known. All that the Commission who subsequently sat to try the conspirators were able to discover was that the Cardinal had been taken to the dungeon beneath the north tower, and there tortured horribly for several days, and afterwards burned at the stake in the courtyard, the fire being ignited by Lord Glencardine himself, and the dead Cardinal's ashes afterwards scattered to the winds."

"A terrible revenge!" exclaimed the girl with a shudder. "They were veritable fiends in those days."

"They were," he laughed, rehanging the frame upon the wall. "Some historians have, of course, declared that Setoun was murdered at Mains Castle, and others declare Cortachy to have been the scene of the assassination; but the truth that it occurred at Glencardine is proved by a quantity of the family papers which, when your father purchased Glencardine, came into his possession. You ought to search through them."

"I will. I had no idea dad possessed any of the Glencardine papers," she declared, much interested in that story of the past. "Perhaps from them I may be able to glean something further regarding the strange Whispers of Glencardine."

"Make whatever searches you like, dearest," he said in all earnestness, "but never attempt to investigate the Whispers themselves." And as they were alone, he took her little hand in his, and looking into her face with eyes of love, pressed her to promise him never to disregard his warning.

She told him nothing of her own weird experience. He was ignorant of the fact that she had actually heard the mysterious Whispers, and that, as a consequence, a great evil already lay upon her.

CHAPTER XV

FOLLOWS FLOCKART'S FORTUNES

One evening, a few days later, Gabrielle, seated beside her father at his big writing-table, had concluded reading some reports, and had received those brief, laconic replies which the blind man was in the habit of giving, when she suddenly asked, "I believe, dad, that you have a quantity of the Glencardine papers, haven't you? If I remember aright, when you bought the castle you made possession of these papers a stipulation."

"Yes, dear, I did," was his answer. "I thought it a shame that the papers of such a historic family should be dispersed at Sotheby's, as they no doubt would have been. So I purchased them."

"You've never let me see them," she said. "As you know, you've taught me so much antiquarian knowledge that I'm becoming an enthusiast like yourself."

"You can see them, dear, of course," was his reply. "They are in that big ebony cabinet at the end of the room yonder - about two hundred charters, letters, and documents, dating from 1314 down to 1695."

"I'll go through them to-morrow," she said. "I suppose they throw a good deal of light upon the history of the Grahams and the actions of the great Lord Glencardine?"

"Yes; but I fear you'll find them very difficult to read," he remarked. "Not being able to see them for myself, alas! I had to send them to London to be deciphered."

"And you still have the translations?"

"Unfortunately, no, dear. Professor Petre at Oxford, who is preparing his great work on Glencardine, begged me to let him see them, and he still has them."

"Well," she laughed, "I must therefore content myself with the originals, eh? Do they throw any further light upon the secret agreement in 1644 between the great Marquess of Glencardine, whose home was here, and King Charles?"

"Really, Gabrielle," laughed the old antiquary, "for a girl, your recollection of abstruse historical points is wonderful."

"Not at all. There was a mystery, I remember, and mysteries always attract me."

"Well," he replied after a few moments' hesitation, "I fear you will not find the solution of that point, or of any other really important point, contained in any of the papers. The most interesting records they contain are some relating to Alexander Senescallus (Stewart), the fourth son of Robert II., who was granted in 1379 a Castle of Garth. He was a reprobate, and known as the Wolf of Badenoch. On his father's accession in 1371, he was granted the charters of Badenoch, with the Castle of Lochindorb and of Strathavon; and at a slightly later date he was granted the lands of Tempar, Lassintulach, Tulachcroske, and Gort (Garth). As you know, many traditions regarding him still survive; but one fact contained in yonder papers is always interesting, for it shows that he was confined in the dungeon of the old keep of Glencardine until Robert III. released him. There are also a quantity of interesting facts regarding 'Red Neil,' or Neil Stewart of Fothergill, who was Laird of Garth, which will some day be of value to future historians of Scotland."

"Is there anything concerning the mysterious fate of Cardinal Setoun within Glencardine?" asked the girl, unable to curb her curiosity.

"No," he replied in a manner which was almost snappish. "That's a mere tradition, my dear - simply a tale invented by the country-folk. It seems to have been imagined in order to associate it with the mysterious Whispers which some superstitious people claim to have heard. No old castle is complete nowadays without its ghost, so we have for our share the Lady of Glencardine and the Whispers," he laughed.

"But I thought it was a matter of authenticated history that the Cardinal was actually enticed here, and disappeared!" exclaimed the girl. "I should have thought that the Glencardine papers would have referred to it," she added, recollecting what Walter had told her.

"Well, they don't; so why worry your head, dear, over a mere fable? I have already gone very carefully into all the facts that are proved, and have come to the conclusion that the story of the torture of his Eminence is a fairy-tale, and that the supernatural Whispers have only been heard in imagination."

She was silent. She recollected that sound of murmuring voices. It was certainly not imagination.

"But you'll let me have the key of the cabinet, won't you, dad?" she asked, glancing across to where stood a beautiful old Florentine cabinet of ebony inlaid with ivory, and reaching almost to the ceiling.

"Certainly, Gabrielle dear," was the reply of the expressionless man. "It is upstairs in my room. You shall have it to-morrow."

And then he lapsed again into silence, reflecting whether it were not best to secure certain parchment records from those drawers before his daughter investigated them. There was a small roll of yellow parchment, tied with modern tape, which he was half-inclined to conceal from her curious gaze. Truth to tell, they constituted a record of the torture and death of Cardinal Setoun much in the same manner as Walter Murie had described to her. If she read that strange chronicle she might, he feared, be impelled to watch and endeavour to hear the fatal Whispers.

Strange though it was, yet those sounds were a subject which caused him daily apprehension. Though he never referred to them save to ridicule every suggestion of their existence, or to attribute the weird noises to the wind, yet never a day passed but he sat calmly reflecting. That one matter which his daughter knew above all others caused him the most serious thought and apprehension - a fear which had become doubly increased since she had referred to the curious and apparently inexplicable phenomenon. He, a refined, educated man of brilliant attainments, scouted the idea of any supernatural agency. To those who had made mention of the Whispers - among them his friend Murie, the Laird of Connachan; Lord Strathavon, from whom he had purchased the estate; and several of the neighbouring landowners - he had always expressed a hope that one day he might be fortunate enough to hear the whispered counsel of the Evil One, and so decide for himself its true cause. He pretended always to treat the affair with humorous incredulity, yet at heart he was sorely troubled.

If his young wife's remarkable friendship with the man Flockart often caused him bitter thoughts, then the mysterious Whispers and the fatality so strangely connected with them were equally a source of constant inquietude.

A few days later Flockart, with clever cunning, seemed to alter his ingenious tactics completely, for suddenly he had commenced to bestir himself in Sir Henry's interests. One morning after breakfast, taking the Baronet by the arm, he led him for a stroll along the drive, down to the lodge-gates, and back, for the purpose, as he explained, of speaking with him in confidence.

William Le Queux

At first the blind man was full of curiosity as to the reason of this unusual action, as those deprived of sight usually are.

"I know, Sir Henry," Flockart said presently, and not without hesitation, "that certain ill-disposed people have endeavoured to place an entirely wrong construction upon your wife's friendship towards me. For that reason I have decided to leave Glencardine, both for her sake and for yours."

"But, my dear fellow," exclaimed the blind man, "why do you suggest such a thing?"

"Because your wife's enemies have their mouths full of scandalous lies," he replied. "I tell you frankly, Sir Henry, that my friendship with her ladyship is a purely platonic one. We were children together, at home in Bedford, and ever since our schooldays I have remained her friend."

"I know that," remarked the old man quietly. "My wife told me that when you dined with us on several occasions at Park Street. I have never objected to the friendship existing between you, Flockart; for, though I have never seen you, I have always believed you to be a man of honour."

"I feel very much gratified at those words, Sir Henry," he said in a deep, earnest voice, glancing at the grey, dark-spectacled face of the fragile man whose arm he was holding. "Indeed, I've always hoped that you would repose sufficient confidence in me to know that I am not such a blackguard as to take any advantage of your cruel affliction."

The blind Baronet sighed. "Ah, my dear Flockart! all men are not honourable like yourself. There are many ready to take advantage of my lack of eyesight. I have experienced it, alas! in business as well as in my private life."

The dark-faced man was silent. He was playing an ingenious, if dangerous, game. The Baronet had referred to business - his mysterious business, the secret of which he was now trying his best to solve. "Yes," he said at length, "I suppose the standard of honesty in business is nowadays just about as low as it can possibly be, eh? Well, I've never been in business myself, so I don't know. In the one or two small financial deals in which I've had a share, I've usually been 'frozen out' in the end."

"Ah, Flockart," sighed the Laird of Glencardine, "you are unfortunately quite correct. The so-called smart business man is the one who robs his neighbour without committing the sin of being found out."

This remark caused the other a twinge of conscience. Did he intend to convey any hidden meaning? He was full of cunning and cleverness. "Well," Flockart exclaimed, "I'm truly gratified to think that I retain your confidence, Sir Henry. If I have in the past been able to be of any little service to Lady Heyburn, I assure you I am only too delighted. Yet I think that in the face of gossip which some of your neighbours here are trying to spread - gossip started, I very much fear, by Miss Gabrielle - my absence from Glencardine will be of distinct advantage to all concerned. I do not, my dear Sir Henry, desire for one single moment to embarrass you, or to place her ladyship in any false position. I -"

"But, my dear fellow, you've become quite an institution with us!" exclaimed Sir Henry in dismay. "We should all be lost without you. Why, as you know, you've done me so many kindnesses that I can never sufficiently repay you. I don't forget how, through your advice, I've been able to effect quite a number of economies at Caistor, and how often you assist my wife in various ways in her social duties."

"My dear Sir Henry," he laughed, "you know I'm always ready to serve either of you whenever it lies in my power. Only - well, I feel that I'm in your wife's company far too much, both here and in Lincolnshire. People are talking. Therefore, I have decided to leave her, and my decision is irrevocable."

"Let them talk. If I do not object, you surely need not."

"But for your wife's sake?"

"I know - I know how cruel are people's tongues, Flockart," remarked the old man.

"Yes; and the gossip was unfortunately started by Gabrielle. It was surely very unwise of her."

"Ah!" sighed the other, "it is the old story. Every girl becomes jealous of her step-mother. And she's only a child, after all," he added apologetically.

"Well, much as I esteem her, and much as I admire her, I feel, Sir Henry, that she had no right to bring discord into your house. I hope you will permit me to say this, with all due deference to the fact that she's your daughter. But I consider her conduct in this matter has been very unfriendly."

Again the Baronet was silent, and his companion saw that he was reflecting deeply. "How do you know that the scandal was started by her?" he asked presently, in a low, rather strained voice.

"Young Paterson told me so. It appears that when she was staying with them over at Tullyallan she told his mother all sorts of absurd stories. And Mrs. Paterson who, as you know, is a terrible gossip - told the Reads of Logie and the Redcastles, and in a few days these fictions, with all sorts of embroidery, were spread half over Scotland. Why, my friend Lindsay, the member for Berwick, heard some whispers the other day in the Carlton Club! So, in consequence of that, Sir Henry, I'm resolved, much against my will and inclination, I assure you, to end my friendship with your wife."

"All this pains me more than I can tell you," declared the old man. "The more so, too, that Gabrielle should have allowed her jealousy to lead her to make such false charges."

"Yes. In order not to pain you. I have hesitated to tell you this for several weeks. But I really thought that you ought at least to know the truth, and who originated the scandal. And so I have ventured to-day to speak openly, and to announce my departure," said the wily Flockart. He was putting to the test the strength of his position in that household. He had an ulterior motive, one that was ingenious and subtle.

"But you are not really going?" exclaimed the other. "You told me the other day something about my factor Macdonald, and your suspicions of certain irregularities."

"My dear Sir Henry, it will be far better for us both if I leave. To remain will only be to lend further colour to these scandalous rumours. I have decided to leave your house."

"You believe that Macdonald is dishonest, eh?" inquired the afflicted man quickly.

"Yes, I'm certain of it. Remember, Sir Henry, that when one is dealing with a man who is blind, it is sometimes a great temptation to be dishonest."

"I know, I know," sighed the other deeply. They were at a bend in the drive where the big trees met overhead, forming a leafy tunnel. The ascent was a trifle steep, and the Baronet had paused for a few seconds, leaning heavily upon the arm of his friend.

"Oh, pardon me!" exclaimed Flockart suddenly, releasing his arm. "Your watch-chain is hanging down. Let me put it right for you." And for a few seconds he fumbled at the chain, at the same time holding something in the palm of his left hand. "There, that's right," he said a few minutes later. "You caught it somewhere, I expect."

"On one of the knobs of my writing-table perhaps," said the other. "Thanks. I sometimes inadvertently pull it out of my pocket."

A faint smile of triumph passed across the dark, handsome face of the man, who again took his arm, as at the same time he replaced something in his own jacket-pocket. He had in that instant secured what he wanted.

"You were saying with much truth, my dear Flockart, that in dealing with a man who cannot see there is occasionally a temptation towards dishonesty. Well, this very day I intend to have a long chat with my wife, but before I do so will you promise me one thing?"

"And what is that?" asked the man, not without some apprehension.

"That you will remain here, disregard the gossip that you may have heard, and continue to assist me in my helplessness in making full and searching inquiry into Macdonald's alleged defalcations."

The man reflected for a few seconds, with knit brows. His quick wits were instantly at work, for he saw with the utmost satisfaction that he had been entirely successful in disarming all suspicion; therefore his next move must be the defeat of that man's devoted defender, Gabrielle, the one person who stood between his own penniless self and fortune.

"I really cannot at this moment make any promise, Sir Henry," he remarked at last. "I have decided to go."

"But defer your decision for the present. There is surely no immediate hurry for your departure! First let me consult my wife," urged the Baronet, putting out his hand and groping for that of Flockart, which he pressed warmly as proof of his continued esteem. "Let me talk to Winifred. She shall decide whether you go or whether you shall stay."

CHAPTER XVI

SHOWS A GIRL'S BONDAGE

Walter Murie had chosen politics as a profession long ago, even when he was an undergraduate. He had already eaten his dinners in London, and had been called to the Bar as the first step towards a political career. He had a relative in the Foreign Office, while his uncle had held an Under-Secretaryship in the late Government. Therefore he had influence, and hoped by its aid to secure some safe seat. Already he had studied both home and foreign affairs very closely, and had on two occasions written articles in the *Times* upon that most vexed and difficult question, the pacification of Macedonia. He was a very fair speaker, too, and on several occasions he had seconded resolutions and made quite clever speeches at political gatherings in his own county, Perthshire. Indeed, politics was his hobby; and, with money at his command and influence in high quarters, there was no reason why he should not within the next few years gain a seat in the House. With Sir Henry Heyburn he often had long and serious chats. The brilliant politician, whose career had so suddenly and tragically been cut short, gave him much good advice, pointing out the special questions he should study in order to become an authority. This is the age of specialising, and in politics it is just as essential to be a specialist as it is in the medical, legal, or any other profession.

In a few days the young man was returning to his dingy chambers in the Temple, to pore again over those mouldy

William Le Queux

tomes of law; therefore almost daily he ran over to Glencardine to chat with the blind Baronet, and to have quiet walks with the sweet girl who looked so dainty in her fresh white frocks, and whose warm kisses were so soft and caressing.

Surely no pair, even in the bygone days of knight and dame, the days of real romance, were more devoted to each other. With satisfaction he saw that Gabrielle's apparent indifference had now worn off. It had been but the mask of a woman's whim, and as such he treated it.

One afternoon, after tea out on the lawn, they were walking together by the bypath to the lodge in order to meet Lady Heyburn, who had gone into the village to visit a bedridden old lady. Hand-in-hand they were strolling, for on the morrow he was going south, and would probably be absent for some months.

The girl had allowed herself to remain in her lover's arms in one long kiss of perfect ecstasy. Then, with a sigh of regret, she had held his hand and gone forward again without a word. When Walter had left, the sun of her young life would have set, for after all it was not exactly exciting to be the eyes and ears of a man who was blind. And there was always at her side that man whom she hated, and who, she knew, was her bitterest foe - James Flockart.

Of late her father seemed to have taken him strangely into his confidence. Why, she could not tell. A sudden change of front on the Baronet's part was unusual; but as she watched with sinking heart she could not conceal from herself the fact that Flockart now exercised considerable influence over her father - an influence which in some matters had already proved to be greater than her own.

It was of this man Walter spoke. "I have a regret, dearest - nay, more than a regret, a fear - in leaving you here alone," he exclaimed in a low, distinct voice, gazing into the blue, fathomless depths of those eyes so very dear to him.

"A fear! Why?" she asked in some surprise, returning his look.

"Because of that man - your mother's friend," he said. "Recently I have heard some curious tales concerning him. I really wonder why Sir Henry still retains him as his guest."

"Why need we speak of him?" she exclaimed quickly, for the subject was distasteful.

"Because I wish you to be forewarned," he said in a serious voice. "That man is no fitting companion for you. His past is too well known to a certain circle."

"His past!" she echoed. "What have you discovered concerning him?"

Her companion did not answer for a few moments. How could he tell her all that he had heard? His desire was to warn her, yet he could not relate to her the allegations made by certain persons against Flockart.

"Gabrielle," he said, "all that I have heard tends to show that his friendship for you and for your father is false; therefore avoid him - beware of him."

"I - I know," she faltered, lowering her eyes. "I've felt that was the case all along, yet I -"

"Yet what?" he asked.

"I mean I want you to promise me one thing, Walter," she said quickly. "You love me, do you not?"

"Love you, my own darling! How can you ask such a question? You surely know that I do!"

"Then, if you really love me, you will make me a promise."

"Of what?"

"Only one thing - one little thing," she said in a low, earnest voice, looking straight into his eyes. "If - if that man ever makes an allegation against me, you won't believe him?"

"An allegation! Why, darling, what allegation could such a man ever make against you?"

"He is my enemy," she remarked simply.

"I know that. But what charge could he bring against you? Why, if even he dared to utter a single word against you, I - I'd wring the ruffian's neck!"

"But if he did, Walter, you wouldn't believe him, would you?"

"Of course I wouldn't."

"Not - not if the charge he made against me was a terrible one - a - a disgraceful one?" she asked in a strained voice after a brief and painful pause.

"Why, dearest!" he cried, "what is the matter? You are really not yourself to-day. You seem to be filled with a graver apprehension even than I am. What does it mean? Tell me."

"It means, Walter, that that man is Lady Heyburn's friend; hence he is my enemy."

"And what need you fear when you have me as your friend?"

"I do not fear if you will still remain my friend - always - in face of any allegation he makes."

"I love you, darling. Surely that's sufficient guarantee of my friendship?"

"Yes," she responded, raising her white, troubled face to his while he bent and kissed her again on the lips. "I know that I am yours, my own well-beloved; and, as yours, I will not fear."

"That's right!" he exclaimed, endeavouring to smile. "Cheer up. I don't like to see you on this last day down-hearted and apprehensive like this."

"I am not so without cause."

"Then, what is the cause?" he demanded. "Surely you can repose confidence in me?"

Again she was silent. Above them the wind stirred the leaves, and through the high bracken a rabbit scuttled at their feet. They were alone, and she stood again locked in her lover's fond embrace.

"You have told me yourself that man Flockart is my enemy," she said in a low voice.

"But what action of his can you fear? Surely you should be forearmed against any evil he may be plotting. Tell me the truth, and I will go myself to your father and denounce the fellow before his face!"

"Ah, no!" she cried, full of quick apprehension. "Never think of doing that, Walter!"

"Why? Am I not your friend?"

"Such a course would only bring his wrath down upon my head. He would retaliate quickly, and I alone would suffer."

"But, my dear Gabrielle," he exclaimed, "you really speak in enigmas. Whatever can you fear from a man who is known to be a blackguard - whom I could now, at this very moment, expose in such a manner that he would never dare to set foot in Perthshire again?"

"Such a course would be most injudicious, I assure you. His ruin would mean - it would mean - my - own!"

"I don't follow you."

"Ah, because you do not know my secret - you -"

"Your secret!" the young man gasped, staring at her, yet still holding her trembling form in his strong arms. "Why, what do you mean? What secret?"

"I - I cannot tell you!" she exclaimed in a hard, mechanical voice, looking straight before her.

"But you must," he protested.

"I - I asked you, Walter, to make me a promise," she said, her voice broken by emotion - "a promise that, for the sake of the love you bear for me, you will not believe that man, that you will disregard any allegation against me."

"And I promise, on one condition, darling - that you tell me in confidence what I, as your future husband, have a just right to know - the nature of this secret of yours."

"Ah, no!" she cried, unable longer to restrain her tears, and burying her pale, beautiful face upon his arm. "I - I was foolish to have spoken of it," she sobbed brokenly: "I ought to have kept it to myself. It is - it's the one thing that I can never reveal to you - to you of all men!"

CHAPTER XVII

DESCRIBES A FRENCHMAN'S VISIT

"Monsieur Goslin, Sir Henry," Hill announced, entering his master's room one morning a fortnight later, just as the blind man was about to descend to breakfast. "He's in the library, sir."

"Goslin!" exclaimed the Baronet, in great surprise. "I'll go to him at once; and Hill, serve breakfast for two in the library, and tell Miss Gabrielle that I do not wish to be disturbed this morning."

"Very well, Sir Henry;" and the man bowed and went down the broad oak staircase.

"Goslin here, without any announcement!" exclaimed the Baronet, speaking to himself. "Something must have happened. I wonder what it can be." He tugged at his collar to render it more comfortable; and then, with a groping hand on the broad balustrade, he felt his way down the stairs and along the corridor to the big library, where a stout, grey-haired Frenchman came forward to greet him warmly, after carefully closing the door.

"Ah, *mon cher ami!*" he began; and, speaking in French, he inquired eagerly after the Baronet's health. He was rather long-faced, with beard worn short and pointed, and his dark, deep-set eyes and his countenance showed a fund of good humour.

"This visit is quite unexpected," exclaimed Sir Henry. "You were not due till the 20th."

"No; but circumstances have arisen which made my journey imperative, so I left the Gare du Nord at four yesterday afternoon, was at Charing Cross at eleven, had half-an-hour to catch the Scotch express at King's Cross, and here I am."

"Oh, my dear Goslin, you always move so quickly! You're simply a marvel of alertness."

The other smiled, and, with a shrug of the shoulders, said, "I really don't know why I should have earned a reputation as a rapid traveller, except, perhaps, by that trip I made last year, from Paris to Constantinople, when I remained exactly thirty-eight minutes in the Sultan's capital. But I did my business there, nevertheless, even though I got through quicker than *messieurs les touristes* of the most estimable Agence Cook."

"You want a wash, eh?"

"Ah, no, my friend. I washed at the hotel in Perth, where I took my morning coffee. When I come to Scotland I carry no baggage save my tooth-brush in my pocket, and a clean collar across my chest, its ends held by my braces."

The Baronet laughed heartily. His friend was always most resourceful and ingenious. He was a mystery to all at Glencardine, and to Lady Heyburn most of all. His visits were always unexpected, while as to who he really was, or whence he came, nobody - not even Gabrielle herself - knew. At times the Frenchman would take his meals alone with Sir Henry in the library, while at others he would lunch with her ladyship and her guests. On these latter occasions he proved himself a most amusing cosmopolitan, and at the same time exhibited an extreme courtliness towards every one. His manner was quite charming, yet his presence there was always puzzling, and had given rise to considerable speculation.

Hill came in, and after helping the Frenchman to take off his heavy leather-lined travelling-coat, laid a small table for two and prepared breakfast.

Then, when he had served it and left, Goslin rose, and, crossing to the door, pushed the little brass bolt into its socket. Returning to his chair opposite the blind man (whose food Hill had already cut up for him), he exclaimed in a very calm, serious voice, speaking in French, "I want you to hear what I have to say, Sir Henry, without exciting yourself unduly. Something has occurred - something very strange and remarkable."

The other dropped his knife, and sat statuesque and expressionless. "Go on," he said hoarsely. "Tell me the worst at once."

"The worst has not yet happened. It is that which I'm dreading."

"Well, what has happened? Is - is the secret out?"

"The secret is safe - for the present."

The blind man drew a long breath. "Well, that's one thing to be thankful for," he gasped. "I was afraid you were going to tell me that the facts were exposed."

"They may yet be exposed," the mysterious visitor exclaimed. "That's where lies the danger."

"We have been betrayed, eh? You may as well admit the ugly truth at once, Goslin!"

"I do not conceal it, Sir Henry. We have."

"By whom?"

"By somebody here - in this house."

"Here! What do you mean? Somebody in my own house?"

"Yes. The Greek affair is known. They have been put upon their guard in Athens."

"By whom?" cried the Baronet, starting from his chair.

"By somebody whom we cannot trace - somebody who must have had access to your papers."

"No one has had access to my papers. I always take good care of that, Goslin - very good care of that. The affair has leaked out at your end, not at mine."

"At our end we are always circumspect," the Frenchman said calmly. "Rest assured that nobody but we ourselves are aware of our operations or intentions. We know only too well that any revelation would assuredly bring upon us - disaster."

"But a revelation has actually been made!" exclaimed Sir Henry, bending forward. "Therefore the worst is to be feared."

"Exactly. That is what I am endeavouring to convey."

"The betrayal must have come from your end, I expect; not from here."

"I regret to assert that it came from here - from this very room."

"How do you know that?"

"Because in Athens they have a complete copy of one of the documents which you showed me on the last occasion I was here, and which we have never had in our possession."

The blind man was silent. The allegation admitted of no argument.

"My daughter Gabrielle is the only person who has seen it, and she understands nothing of our affairs, as you know quite well."

"She may have copied it."

"My daughter would never betray me, Goslin," said Sir Henry in a hard, distinct voice, rising from the table and slowly walking down the long, book-lined room.

"Has no one else been able to open your safe and examine its contents?" asked the Frenchman, glancing over to the small steel door let into the wall close to where he was sitting.

"No one. Though I'm blind, do you consider me a fool? Surely I recognise only too well how essential is secrecy. Have I not always taken the most extraordinary precautions?"

"You have, Sir Henry. I quite admit that. Indeed, the precautions you've taken would, if known to the world, be regarded - well, as simply amazing."

"I hope the world will never know the truth."

"It will know the truth. They have the copies in Athens. If there is a traitor - as we have now proved the existence of one - then we can never in future rest secure. At any moment another exposure may result, with its attendant disaster."

The Baronet halted before one of the long windows, the morning sunshine falling full upon his sad, grey face. He drew a long sigh and said, "Goslin, do not let us discuss the future. Tell me exactly what is the present situation."

"The present situation," the Frenchman said in a dry, matter-of-fact voice, "is one full of peril for us. You have, over there in your safe, a certain paper - a confidential report which you received direct from Vienna. It was brought to you by special messenger because its nature was not such as should be sent through the post. A trusted official of the Austrian Ministry of Foreign Affairs brought it here. To whom did he deliver it?"

"To Gabrielle. She signed a receipt."

"And she broke the seals?"

"No. I was present, and she handed it to me. I broke the seals myself. She read it over to me."

"Ah!" ejaculated the Frenchman suspiciously. "It is unfortunate that you are compelled to entrust our secrets to a woman."

"My daughter is my best friend; indeed, perhaps my only friend."

"Then you have enemies?"

"Who has not?"

"True. We all of us have enemies," replied the mysterious visitor. "But in this case, how do you account for that report falling into the hands of the people in Athens? Who keeps the key of the safe?"

"I do. It is never out of my possession."

"At night what do you do with it?"

"I hide it in a secret place in my room, and I sleep with the door locked."

"Then, as far as you are aware, nobody has ever had possession of your key - not even mademoiselle your daughter?"

"Not even Gabrielle. I always lock and unlock the safe myself."

"But she has access to its contents when it is open," the visitor remarked. "Acting as your secretary, she is, of course, aware of a good deal of your business."

"No; you are mistaken. Have we not arranged a code in order to prevent her from satisfying her woman's natural inquisitiveness?"

"That's admitted. But the document in question, though somewhat guarded, is sufficiently plain to any one acquainted with the nature of our negotiations."

The blind man crossed to the safe, and with the key upon his chain opened it, and, after fumbling in one of the long iron drawers revealed within, took out a big oblong envelope, orange-coloured, and secured with five black seals, now, however, broken.

This he handed to his friend, saying, "Read it again, to refresh your memory. I know myself what it says pretty well by heart."

Monsieur Goslin drew forth the paper within and read the lines of close, even writing. It was in German. He stood near the window as he read, while Sir Henry remained near the open safe.

Hill tapped at the bolted door, but his master replied that he did not wish to be disturbed. "Yes," the Frenchman said at last, "the copy they have in Athens is exact - word for word."

"They may have obtained it from Vienna."

"No; it came from here. There are some pencilled comments in your daughter's handwriting."

"They were dictated by me."

"Exactly. And they appear in the copy now in the hands of the people in Athens! Thus it is doubly proved that it was this actual document which was copied. But by whom?"

"Ah!" sighed the helpless man, his face drawn and paler than usual, "Gabrielle is the only person who has had sight of it."

"Mademoiselle surely could not have copied it," remarked the Frenchman. "Has she a lover?"

"Yes; the son of a neighbour of mine, a very worthy young fellow."

Goslin grunted dubiously. It was apparent that he suspected her of trickery. Information such as had been supplied to the Greek Government would, he knew, be paid for, and at a high price. Had mademoiselle's lover had a hand in that revelation?

"I would not suggest for a single moment, Sir Henry, that mademoiselle your daughter would act in any way against your personal interests; but -"

"But what?" demanded the blind man fiercely, turning towards his visitor.

"Well, it is peculiar - very peculiar - to say the least."

Sir Henry was silent. Within himself he was compelled to admit that certain suspicion attached to Gabrielle. And yet was she not his most devoted - nay, his only - friend? "Some one has copied the report - that's evident," he said in a low, hard voice, reflecting deeply.

"And by so doing has placed us in a position of grave peril, Sir Henry - imminent peril," remarked the visitor. "I see in this an attempt to obtain further knowledge of our affairs. We have a secret enemy, who, it seems, has found a vulnerable point in our armour."

"Surely my own daughter cannot be my enemy?" cried the blind man in dismay.

"You say she has a lover," remarked the Frenchman, speaking

slowly and with deliberation. "May not he be the instigator?"

"Walter Murie is upright and honourable," replied the blind man. "And yet -" A long-drawn sigh prevented the conclusion of that sentence.

"Ah, I know!" exclaimed the mysterious visitor in a tone of sympathy. "You are uncertain in your conclusions because of your terrible affliction. Sometimes, alas! my dear friend, you are imposed upon, because you are blind."

"Yes," responded the other, bitterly. "That is the truth, Goslin. Because I cannot see like other men, I have been deceived - foully and grossly deceived and betrayed! But - but," he cried, "they thought to ruin me, and I've tricked them, Goslin - yes, tricked them! Have no fear. For the present our secrets are our own!"

CHAPTER XVIII

REVEALS THE SPY

The Twelfth - the glorious Twelfth - had come and gone. "The rush to the North" had commenced from London. From Euston, St. Pancras, and King's Cross the night trains for Scotland had run in triplicate, crowded by men and gun-cases and kit-bags, while gloomy old Perth station was a scene of unwonted activity each morning.

At Glencardine there were little or no grouse; therefore it was not until later that Sir Henry invited his usual party.

Gabrielle had been south to visit one of her girlfriends near Durham, and the week of her absence her afflicted father had spent in dark loneliness, for Flockart had gone to London, and her ladyship was away on a fortnight's visit to the Pelhams, down at New Galloway.

On the last day of August, however, Gabrielle returned, being followed a few hours later by Lady Heyburn, who had travelled up by way of Stirling and Crieff Junction, while that same night eight men forming the shooting-party arrived by the day express from the south.

The gathering was a merry one. The guests were the same who came up there every year, some of them friends of Sir Henry in the days of his brilliant career, others friends of his wife. The shooting at Glencardine was always excellent; and Stewart, wise and serious, had prophesied first-class sport.

Walter Murie was in London. While Gabrielle had been at Durham he had travelled up there, spent the night at the "Three Tuns," and met her next morning in that pretty wooded walk they call "the Banks." Devoted to her as he was, he could not bear any long separation; while she, on her part, was gratified by this attention. Not without some difficulty did she succeed in getting away from her friends to meet him, for a provincial town is not like London, and any stranger is always in the public eye. But they spent a delightful couple of hours together, strolling along the footpath through the meadows in the direction of Finchale Priory. There were no eavesdroppers; and he, with his arm linked in hers, repeated the story of his all-conquering love.

She listened in silence, then raising her fine clear eyes to his, said, "I know, Walter - I know that you love me. And I love you also."

"Ah," he sighed, "if you would only be frank with me, dearest - if you would only be as frank with me as I am with you!"

Sadly she shook her head, but made no reply. He saw that a shadow had clouded her brow, that she still clung to her strange secret; and at length, when they retraced their steps back to the city, he reluctantly took leave of her, and half-an-hour later was speeding south again towards York and King's Cross.

The opening day of the partridge season proved bright and pleasant. The men were out early; and the ladies, a gay party, including Gabrielle, joined them at luncheon spread on a mossy bank about three miles from the castle. Several of the male guests were particularly attentive to the dainty, sweet-faced girl whose charming manner and fresh beauty attracted them. But Gabrielle's heart was with Walter always. She loved him. Yes, she told herself so a dozen times each day. And yet was not the barrier between them insurmountable? Ah, if he only knew! If he only knew!

The blind man was left alone nearly the whole of that day. His daughter had wanted to remain with him, but he would not hear of it. "My dear child," he had said, "you must go out and lunch. You really must assist your mother in entertaining the people."

"But, dear dad, I much prefer to remain with you and help you," she protested. "Yesterday the Professor sent you five more bronze matrices of ecclesiastical seals. We haven't yet examined them."

"We'll do so to-night, dear," he said. "You go out to-day. I'll amuse myself all right. Perhaps I'll go for a little walk."

Therefore the girl had, against her inclination, joined the luncheon-party, where foremost of all to have her little attentions was a rather foppish young stockbroker named Girdlestone, who had been up there shooting the previous year, and had on that occasion flirted with her furiously.

During her absence her father tried to resume his knitting - an occupation which he had long ago been compelled to resort to in order to employ his time; but he soon put it down with a sigh, rose, and taking his soft brown felt-hat and stout stick, tapped his way along through the great hall and out into the park.

He felt the warmth upon his cheek as he passed slowly along down the broad drive. "Ah," he murmured to himself, "if only I could once again see God's sunlight! If I could only see the greenery of nature and the face of my darling child!" and he sighed brokenly, and went on, his chin sunk upon his breast, a despairing, hopeless man. Surely no figure more pathetic than his could be found in the whole of Scotland. Upon him had been showered honour, great wealth, all indeed that makes life worth living, and yet, deprived of sight, he existed in that world of darkness, deceived and plotted against by all about him. His grey countenance was hard and thoughtful as he passed slowly along tapping the ground before him, for he was thinking - ever thinking - of the declaration of his French visitor. He had been betrayed. But by whom?

His thoughts were wandering back to those days when he could see - those well-remembered days when he had held the House in silence by his brilliant oratory, and when the papers next day had leading articles concerning his speeches. He recollected his time-mellowed old club in St. James's Street - Boodle's - of which he had been so fond. Then came his affliction. The thought of it all struck him suddenly; and, clenching his hands, he murmured some inarticulate words through his teeth. They sounded strangely like a threat. Next instant, however, he laughed bitterly to himself the dry, harsh laugh of a man into whose very soul the iron had entered.

In the distance he could hear the shots of his guests, those men who accepted his hospitality, and who among themselves agreed that he was "a terrible bore, poor old fellow!" They came up there - with perhaps two exceptions - to eat his dinners, drink his choice wines, and shoot his birds, but begrudged him more than ten minutes or so of their company each day. In the billiard-room of an evening, as he sat upon one of the long lounges, they would perhaps deign to chat with him; but, alas! He knew that he was only as a wet blanket to his wife's guests, hence he kept himself so much to the library - his own domain.

That night he spent half-an-hour in the billiard-room in order to hear what sport they had had, but very soon escaped, and with Gabrielle returned again to the library to fulfil his promise and examine the seal-matrices which the Professor had sent.

To where they sat came bursts of boisterous laughter and of the waltz-music of the pianola in the hall, for in the shooting season the echoes of the fine mansion were awakened by the merriment of as gay a crowd as any who assembled in the Highlands.

Sir Henry heard it. The sounds jarred upon his nerves. Mirth such as theirs was debarred him for ever, and he had now become gloomy and misanthropic. He sat fingering those big oval matrices of bronze, listening to Gabrielle's voice deciphering the inscriptions, and explaining what was meant and what was possibly their history. One which Sir Henry declared to be the gem of them all bore the _manus Dei_ for device, and was the seal of Archbishop Richard (1174-84). Several documents bearing impressions of this seal were, he said, preserved at Canterbury and in the British Museum, but here the actual seal itself had come to light.

With all the enthusiasm of an expert he lingered over the matrice, feeling it carefully with the tips of his fingers, and tracing the device with the nail of his forefinger. "Splendid!" he declared. "The lettering is a most excellent specimen of early Lombardic." And then he gave the girl the titles of several works, which she got down from the shelves, and from which she read extracts after some careful search.

The sulphur-casts sent with the matrices she placed carefully with her father's collection, and during the remainder of the evening they were occupied in replying to several letters regarding estate matters.

At eleven o'clock she kissed her father good-night and passed out to the hall, where the pianola was still going, and where the merriment was still in full swing. For a quarter of an hour she was compelled to remain with the insipid young ass Bertie Girdlestone, a man who patronised musical comedy nightly, and afterwards supped regularly at the "Savoy"; then she escaped at last to her room.

Exchanging her pretty gown of turquoise chiffon for an easy wrap, she took up a novel, and, switching on her green-shaded reading-lamp, sat down to enjoy a quiet hour before retiring. Quickly she became engrossed in the story, and though the stable-chimes sounded each half-hour she remained undisturbed by them.

It was half-past two before she had reached the happy *denouement* of the book, and, closing it, she rose to take off her trinkets. Having divested herself of bracelets, rings, and necklet, she placed her hands to her ears. There was only one ear-ring; the other was missing! They were sapphires, a present from Walter on her last birthday. He had sent them to her from Yokohama, and she greatly prized them. Therefore, at risk of being seen in her dressing-gown by any of the male guests who might still be astir - for she knew they always played billiards until very late - she took off her little blue satin slippers and stole out along the corridor and down the broad staircase.

The place was in darkness; but she turned on the light, and again when she reached the hall.

She must have dropped her ear-ring in the library; of that she felt sure. Servants were so careless that, if she left it, it might easily be swept up in the morning and lost for ever. That thought had caused her to search for it at once.

As she approached the library door she thought she heard the sound as of some one within. On her opening the door, however, all was in darkness. She laughed at her apprehension.

In an instant she touched the switch, and the place became flooded by a soft, mellow light from lamps cunningly concealed behind the bookcases against the wall. At the same moment, however, she detected a movement behind one of the bookcases against which she stood. With sudden resolution and fearlessness, she stepped forward to ascertain its cause. Her eyes at that instant fell upon a sight which caused her to start and stand dumb with amazement. Straight before her the door of her father's safe stood open. Beside it, startled at the sudden interruption, stood a man in evening-dress, with a small electric lamp in his clenched hand. A pair of dark, evil eyes met hers in defiance - the eyes of James Flockart.

"You!" she gasped.

"Yes," he laughed dryly. "Don't be afraid. It's only I. But, by Jove! how very charming you look in that gown! I'd love to get a snapshot of you just as you stand now."

"What are you doing there, examining my father's papers?" she demanded quickly, her small hands clenched.

"My dear girl," he replied with affected unconcern, "that's my own business. You really ought to have been in bed long ago. It isn't discreet, you know, to be down here with me at this hour!"

"I demand to know what you are doing here!" she cried firmly.

"And, my dear little girl, I refuse to tell you," was his decisive answer.

"Very well, then I shall alarm the house and explain to my father what I have discovered."

CHAPTER XIX

SHOWS GABRIELLE DEFIANT

Gabrielle crossed quickly to one of the long windows, which she unbolted and flung open, expecting to hear the shrill whir of the burglar-alarm, which, every night, Hill switched on before retiring.

"My dear little girl!" exclaimed the man, smiling as he strolled leisurely across to her with a cool, perfect unconcern which showed how completely he was master, "why create such a beastly draught? Nothing will happen, for I've already seen to those wires."

"You're a thief!" she cried, drawing herself up angrily. "I shall go straight to my father and tell him at once."

"You are at perfect liberty to act exactly as you choose," was Flockart's answer, as he bowed before her with irritating mock politeness. "But before you go, pray allow me to finish these most interesting documents, some of which, I believe, are in your very neat handwriting."

"My father's business is his own alone, and you have no right whatever to pry into it. I thought you were posing as his friend!" she cried in bitter protest, as she stood with both her hands clenched.

"I am his friend," he declared. "Some day, Gabrielle, you will know the truth of how near he is to disaster, and how I am risking much in an endeavour to save him."

"I don't believe you!" she exclaimed in undisguised disgust. "In your heart there is not one single spark of sympathy with him in his affliction or with me in my ghastly position!"

"Your position is only your own seeking, my dear child," was his cold response. "I gave you full warning long ago. You can't deny that."

"You conspired with Lady Heyburn against me!" she cried. "I have discovered more about it than you think; and I now openly defy you, Mr. Flockart. Please understand that."

"Good!" he replied, still unruffled. "I quite understand. You will pardon my resuming, won't you?" And walking back to the open safe, he drew forth a small bundle of papers from a drawer. Then he threw himself into a leather arm-chair, and proceeded to untie the tape and examine the documents one by one, as though in eager search of something.

"Though Lady Heyburn may be your friend, I am quite sure even she would never for a moment countenance such a dastardly action as this!" cried the girl, crimsoning in anger. "You come here, accept my father's hospitality, and make pretence of being his friend and adviser; yet you are conspiring against him, as you have done against myself!"

"So far as you yourself are concerned, my dear Gabrielle," he laughed, without deigning to look up from the papers he was scanning, "I offered you my friendship, but you refused it."

"Friendship!" she cried, in sarcasm. "Your friendship, Mr. Flockart! What, pray, is it worth? You surely know what people are saying - the construction they are placing upon your friendship for Lady Heyburn?"

"The misconstruction, you mean," he exclaimed airily,

correcting her. "Well, to me it matters not a single jot. The world is always ill-disposed and ill-natured. A woman can surely have a male friend without being subject to hostile and venomous criticism?"

"When the male friend is an honest man," said the girl meaningly.

He shrugged his shoulders and continued reading, as though utterly disregarding her presence.

What should she do? How should she act? She knew quite well that from those papers he could gather no knowledge of her father's affairs, unless he held some secret knowledge of the true meaning of those cryptic terms and allusions. To her they were all as Hebrew.

Only that very day Monsieur Goslin had again made one of those unexpected visits, remaining from eleven in the morning until three; afterwards taking his leave, and driving back in the car to Auchterarder Station. She had not seen him; but he had brought from Paris for her a big box of chocolates tied with violet ribbons, as had been his habit for quite a couple of years past. She was a particular favourite with the polite, middle-aged Frenchman.

Her father's demeanour was always more thoughtful and serious after the stranger's visits. Business matters put before him by his visitor always, it seemed, required much deep thought and ample consideration.

Some papers brought to her father by Goslin she had placed in the safe earlier that evening, and these, she recognised, were now in Flockart's hands. She had not read them herself, and had no idea of their contents. They were, to her, never interesting.

"Mr. Flockart," she exclaimed very firmly at last, "I ask you to kindly replace those papers in my father's safe, relock it, and hand me the key."

"That I certainly refuse to do," was the man's defiant reply, bowing as he spoke.

"You would prefer, then, that I should go up to my father and explain all I have seen?"

"I repeat what I have already said. You are perfectly at liberty to tellwhom you like. It makes no difference whatever to me. And, well, I don't want to be disturbed just now." Rising, he walked across to the writing-table, and taking a piece of note-paper bearing the Heyburn crest, rapidly pencilled some memoranda upon it. He was, it seemed, taking a copy of one of the documents.

Suddenly she sprang towards him, crying, "Give me that paper! Give it to me at once, I say! It is my father's."

He straightened himself from the table, pulled down his white dress-vest with its amethyst buttons, and, looking straight into her face, ordered her to leave the room.

"I shall not go," she answered boldly. "I have discovered a thief in my father's house; therefore my duty is to remain here."

"No. Surely your duty is to go upstairs and tell him;" and he bent again, resuming his rapid memoranda. "Well," he asked defiantly, a few moments later, seeing that she had not moved, "aren't you going?"

"I shall not leave you here alone."

"Don't. I might run away with some of the ornaments."

"Oh, yes!" exclaimed the girl bitterly, "you taunt me because you are well aware of my helplessness - of what occurred on that never-to-be-forgotten afternoon - of how completely you have me in your power! I see it all. You defy me, well knowing

The House Of Whispers   151

that you could, in a moment, bring upon me a vengeance terrible and complete. It is all horrible!" she cried, covering her face with her hands. "I know that I am in your power. And you have no pity, no remorse."

"I gave you full warning," he declared, placing the papers upon the table and looking at her. "I gave you your choice. You cannot blame me. You had ample time and opportunity."

"But I still have one man who loves me - a man who will yet stand my friend and defend me, even against you!"

"Walter Murie!" he laughed, with a quick gesture of disregard. "You believe him to be your friend? Recollect, my dear Gabrielle, that men are deceivers ever."

"So it seems in your case," she exclaimed with poignant bitterness. "You have brought scandalous comment upon my father's name, and yet you are utterly unconcerned."

"Because, as I have already told you, your father is my friend."

"And it is his money which you spend so freely," she said, in a low, hard voice of reproach. "It comes from him."

"His money!" he exclaimed quickly. "What do you mean? What do you imply?"

"Simply that among my father's accounts a short time back I found two cheques drawn by Lady Heyburn in your favour."

"And you told your father of them, of course!" he exclaimed with sarcasm. "A remarkable discovery, eh?"

"I told him nothing," was her bold reply. "Not because I wished to shield you, but because I did not wish to pain him unduly. He has worries sufficient, in all conscience."

"Your devotion is really most charming," the man declared

calmly, leaning against the table and examining her critically from head to foot. "Sir Henry believes in you. You are his dutiful daughter - pure, good, and all that!" he sneered. "I wonder what he would say if he - well, if he knew just a little of the truth, of what happened that day at Chantilly?"

"The truth! Ah, and you would tell him - you!" she gasped in a broken voice, her sweet, innocent face blanched to the lips in an instant. "You would drag my good name into the mire, and blast my life for ever with just as little compunction as you would shoot a rabbit. I know - I know you only too well, Mr. Flockart! I stand in your way; I am in your way as well as in Lady Heyburn's. You are only awaiting an opportunity to wreck my life and crush me! Once I am away from here, my poor father will be helpless in your hands!"

"Dear me," he sneered, "how very tragic you are becoming! That dressing-gown really makes you appear quite like a heroine of provincial melodrama. I ought now to have a revolver and threaten you, and then this scene would be complete for the stage - wouldn't it? But for goodness' sake don't remain here in the cold any longer, my dear little girl. Run off to bed, and forget that to-night you've been walking in your sleep."

"Not until I see that safe relocked and you give me the false key of yours. If you will not, then you shall this very night have an opportunity of telling the truth to my father. I am prepared to bear my shame and all its consequences -"

The words froze upon her pale lips. On the lawn outside the half-open glass door there was at that moment a light movement - the tapping of a walking-stick!

"Hush!" cried Flockart. "Remember what I can tell him - if I choose!"

In an instant she saw the fragile figure of her father, in soft felt-hat and black coat, creeping almost noiselessly past the window. He had been out for one of his nocturnal walks, for he sometimes went out alone when suffering from insomnia. He had just returned.

The blind man went forward only a few paces farther; but, finding that he had proceeded too far, he returned and discovered the open door. Near it stood the pair, not daring now to move lest the blind man's quick ears should detect their footsteps.

"Gabrielle! Gabrielle, my dear!" exclaimed the Baronet.

But though her heart beat quickly, the girl did not reply. She knew, however, that the old man could almost read her innermost thoughts. The ominous words of Flockart rang in her ears. Yes, he could tell a terrible and awful truth which must be concealed at all hazards.

"I felt sure I heard Gabrielle's voice. How curious!" murmured the old man, as his feet fell noiselessly upon the thick Turkey carpet. "Gabrielle, dear!" he called. But his daughter stood there breathless and silent, not daring to move a muscle. Plain it was that while passing across the lawn outside he heard her voice. He had overheard her declaration that she was prepared to bear the consequences of her disgrace.

Across the room the blind man groped, his hand held before him, as was his habit. "Strange! Remarkably strange!" he remarked to himself quite aloud. "I'm never mistaken in Gabrielle's voice. Gabrielle, dear, where are you? Why don't you speak? It's too late to-night to play practical jokes."

Flockart knew that he had left the safe-door open, yet he dared not move across the room to close it. The sightless man would detect the slightest movement in that dead silence of the night. With great care he left the girl's side, and a single stride brought him to the large writing-table, where he secured the document, together with the pencilled memoranda of its purport, both of which he slipped into his pocket unobserved.

Gabrielle dared not breathe. Her discovery there meant her ruin.

The man who held her in his toils cast her an evil, threatening glance, raising his clenched fist in menace, as though daring her to make the slightest movement. In his dark eyes showed a sinister expression, and his nether lip was hard. She was, alas! utterly and completely in his power.

The safe was some distance away, and in order to reach and close it he would be compelled to pass the man in blue spectacles now standing, puzzled and surprised, in the centre of the great book-lined apartment. Both of them could escape by the open window, but to do so would be to court discovery should the Baronet find his safe standing open. In that case the alarm would be raised, and they would both be found outside the house, instead of within.

Slowly the old man drew his thin hand across his furrowed brow, and then, as a sudden recollection dawned upon him, he cried, "Ah, the window! Why, that's strange! When I went out I closed it! But it was open - open - as I came in! Some one - some one has entered here in my absence!"

With both his thin, wasted hands outstretched, he walked quickly to his safe, cleverly avoiding the furniture in his course, and next second discovered that the iron door stood wide open.

"Thieves!" he gasped aloud hoarsely as the truth dawned upon him. "My papers! Gabrielle's voice! What can all this mean?" And next moment he opened the door, crying, "Help!" and endeavouring to alarm the household.

In an instant Flockart dashed forward towards the safe, and, without being observed by Gabrielle, had slipped the key into his own pocket.

"Gabrielle," cried the blind man, "you are here in the room. I know you are. You cannot deceive me. I smell that new scent, which your aunt Annie sent you, upon your handkerchief. Why don't you speak to me?"

"Yes, dad," she answered at last, in a low, strained voice, "I - I am here."

"Then what is meant by my safe being open?" he asked sternly, as all that Goslin had told him a little while before flashed across his memory. "Why have you obtained a key to it?"

"I have no key," was her quick answer.

"Come here," he said. "Let me take your hand."

With great reluctance, her eyes fixed upon Flockart's face, she did as she was bid, and as her father took her soft hand in his, he said in a stern, harsh tone, full of suspicion and quite unusual to him, "You are trembling, Gabrielle - trembling, because - because of my unexpected appearance, eh?"

The fair girl with the sweet face and dainty figure was silent. What could she reply?

CHAPTER XX

TELLS OF FLOCKART'S TRIUMPH

"What are you doing here at this hour?" Gabrielle's father demanded slowly, releasing her hand. "Why are you prying into my affairs?" He had not detected Flockart's presence, and believed himself alone with his daughter.

The man's glance again met Gabrielle's, and she saw in his eyes a desperate look. To tell the truth would, she knew, alas! cause the exposure of her secret and her disgrace. On both sides had she suddenly become hemmed in by a deadly peril.

"Dad," she cried suddenly, "do I not know all about your affairs already? Do I not act as your secretary? With what motive should I open your safe?"

Without response, the blind man moved back to the open door, and, placing his hand within, fingered one of the long iron drawers. It was unlocked, and he drew it forth. Some papers were within - blue, legal-looking papers which his daughter had never seen. "Yes," he exclaimed aloud, "just as I thought. This drawer has been opened, and my private affairs pried into. Tell me, Gabrielle, where is young Murie just at present?"

"In Paris, I believe. He left London unexpectedly three days ago."

"Paris!" echoed the old man. "Ah," he added, "Goslin was right - quite right. And so you, my daughter, in whom I placed all my trust - my - my only friend - have betrayed me!" he added brokenly.

"I have not betrayed you, dear father," was her quick protest. "To whom do you allege I have exposed your affairs?"

"To your lover, Walter."

To Flockart, whose wits were already at work upon some scheme to extricate himself, there came at that instant a sudden suggestion. He spoke, causing the old man to start suddenly and turn in the direction of the speaker.

As the words left his lips he raised a threatening finger towards Gabrielle, a sign of silence to her of which the old man was unfortunately in ignorance.

"I think, Sir Henry, that I ought to speak - to tell you the truth, painful though it may be. Five minutes ago I came down here in order to get a telegraph-form, as I wanted to send a wire at the earliest possible moment to-morrow, when, to my surprise, I saw a light beneath the door. I -"

"Oh, no, no!" gasped the girl, in horrified protest. "It's a lie!"

"I crept in quietly, and was very surprised to find Gabrielle with the safe open, and alone. I had expected that she was sitting up late, working with you. But she seemed to be examining and reading some papers she took from a drawer. Forgive me for telling you this, but the truth must now be made plain. I startled her by my sudden presence; and, pointing out the dishonour of copying her father's papers, no matter for what purpose, I compelled her to return the documents to their place. I fold her frankly that it was my duty, as your friend, to inform you of the incident; but she implored me, for the sake of her lover, to remain silent."

"Mr. Flockart!" cried the girl, "how dare you say such a thing when you know it to be an untruth; when -"

"Enough!" exclaimed her father bitterly. "I'm ashamed of you, Gabrielle. I -"

"I would beg of you, Sir Henry, not further to distress yourself," Flockart interrupted. "Love, as you know, often prompts both men and women to commit acts of supreme folly."

"Folly!" echoed the blind man. "This is more than folly! Gabrielle and her lover have conspired to bring about my ruin. I have had suspicions for several weeks; now, alas! they are confirmed. Walter Murie is in Paris at this moment in order to make money out of the secret knowledge which Gabrielle obtains for him. My own daughter is responsible for my betrayal!" he added, in a voice broken by emotion.

"No, no, Sir Henry!" urged Flockart. "Surely the outlook is not so black as you foresee. Gabrielle has acted injudiciously; but surely she is still devoted to you and your interests."

"Yes," cried the girl in desperation, "you know I am, dad. You know that I -"

"It is useless, Flockart, for you to endeavour to seek forgiveness for Gabrielle," declared her father in a firm, harsh voice, "Quite useless. She has even endeavoured to deny the statement you have made - tried to deny it when I actually heard with my own ears her defiant declaration that she was prepared to bear her shame and all its consequences! Let her do so, I say. She shall leave Glencardine to-morrow, and have no further opportunity to conspire against me."

"Oh, father, what are you saying?" she cried in despair, bursting into tears. "I have not conspired."

"I am saying the truth," went on the blind man. "You and

your lover have formed another clever plot, eh? Because I have not sight to watch you, you will copy my business reports and send them to Walter Murie, who hopes to place them in a certain channel where he can receive payment. This is not the first time my business has leaked out from this room. Only a short time ago certain confidential documents were offered to the Greek Government, but fortunately they were false ones prepared on purpose to trick any one who had designs upon my business secrets."

"I swear I am in ignorance of it all."

"Well, I have now told you plainly," the old man said. "I loved you, Gabrielle, and until this moment foolishly believed that you were devoted to me and to my interests. I trusted you implicitly, but you have betrayed me into the hands of my enemies - betrayed me," he wailed, "in such a manner that only ruin may face me. I tell you the hard and bitter truth. I am blind, and ever since your return from school you have acted as my secretary, and I have looked at the world only through your eyes. Ah," he sighed, "but I ought to have known! I should never have trusted a woman, even though she be my own daughter."

The girl stood with her blanched face covered by her hands. To protest, to declare that Flockart's story was a lie, was, she saw, all to no purpose. Her father had overheard her bold defiance and had, alas! Most unfortunately taken it as an admission of her guilt.

Flockart stood motionless but watchful; yet by the few words he uttered he succeeded in impressing the blind man with the genuineness of his friendship both for father and for daughter. He urged forgiveness, but Sir Henry disregarded all his appeals.

"No," he declared. "It is fortunate indeed, Flockart, that you made this discovery, and thus placed me upon my guard." The poor deluded man little dreamt that on the occasion when

Flockart had taken him down the drive to announce his departure from Glencardine on account of the gossip, and had drawn Sir Henry's attention to his hanging watch-chain, he had succeeded in cleverly obtaining two impressions of the safe-key attached. In his excitement, it had never occurred to him to ask his daughter by what means she had been able to open that steel door.

"Dad," she faltered, advancing towards him and placing her soft, tender hand upon his shoulder, "won't you listen to reason? I assure you I am quite innocent of any attempt or intention to betray you. I know you have many enemies;" and she glanced quickly in Flockart's direction. "Have we not often discussed them? Have I not kept eyes and ears open, and told you of all I have seen and learnt? Have -"

"You have seen and learnt what is to my detriment," he answered. "All argument is useless. A fortnight or so ago, by your aid, my enemies secured a copy of a certain document which has never left yonder safe. To-night Mr. Flockart has discovered you again tampering with my safe, and with my own ears I heard you utter defiance. You are more devoted to your lover than to me, and you are supplying him with copies of my papers."

"That is untrue, dad," protested the girl reproachfully.

But her father shook her hand roughly from his shoulder, saying, "I have already told you my decision, which is irrevocable. To-morrow you shall leave Glencardine and go to your aunt Emily at Woodnewton. You won't have much opportunity for mischief in that dull little Northampton village. I won't allow you to remain under my roof any longer; you are too ungrateful and deceitful, knowing as you do the misery of my affliction."

"But, father -"

"Go to your room," he ordered sternly. "Tomorrow I will

speak with your mother, and we shall then decide what shall be done. Only, understand one thing: in the future you are not my dear daughter that you have been in the past. I - I have no daughter," he added in a voice harsh yet broken by emotion, "for you have now proved yourself an enemy worse even than those who for so many years have taken advantage of my helplessness."

"Ah, dad, dad, you are cruel!" she cried, bursting again into a torrent of tears. "You are too cruel! I have done nothing!"

"Do you call placing me in peril nothing?" he retorted bitterly. "Go to your room at once. Remain with me, Flockart. I want to speak to you."

The girl saw herself convicted by those unfortunate words she had used - words meant in defiance of her arch-enemy Flockart, but which had placed her in ignominy and disgrace. Ah, if she could only stand firm and speak the ghastly truth! But, alas! she dared not. Flockart, the man who held her in his power, the man whom she knew to be her father's bitterest opponent, a cheat and a fraud, stood there triumphant, with a smile upon his lips; while she, pure, honest, and devoted to that afflicted man, was denounced and outcast. She raised her voice in one last word of faint protest.

But her father, angered and grieved, turned fiercely upon her and ordered her from his presence. "Go," he said, "and do not come near me again until your boxes are packed and you are ready to leave Glencardine."

"You speak as though I were a servant whom you've discharged," she said bitterly.

"I am speaking to my enemy, not to my daughter," was his hard response.

She raised her eyes to Flockart, and saw upon his dark face a hard, sphinx-like look. What hope of salvation could she ever expect from that man - the man who long ago had sought to estrange her from her father so that he might work his own ends? It was upon her tongue to turn upon him and relate the whole infamous truth. Yet so friendly had the two men become of late that she feared, even if she did so, that her father would only see in the revelation an attempt at reprisal. Besides, what if Flockart spoke? What if he told the awful truth? Her own dear father, whom she loved so well, even though he had misjudged her, would be dragged into the mire. No, she was the victim of that man, who was a past-master of the art of subterfuge; the man who, for years, had lived by his wits and preyed upon society.

"Leave us, and go to your room," again commanded her father.

She looked sadly at the white, bespectacled countenance which she loved so well. Her soft hand once more sought his; but he cast it from him, saying, "Enough of your caresses! You are no longer my daughter! Leave us!" And then, seeing all protest in vain, she sighed, turned very slowly, and with a last, lingering look upon the helpless man to whom she had been so devoted, and who now so grossly misjudged her, she tottered out, closing the door behind her.

"Has she gone?" asked Sir Henry a moment later.

Flockart responded in the affirmative, laying his hand upon the shoulder of his agitated host, and urging him to remain calm.

"That's all very well, my dear Flockart," he cried; "but you don't know what she has done. She exposed a week or so ago a most confidential arrangement with the Greek Government, a revelation which might have involved me in the loss of over a hundred thousand."

"Then it's fortunate, perhaps, that I discovered her to-night," replied his guest. "All this must be very painful to you,

Sir Henry."

"Very. I shall not give her another opportunity to betray me, Flockart, depend upon that," the elder man said. "My wife warned me against Gabrielle long ago. I now see that I was a fool for not taking her advice."

"Certainly it's a curious fact that Walter Murie is in Paris," remarked the other. "Was the revelation of your financial dealings made in Paris, do you know?"

"Yes, it was," snapped the blind man. "I believed Walter to be quite a good young fellow."

"Ah, I knew different, Sir Henry. His life up in London was not - well, not exactly all that it should be. He's in with a rather shady crowd."

"You never told me so."

"Because you did not believe me to be your friend until quite recently. I hope I have now proved what I have asserted. If I can do anything to assist you I am only too ready. I assure you that you have only to command me."

Sir Henry reflected deeply for a few moments. The discovery that his daughter was playing him false caused within him a sudden revulsion of feeling. Unfortunately, he could not see the expression upon the countenance of his false friend. He was wondering at that moment whether he might entrust to him a somewhat delicate mission.

"Gabrielle shall not return here," her father said, as though speaking to himself.

"That is a course which I would most strongly advise. Send the girl away," urged the other. "Evidently she has grossly betrayed you."

William Le Queux

"That I certainly intend doing," was the answer. "But I wonder, Flockart, if I might take you at your word, and ask you to do me a favour? I am so helpless, or I would not think of troubling you."

"Only tell me what you wish, and I will do it with pleasure."

"Very well, then," replied the blind man. "Perhaps I shall want you to go to Paris at once, watch the actions of young Murie, and report to me from time to time. Would you?"

A look of bright intelligence overspread the man's features as a new vista opened before him. Sir Henry was about to take him into his confidence! "Why, with pleasure," he said cheerily. "I'll start to-morrow, and rest assured that I'll keep a very good eye upon the young gentleman. You now know the painful truth concerning your daughter - the truth which Lady Heyburn has told you so often, and which you have never yet heeded."

"Yes, Flockart," answered the afflicted man, taking his guest's hand in warm friendship. "I once disliked you - that I admit; but you were quite frank the other day, and now to-night you have succeeded in making a discovery that, though it has upset me terribly, may mean my salvation."

CHAPTER XXI

THROUGH THE MISTS

Sir Henry refused to speak with his daughter when, on the following morning, she stole in and laid her hand softly upon his arm. He ordered her, in a tone quite unusual, to leave the library. Through the morning hours she had lain awake trying to make a resolve. But, alas! she dared not tell the truth; she was in deadly fear of Flockart's reprisals.

That morning, at nine o'clock, Lady Heyburn and Flockart had held hurried consultation in secret, at which he had explained to her what had occurred.

"Excellent!" she had remarked briefly. "But we must now have a care, my dear friend. Mind the girl does not throw all prudence to the winds and turn upon us."

"Bah!" he laughed, "I don't fear that for a single second." And he left the room again, to salute her in the breakfast-room a quarter of an hour later as though they had not met before that day.

Gabrielle, on leaving her father, went out for a long walk alone, away over the heather-clad hills. For hours she went on - Jock, her Aberdeen terrier, toddling at her side, in her hand a stout ash-stick - regardless of the muddy roads or the wet weather. It was grey, damp, and dismal, one of those days which in the Highlands are often so very cheerless and dispiriting. Yet on, and still on, she went, her mind full of the events of the previous night; full, also, of the dread secret which prevented her from exposing her father's false friend. In order to save her father, should she sacrifice herself - sacrifice her own life? That was the one problem before her.

She saw nothing; she heeded nothing. Hunger or fatigue troubled her not. Indeed, she took no notice of where her footsteps led her. Beyond Crieff she wandered, along the river-bank a short distance, ascending a hill, where a wild and wonderful view spread before her. There she sat down upon a big boulder to rest.

Her hair blown by the chill wind, she sat staring straight before her, thinking - ever thinking. She had not seen Lady Heyburn that day. She had seen no one.

At six o'clock that morning she had written a long letter to Walter Murie. She had not mentioned the midnight incident, but she had, with many expressions of regret, pointed out the futility of any further affection between them. She had not attempted to excuse herself. She merely told him that she considered herself unworthy of his love, and because of that, and that alone, she had decided to break off their engagement.

A dozen times she had reread the letter after she had completed it. Surely it was the letter of a heart-broken and desperate woman. Would he take it in the spirit in which it was meant, she wondered. She loved him - ah, loved him better than any one else in all the world! But she now saw that it was useless to masquerade any longer. The blow had fallen, and it had crushed her. She was powerless to resist, powerless to deny the false charge against her, powerless to tell the truth.

That letter, which she knew must come as a cruel blow to Walter, she had given to the postman with her own hands, and it was now on its way south. As she sat on the summit of that heather-clad hill she was wondering what effect her written words would have upon him. He had loved her so devotedly ever since they had been children together! Well she knew how strong was his passion for her, how his life was at her disposal. She knew that on reading those despairing lines of hers he would be staggered. She recalled the dear face of her soul-mate, his hot kisses, his soft terms of endearment, and alone there, with none to witness her bitter grief, she burst into a flood of tears.

The sad greyness of the landscape was in keeping with her own great sorrow. She had lost all that was dear to her; and, young as she was, with hardly any experience of the world and its ways, she was already the victim of grim circumstance, broken by the grief of a self-renounced love gnawing at her true heart.

The knowledge that Lady Heyburn and Flockart would exult over her downfall and exile to that tiny house in a sleepy little Northamptonshire village did not trouble her. Her enemies had triumphed. She had played the game and lost, just as she might have lost at billiards or at bridge, for she was a thorough sportswoman. She only grieved because she saw the grave peril of her dear father, and because she now foresaw the utter hopelessness of her own happiness.

It was better, she reflected, far better, that she should go into the dull and dreary exile of an English village, with the unexciting companionship of Aunt Emily, an ascetic spinster of the mid-Victorian era, and make pretence of pique with Walter, than to reveal to him the shameful truth. He would at least in those circumstances retain of her a recollection fond and tender. He would not despise nor hate her, as he most certainly would do if he knew the real astounding facts.

How long she remained there, high up, with the chill winds of autumn tossing her silky, light-brown hair, she knew not. Rainclouds were gathering, and the rugged hill before her was now hidden behind a bank of mist. Time had crept on without her heeding it, for what did time now matter to her? What, indeed, did anything matter? Her young life, though she was still in her teens, had ended; or, at least, as far as she was concerned it had. Was she not calmly and coolly contemplating telling the truth and putting an end to her existence after saving her father's honour?

Her sad, tearful eyes gazed slowly about her as she suddenly awakened to the fact that she was far - very far - from home. She had been dazed, unconscious of everything, because of the heavy burden of grief within her heart. But now she looked forth upon the small, grey loch, with its dark fringe of trees, the grey and purple hills beyond, the grey sky, and the grey, filmy mists that hung everywhere. The world was, indeed, sad and gloomy, and even Jock sat looking up at his young mistress as though regarding her grief in wonder.

Now and then distant shots came from across the hills. They were shooting over the Drummond estate, she knew, for she had had an invitation to join their luncheon-party that day. Lady Heyburn and Flockart had no doubt gone.

That, she told herself, was her last day in the Highlands, that picturesque, breezy country she loved so well. It was her last day amid those familiar places where she and Walter had so often wandered together, and where he had told her of his passionate devotion. Well, perhaps it was best, after all. Down south she would not be reminded of him every moment and at every turn. No, she sighed within herself as she rose to descend the hill, she must steel herself against her own sad reflections. She must learn how to forget.

"What will he say?" she murmured aloud as she went down, with Jock frisking and barking before her. "What will he think of me when he gets my letter? He will believe me fickle; he will believe that I have another lover. That is certain. Well, I must allow him to believe it. We have parted, and we must now, alas! remain apart for ever. Probably he will seek from my father the truth concerning my disappearance from Glencardine. Dad will tell him, no doubt. And then - then, what will he believe? He - he will know that I am unworthy to be his wife. Yet - yet is it not cruel that I dare not speak the truth and clear myself of this foul charge of betraying my own dear father? Was ever a girl placed in such a position as myself, I wonder. Has any girl ever loved a man better than I love Walter?" Her white lips were set hard, and her fine eyes became again bedimmed by tears.

It commenced to rain, that fine drizzle so often experienced north of the Tweed. But she heeded not. She was used to it. To get wet through was, to her, quite a frequent occurrence when out fishing. Though there was no path, she knew her way; and, walking through the wet heather, she came after half-an-hour out upon a muddy byroad which led her into the town of Crieff, whence her return was easy; though it was already dusk, and the dressing-bell had gone, before she re-entered the house by the servants' door and slipped unobserved up to her own room.

Elise found her seated in her blue gown before the welcome fire-log, her chin upon her breast. Her excuse was that she felt unwell; therefore one of the maids brought her some dinner on a tray.

Upon the mantelshelf were many photographs, some of them snap-shots of her schoolfellows and souvenirs of holidays, the odds and ends of portraits and scenes which every girl unconsciously collects.

Among them, in a plain silver frame, was the picture of Walter Murie taken in New York only a few weeks before. Upon the frame was engraved, "Gabrielle, from Walter." She took it in her hand, and stood for a long time motionless. Never again, alas! would she look upon that face so dear to her. Her young heart was already broken, because she was held fettered and powerless.

At last she put down the portrait, and, sinking into her chair, sat crying bitterly. Now that she was outcast by her father, to whom she had been always such a close, devoted friend, her life was an absolute blank. At one blow she had lost both lover and father. Already Elise had told her that she had received instructions to pack her trunks. The thin-nosed Frenchwoman was apparently much puzzled at the order which Lady Heyburn had given her, and had asked the girl whom she intended to visit. The maid had asked what dresses she would require; but Gabrielle replied that she might pack what she liked for a long visit. The girl could hear Elise moving about, shaking out skirts, in the adjoining room, and making preparations for her departure on the morrow.

Despondent, hopeless, grief-stricken, she sat before the fire for a long time. She had locked the door and switched off the light, for it irritated her. She loved the uncertain light of dancing flames, and sat huddled there in her big chair for the last time.

She was reflecting upon her own brief life. Scarcely out of the schoolroom, she had lived most of her days up in that dear old place where every inch of the big estate was so familiar to her. She remembered all those happy days at school, first in England, and then in France, with the kind-faced Sisters in their spotless head-dresses, and the quiet, happy life of the convent. The calm, grave face of Sister Marguerite looked down upon her from the mantelshelf as if sympathising with her pretty pupil in those troubles that had so early come to her. She raised her eyes, and saw the portrait. Its sight aroused within her a new thought and fresh recollection. Had not Sister Marguerite always taught her to beseech the Almighty's aid when in doubt or when in trouble? Those grave, solemn words of the Mother Superior rang in her ears, and she fell upon her knees beside her narrow bed in the alcove, and with murmuring lips prayed for divine support and assistance. She raised her sweet, troubled face to heaven and made confession to her Maker.

Then, after a long silence, she struggled again to her feet, more cool and more collected. She took up Walter's portrait, and, kissing it, put it away carefully in a drawer. Some of her little treasures she gathered together and placed with it, preparatory to departure, for she would on the morrow leave Glencardine perhaps for ever.

The stable-clock had struck ten. To where she stood came the strident sounds of the mechanical piano-player, for some of the gay party were waltzing in the hall. Their merry shouts and laughter were discordant to her ears. What cared any of those friends of her step-mother if she were in disgrace and an outcast?

Drawing aside the curtain, she saw that the night was bright and starlit. She preferred the air out in the park to the sounds of gaiety within that house which was no longer to be her home. Therefore she slipped on a skirt and blouse, and, throwing her golf-cape across her shoulders and a shawl over her head, she crept past the room wherein Elise was packing her belongings, and down the back-stairs to the lawn.

The sound the laughter of the men and women of the shooting-party aroused a poignant bitterness within her. As she passed across the drive she saw a light in the library, where, no doubt, her father was sitting in his loneliness, feeling and examining his collection of seal-impressions.

She turned, and, walking straight on, struck the gravelled path which took her to the castle ruins.

Not until the black, ponderous walls rose before her did she awaken to a consciousness of her whereabouts. Then, entering the ruined courtyard, she halted and listened. All was dark. Above, the stars twinkled brightly, and in the ivy the night-birds stirred the leaves. Holding her breath, she strained her ears. Yes, she was not deceived! There were sounds distinct and undeniable. She was fascinated, listening again to those shadow-voices that were always precursory of death - the fatal Whispers.

CHAPTER XXII

BY THE MEDITERRANEAN

It was February - not the foggy, muddy February of dear, damp Old England, but winter beside the bright blue Mediterranean, the winter of the Cote d'Azur.

At the Villa Heyburn - that big, square, white house with the green sun-shutters, surrounded by its great garden full of spreading palms, sweet-smelling mimosa, orange-trees laden with golden fruit, and bright geraniums, up on the Berigo at San Remo - Lady Heyburn had that afternoon given a big luncheon-party. The smartest people wintering in that most sheltered nook of the Italian Riviera had eaten and gossiped and flirted, and gone back to their villas and hotels. Dull persons found no place in Lady Heyburn's circle. Most of the people were those she knew in London or in Paris, including a sprinkling of cosmopolitans, a Russian prince notorious for his losses over at the new *cercle* at Cannes, a divorced Austrian Archduchess, and two or three well-known diplomats.

"Dear old Henry" remained, of course, at Glencardine, as he always did. Lady Heyburn looked upon her winter visit to that beautiful villa overlooking the calm sapphire sea as her annual emancipation. Henry was a dear old fellow, she openly confided to her friends, but his affliction made him terribly trying.

But Jimmy Flockart, the good-looking, amusing, well-dressed

idler, was living down at the "Savoy," and was daily in her company, driving, motoring, picnicking, making excursions in the mountains, or taking trips over to "Monte" by the *train-de-luxe*. He had left the villa early in the afternoon, returned to his hotel, changed his smart flannels for a tweed suit, and, taking a stout stick, had set off alone for his daily constitutional along the sea-road in the direction of that pretty but half-deserted little watering-place, Ospedaletti.

Straight before him, into the unruffled, tideless sea, the sun was sinking in all its blood-red glory as he went at swinging pace along the white, dusty road, past the *octroi* barrier, and out into the country where, on the left, the waves lazily lapped the grey rocks, while upon the right the fertile slopes were covered with carnations and violets growing for the markets of Paris and London. In the air was a delightful perfume, the freshness of the sea in combination with the sweetness of the flowers.

A big red motor-car dashed suddenly round a corner, raising a cloud of dust. An American party were on their way from Genoa to the frontier along the Corniche, one of the most picturesque routes in all the world.

James Flockart had no eyes for beauty. He was too occupied by certain grave apprehensions. That morning he had walked in the garden with Lady Heyburn, and had a long chat with her. Her attitude had been peculiar. He could not make her out. She had begged him to promise to leave San Remo, and when asked to tell the reason of this sudden demand she had firmly refused.

"You must leave here, Jimmy," she had said quite calmly. "Go down to Rome, to Palermo, to Ragusa, or somewhere where you can put in a month or so in comfort. The Villa Igiea at Palermo would suit you quite well - lots of smart people, and very decent cooking."

"Well," he laughed, " as far as hotels go, nothing could be

worse than this place. I'd never put my nose into this hole if it were not for the fact that you come here. There isn't a hotel worth the name. When one goes to Monte, or Cannes, or even decaying Nice, one can get decent cooking. But here - ugh!" and he shrugged his shoulders. "Price higher than the 'Ritz' in Paris, food fourth-rate, rooms cheaply decorated, and a dullness unequalled."

"My dear Jimmy," laughed her ladyship, "you're such a cosmopolitan that you're incorrigible. I know you don't like this place. You've been here six weeks, so go."

"You've had a letter from the old man, eh?"

"Yes, I have," she replied, and he saw that her countenance changed; but she would say nothing more. She had decided that he must leave San Remo, and would hear no argument to the contrary.

The southern sun sank slowly into the sea, now grey but waveless. On the horizon lay the long smoke-trail of a passing steamer eastward bound. He had rounded the steep, rocky headland, and in the hollow before him nestled the little village of Ospedaletti, with its closed casino, its rows of small villas, and its palm-lined *passeggiata*.

A hundred yards farther on he saw the figure of a rather shabby, middle-aged man, in a faded grey overcoat and grey soft felt-hat of the mode usual on the Riviera, but discoloured by long wear, leaning upon the low sea-wall and smoking a cigarette. No other person was in the vicinity, and it was quickly evident from the manner in which the wayfarer recognised him and came forward to meet him with outstretched hand that they had met by appointment. Short of stature as he was, with fair hair, colourless eyes, and a fair moustache, his slouching appearance was that of one who had seen better days, even though there still remained about him a vestige of dandyism. The close observer would, however, detect that his clothes, shabby though they were, were of foreign cut, and that his greeting was of that demonstrative character that betrayed his foreign birth.

"Well, my dear Krail," exclaimed Flockart, after they had shaken hands and stood together leaning upon the sea-wall, "you got my wire in Huntingdon? I was uncertain whether you were at the 'George' or at the 'Fountain,' so I sent a message to both."

"I was at the 'George,' and left an hour after receipt of your wire."

"Well, tell me what has happened. How are things up at Glencardine?"

"Goslin is with the old fellow. He has taken the girl's place as his confidential secretary," was the shabby man's reply, speaking with a foreign accent. "Walter Murie was at home for Christmas, but went to Cairo."

"And how are matters in Paris?"

"They are working hard, but it's an uphill pull. The old man is a craftyold bird. Those papers you got from the safe had been cunningly prepared for anybody who sought to obtain information. The consequence is that we've shown our hand, and heavily handicapped ourselves thereby."

"You told me all that when you were down here a month ago," Flockart said impatiently.

"You didn't believe me then. You do now, I suppose?"

"I've never denied it," Flockart declared, offering the stranger a Russian cigarette from his gold case. "I was completely misled, and by the girl also."

"The girl's influence with her father is happily quite at an end," remarked the shabby man. "I saw her last week in

Woodnewton. The change from Glencardine to an eight-roomed cottage in a village street must be rather severe."

"Only what she deserves," snapped Flockart. "She defied us."

"Granted. But I cannot help thinking that we haven't played a very fair game," said the man. "Remember, she's only a girl."

"But dangerous to us and to our plans, my dear Krail. She knows a lot."

"Because - well, forgive me for saying so, my dear Flockart – because you've been a fool, and have allowed her to know."

"It wasn't I; it was the woman."

"Lady Heyburn! Why, I always believed her to be the soul of discretion."

"She's been too defiant of consequences. A dozen times I've warned her; but she will not heed."

"Then she'll land herself in a deep hole if she isn't careful," replied the foreigner, speaking very fair English. "Does she know I'm here?"

"Of course not. If we're to play the game she must know nothing. She's already inclined to throw prudence to the winds, and to confess all to her husband."

"Confess!" gasped the stranger, paling beneath his rather sallow skin. "*Per Bacco!* she's not going to be such an idiot, surely?"

"We were run so close, and so narrowly escaped discovery after I got at those papers at Glencardine, that she seems to have lost heart," Flockart remarked.

"But if she acted the fool and told Sir Henry, it would mean ruin for us, and that would also mean -"

"It would mean exposure for Gabrielle," interrupted Flockart. "The old man dare not lift his voice for his daughter's sake."

"Ah," exclaimed Krail, "that's just where you've acted injudiciously! You've set him against her; therefore he wouldn't spare her."

"It was imperative. I couldn't afford to be found prying into the old man's papers, could I? I got impressions of his key while walking in the park one day. He's never suspected it."

"Of course not. He believes in you," laughed his friend, "as one of the few upright men who are his friends! But," he added, "you've done wrong, my dear fellow, to trust a woman with a secret. Depend upon it, her ladyship will let you down."

"Well, if she does," remarked Flockart, with a shrug of the shoulders, "she'll have to suffer with me. You know where we should all find ourselves."

The man pulled a wry face and puffed at his cigarette in silence.

"What does the girl do?" asked Flockart a few moments later.

"Well, she seems to have a pretty dull time with the old lady. I stayed at the 'Cardigan Arms' at Woodnewton for two days - a miserable little place - and watched her pretty closely. She's out a good deal, rambling alone across the country with a collie belonging to a neighbouring farmer. She's the very picture of sadness, poor little girl!"

"You seem to sympathise with her, Krail. Why, does she not stand between us and fortune?"

"She'll stand between us and a court of assize if that woman acts the fool!" declared the shabby stranger, who moved so rapidly and whose vigilance seemed unequalled.

"If we go, she shall go also," Flockart declared in a threatening voice.

"But you must prevent such a *contretemps*," Krail urged.

"Ah, it's all very well to talk like that! But you know enough of her ladyship to be aware that she acts on her own initiative."

"That shows that she's no fool," remarked the foreigner quickly. "You who hold her in the hollow of your hand must prevent her from opening up to her husband. The whole future lies with you."

"And what is the future without money? We want a few thousands for immediate necessities, both of us. The woman's allowance from her husband is nowadays a mere bagatelle."

"Because he probably knows that some of her money has gone into your pockets, my dear boy."

"No; he's completely in ignorance of that. How, indeed, could he know? She takes very good care there's no possibility of his finding out."

"Well," remarked the stranger, "that's what I fear has happened, or may one day happen. The fact is, *caro mio*, we are in a quandary at the present moment. You were a bit too confident in dealing with those documents you found at Glencardine. You should have taken her ladyship into your confidence and got her to pump her husband concerning them. If you had, we shouldn't have made the mess of it that we have done."

"I must admit, Krail, that what you say is true," declared the well-dressed man. "You are such a philosopher always! I asked you to come here in secret to explain the exact position."

"It is one of peril. We are checkmated. Goslin holds the whole position in his hands, and will keep it."

"Very fortunately for you he doesn't, though we were very near exposure when I went out to Athens and made a fool of myself upon the report furnished by you."

"I believed it to be a genuine one. I had no idea that the old man was so crafty."

"Exactly. And if he displayed such clever ingenuity and forethought in laying a trap for the inquisitive, is it not more than likely that there may be other traps baited with equal craft and cunning?"

"Then how are we to make the *coup*?" Flockart asked, looking into the colourless eyes of his friend.

"We shall, I fear, never make it, unless -"

"Unless what?" he asked.

"Unless the old man meets with an accident," replied the other, in a low, distinct voice. "*Blind men sometimes do, you know!*"

CHAPTER XXIII

WHICH SHOWS A SHABBY FOREIGNER

Felix Krail, his cigarette held half-way to his lips, stood watching the effect of his insinuation. He saw a faint smile playing about Flockart's lips, and knew that it appealed to him. Old Sir Henry Heyburn had laid a clever trap for him, a trap into which he himself believed that his daughter had fallen. Why should not Flockart retaliate?

The shabby stranger, whose own ingenuity and double-dealing were little short of marvellous, and under whose watchful vigilance the Heyburn household had been ever since her ladyship and her friend Flockart had gone south, stood silent, but in complete satisfaction.

The well-dressed Riviera-lounger - the man so well known at all the various gay resorts from Ventimiglia along to Cannes, and who was a member of the Fetes Committee at San Remo and at Nice - merely exchanged glances with his friend and smiled. Quickly, however, he changed the topic of conversation. "And what's occurring in Paris?"

"Ah, there we have the puzzle!" replied the man Krail, his accent being an unfamiliar one - so unfamiliar, indeed, that those unacquainted with the truth were always placed in doubt regarding his true nationality.

"But you've made inquiry?" asked his friend quickly.

"Of course; but the business is kept far too close. Every precaution is taken to prevent anything leaking out," Krail responded.

"The clerks will speak, won't they?" the other said.

"*Mon cher ami*, they know no more of the business of the mysterious firm of which the blind Baronet is the head than we do ourselves," said Krail.

"They make enormous financial deals, that's very certain."

"Not deals - but *coups* for themselves," he laughed, correcting Flockart. "Recollect what I discovered in Athens, and the extraordinary connection you found in Brussels."

"Ah, yes. You mean that clever crowd - four men and two women who were working the gambling concession from the Dutch Government!" exclaimed Flockart. "Yes, that was a complete mystery. They sent wires in cipher to Sir Henry at Glencardine. I managed to get a glance at one of them, and it was signed 'Metaforos.'"

"That's their Paris cable address," said his companion.

"Surely you, with your network of sources of information, and your own genius for discovering secrets, ought to be able to reveal the true nature of Sir Henry's business. Is it an honest one?" asked Flockart.

"I think not."

"Think! Why, my dear Felix, this isn't like you only to think; you always *know*. You're so certain of your facts that I've always banked upon them."

The other gave his shoulders a shrug of indecision. "It was not a judicious move on your part to get rid of the girl from Glencardine," he said slowly. "While she was there we had a chance of getting at some clue. But now old Goslin has taken her place we may just as well abandon investigation at that end."

"You've failed, Krail, and attribute your failure to me," protested his companion. "How could I risk being ignominiously kicked out of Glencardine as a spy?"

"Whatever attitude you might have taken would have had the same result. We used the information, and found ourselves fooled - tricked by a very crafty old man, who actually prepared those documents in case he was betrayed."

"Admitted," said Flockart. "But even though we made fools of ourselves in Athens, and caused the Greek Government to look upon us as rogues and liars, the girl is suspected; and I for one don't mean to give in before we've secured a nice, snug little sum."

"How are we to do it?"

"By obtaining knowledge of the game being played in Paris, and working in an opposite direction," Flockart replied. "We are agreed upon one point: that for the past few years, ever since Goslin came on the scene, Sir Henry's business - a big one, there is no doubt - has been of a mysterious and therefore shady character. By his confidence in Gabrielle, his care that nobody ever got a chance inside that safe, his regular consultations with Goslin (who travelled from Paris specially to see him), his constant telegrams in cipher, and his refusal to allow even his wife to obtain the slightest inkling into his private affairs, it is shown that he fears exposure. Do you agree?"

"Most certainly I do."

"Well, any man who is in dread of the truth becoming known must be carrying on some negotiations the reverse of creditable. He is the moving spirit of that shady house, without a doubt," declared Flockart, who had so often grasped the blind man's hand in friendship. "In such fear that his transactions should become known, and that exposure might result, he actually had prepared documents on purpose to mislead those who pried into his affairs. Therefore, the instant we discover the truth, fortune will be at our hand. We all want money, you, I, and Lady Heyburn - and money we'll have."

"With these sentiments, my dear friend, I entirely and absolutely agree," remarked the shabby man, lighting a fresh cigarette. "But one fact you seem to have entirely overlooked."

"What?"

"The girl. She stands between you, and she might come back into the old man's favour, you know."

"And even though she did, that makes no difference," Flockart answered defiantly.

"Why?"

"Because she dare not say a single word against me."

Krail looked him straight in the face with considerable surprise, but made no comment.

"She knows better," Flockart added.

"Never believe too much in your own power with a woman, *mon cher ami*," remarked the other dubiously. "She's young, therefore of a romantic turn of mind. She's in love, remember, which makes matters much worse for us."

"Why?"

"Because, being in love, she may become seized with a sentimental fit. This ends generally in a determination of self-sacrifice; and in such case she would tell the truth in defiance of you, and would be heedless of her own danger."

Flockart drew a long breath. What this man said was, he knew within his own heart, only too true of the girl towards whom they had been so cruel and so unscrupulous. His had been a lifelong scheme, and as part of his scheme in conjunction with the woman who was Sir Henry's wife, it had been unfortunately compulsory to sacrifice the girl who was the blind man's right hand.

Yes, Gabrielle was deeply in love with Walter Murie - the man upon whom Sir Henry now looked as his enemy, and who would have exposed him to the Greek Government if the blind man had not been too clever. The Baronet, after his daughter's confession, naturally attributed her curiosity to Walter's initiative, the more especially that Walter had been in Paris, and, it was believed, in Athens also.

The pair were, however, now separated. Krail, in pursuit of his diligent inquiries, had actually been in Woodnewton, and seen the lonely little figure, sad and dejected, taking long rambles accompanied only by a farmer's sheep-dog. Young Murie had not been there; nor did the pair now correspond. This much Krail had himself discovered.

The problem placed before Flockart by his shabby friend was a somewhat disconcerting one. On the one hand, Lady Heyburn had urged him to leave the Riviera, without giving him any reason, and on the other, he had the ever-present danger of Gabrielle, in a sudden fit of sentimental self-sacrifice, "giving him away." If she did, what then? The mere suggestion caused him to bite his nether lip.

Krail knew a good deal, but he did not know all. Perhaps it was as well that he did not. There is a code of honour among adventurers all the world over; but few of them can resist the practice of blackmail when they chance to fall upon evil days.

"Yes," Flockart said reflectively, as at Krail's suggestion they turned and began to descend the steep hill towards Ospedaletti, "perhaps it's a pity, after all, that the girl left Glencardine. Yet surely she's safer with her aunt?"

"She was driven from Glencardine!"

"By her father."

"You sacrificed her in order to save yourself. That was but natural. It's a pity, however, you didn't take my advice."

"I suggested it to Lady Heyburn. But she would have nothing to do with it. She declared that such a course was far too dangerous."

"Dangerous!" echoed the shabby man. "Surely it could not have placed either of you in any greater danger than you are in already?"

"She didn't like it."

"Few people do," laughed the other. "But, depend upon it, it's the only way. She wouldn't, at any rate, have had an opportunity of telling the truth."

Flockart pulled a wry face, and after a silence of a few moments said, "Don't let us discuss that. We fully considered all the pros and cons, at the time."

"Her ladyship is growing scrupulously honest of late," sneered his companion. "She'll try to get rid of you very soon, I expect."

The latter sentence was more full of meaning than the speaker dreamed. The words, falling upon Flockart's ears, caused him to wince. Was her ladyship really trying to rid herself of his influence? He laughed within himself at the thought of her endeavouring to release herself from the bond. For her he had never, at any moment, entertained either admiration or affection. Their association had always been purely one of business - business, be it said, in which he made the profits and she the losses.

"It would hardly be an easy matter for her," replied the easy-going, audacious adventurer.

"She seems to be very popular up at Glencardine," remarked the foreigner, "because she's extravagant and spends money in the neighbourhood, I suppose. But the people in Auchterarder village criticise her treatment of Gabrielle. They hear gossip from the servants, I expect."

"They should know of the girl's treatment of her stepmother," exclaimed Flockart. "But there, villagers are always prone to listen to and embroider any stories concerning the private life of the gentry. It's just the same in Scotland as in any other country in the world."

"Ah!" continued Flockart, "in Scotland the old families are gradually decaying, and their estates are falling into the hands of blatant parvenus. Counter-jumpers stalk deer nowadays, and city clerks on their holidays shoot over peers' preserves. The humble Scot sees it all with regret, because he has no real liking for this latter-day invasion by the newly-rich English. Cotton-spinners from Lancashire buy deer-forests, and soap-boilers from Limehouse purchase castles with family portraits and ghosts complete."

"Ah! speaking of the supernatural," exclaimed Krail suddenly, "do you know I had a most extraordinary and weird experience when at Glencardine about three weeks ago. I actually heard the Whispers!"

Flockart stared hard at the man at his side, and, laughing outright, said, "Well, that's the best joke I've heard to-day. You, of all men, to be taken in by a mere superstition."

"But, my dear friend, I heard them," said Krail. "I swear I

ctually heard them! And I - well, I admit to you, even though you may laugh at me for being a superstitious fool - I somehow anticipate that something uncanny is about to happen to me."

"You're going to die, like all the rest of them, I suppose," laughed his friend, as they descended the dusty, winding road that led to the palm-lined promenade of the quiet little Mediterranean watering-place.

CHAPTER XXIV

"WHEN GREEK MEETS GREEK"

On their left were several white villas, before which pink and scarlet geraniums ran riot, with spreading mimosas golden with their feathery blossom, for Ospedaletti makes a frantic, if vain, bid for popularity as a winter-resort. Its deadly dullness, however, is too well known to the habitue of the Riviera; and its casino, which never obtained a licence, imparts to it the air of painful effort at gaiety.

"Well," remarked the shabby man as they passed along and out upon the sea-road in the direction of Bordighera, "I always looked upon what the people at Auchterarder said regarding the Whispers as a mere myth. But now, having heard them with my own ears, how can I have further doubt?"

"I've listened in the Castle ruins a good many times, my dear Krail," replied the other, "but I've never heard anything more exciting than an owl. Indeed, Lady Heyburn and I, when there was so much gossip about the strange noises some two years ago, set to work to investigate. We went there at least a dozen times, but without result; only both of us caught bad colds."

"Well," exclaimed Krail, "I used to ridicule the weird stories I heard in the village about the Devil's Whisper, and all that. But by mere chance I happened to be at the spot one bright night, and I heard distinct whisperings, just as had been described to me. They gave me a very creepy feeling, I can assure you."

"Bosh! Now, do you believe in ghosts, you man-of-the-world that you are, my dear Felix?"

"No. Most decidedly I don't."

"Then what you've heard is only in imagination, depend upon it. The supernatural doesn't exist in Glencardine, that's quite certain," declared Flockart. "The fact is that there's so much tradition and legendary lore connected with the old place, and its early owners were such a set of bold and defiant robbers, that for generations the peasantry have held it in awe. Hence all sorts of weird and terrible stories have been invented and handed down, until the present age believes them to be based upon fact."

"But, my dear friend, I actually heard the Whispers - heard them with my own ears," Krail asserted. "I happened to be about the place that night, trying to get a peep into the library, where Goslin and the old man were, I believe, busy at work. But the blinds fitted too closely, so that I couldn't see inside. The keeper and his men were, I knew, down in the village; therefore I took a stroll towards the ruins, and, as it was a beautiful night, I sat down in the courtyard to have a smoke. Then, of a sudden, I heard low voices quite distinctly. They startled me, for not until they fell upon my ears did I recall the stories told to me weeks before."

"If Stewart or any of the under-keepers had found you prowling about the Castle grounds at that hour they might have asked you awkward questions," remarked Flockart.

"Oh," laughed the other, "they all know me as a visitor to the village fond of walking exercise. I took very good care that they should all know me, so that as few explanations as possible would be necessary. As you well know, the secret of all my successes is that I never leave anything to chance."

"To go peeping about outside the house and trying to took in at lighted windows sounds a rather injudicious proceeding," his companion declared.

"Not if proper precautions are taken, as I took them. I was weeks inthat terribly dull Scotch village, but nobody suspected my real mission. I made quite a large circle of friends at the 'Star,' who all elieved me to be a foreign ornithologist writing a book upon the birds of Scotland. Trust me to tell people a good story."

"Well," exclaimed Flockart, after a long silence, "those Whispers are certainly a mystery, more especially if you've actually heard them. On two or three occasions I've spoken to Sir Henry about them. He ridicules the idea, yet he admitted to me one evening that the voices had really been heard. I declared that the most remarkable fact was the sudden death of each person who had listened and heard them. It is a curious phenomenon, which certainly should be investigated."

"The inference is that I, having listened to the ghostly voices, am doomed to a sudden and violent end," remarked the shabby stranger quite gloomily.

Flockart laughed. "Really, Felix, this is too funny!" he said. "Fancy your taking notice of such old wives' fables! Why, my dear fellow, you've got many years of constant activity before you yet. You must return to Paris in the morning, and watch in patience."

"I have watched, but discovered nothing."

"Perhaps I'll come and assist you; most probably I shall."

"No, don't! As soon as you leave San Remo Sir Henry will know, and he might suspect."

"Suspect what?"

"That you are in search of the truth, and of fortune in consequence."

"He believes in me. Only the other day I had a letter from him written in Goslin's hand, repeating the confidence he reposes in me."

"Exactly. You must remain down here for the present."

Flockart recollected the puzzling decision of Lady Heyburn, and remained silent.

"Our chief peril is still the one which has faced us all along," went on the man in the grey hat - "the peril that the girl may tell about that awkward affair at Chantilly."

"She dare not," Flockart assured him quickly.

Krail shook his head dubiously. "She's leading a lonely life. Her heart is broken, and she believes herself, as every other young girl does, to be without a future. Therefore, she's brooding over it. One never knows in such cases when a girl may fling all prudence to the winds," he said. "If she did, then nothing could save us."

"That's just what her ladyship said the other day," answered Flockart, tossing away his cigarette. "But you don't know that I hold her irrevocably. She dare not say a single word. If she dare, why did she not tell the truth about the safe?"

"Probably because it was all too sudden. She now finds life in that dismal little village intolerable. She's a girl of spirit, you know, and has always been used to luxury and freedom. To live with an old woman in a country cottage away from all her friends must be maddening. No, my dear James, in this you've acted most injudiciously. You were devoid of your usual foresight. Depend upon it, a very serious danger threatens. She will speak."

"I tell you she dare not. Rest your mind assured."

"She will."

"*She shall not!*"

"How, pray, can you close her mouth?" asked the foreigner.

Flockart's eyes met his. In them was a curious expression, almost a glitter.

Krail understood. He shrugged his shoulders, but uttered no word. His gesture was, however, that of one unconvinced. Adventurer as he was, ingenious and unscrupulous, he lived from hand to mouth. Sometimes he made a big *coup* and placed himself in funds. But following such an event he was open-handed and generous to his friends, extravagant in his expenditure; and very soon found himself under the necessity to exercise his wits in order to obtain the next louis. He had known Flockart for years as one of his own class. They had first met long ago on board a Castle liner homeward bound from Capetown, where both found themselves playing a crooked game. A friendship begotten of dishonesty had sprung up between them, and in consequence they had thrown in their lot together more than once with considerable financial advantage.

The present affair was, however, not much to Krail's liking, and this he had more than once told his friend. It was quite possible that if they could discover the mysterious source of this blind man's wealth they might, by judiciously levying blackmail through a third party, secure a very handsome income which he was to share with Flockart and her ladyship.

The last-named Krail had always admitted to be one of the cleverest women he had ever met. His only surprise had been that she, as Sir Henry's wife, was unable to get at the facts which were so cleverly withheld. It only showed, however, that the Baronet, though deprived of eyesight, was even more clever than the unscrupulous woman he had so foolishly married.

Krail held Lady Heyburn in distinct distrust. He had once had dealings with her which had turned out the reverse of satisfactory. Instinctively he knew that, in order to save herself, if exposure ever came, she would "give him away" without the least compunction.

What had puzzled him for several years, and what, indeed, had puzzled other people, was the reason of the close friendship between Flockart and the Baronet's wife. It was certainly not affection. He knew Flockart intimately, and had knowledge of his private affairs; therefore he was well aware of the existence of an unknown and rather insignificant woman to whom he was in secret devoted.

No; the bond between the pair was an entirely mysterious one. He knew that on more than one occasion, when Flockart's demands for money had been a little too frequent, she had resisted and attempted to withdraw from further association with him. Yet by a single word, or even a look, he could compel her to disgorge the funds he needed, for she had even handed him some of her trinkets to pawn until she could obtain further funds from Sir Henry to redeem them.

As they walked together along the white Corniche Road, their faces set towards the gorgeous southern afterglow, while the waves lapped lazily on the grey rocks, all these puzzling thoughts recurred to Krail.

"Lady Heyburn seems still to remain your very devoted friend," he remarked at last with a meaning smile. "I see from the *New York Herald* what pleasant parties she gives, and how she is the heart and soul of social merriment in San Remo. By Jove, James! you're a lucky man to possess such a popular hostess as friend."

"Yes," laughed Flockart, "Winnie is a regular pal. Without her I should have been broken long ago. But she's always ready to help me along."

"People have already remarked upon your remarkable friendship," said his friend, "and many ill-natured allegations have been made."

"Oh, yes, I'm quite well aware of that, my dear fellow. It has pained me more than enough. You yourself know that, as far as affection goes, I've never in my life entertained a spark of it for Winnie. We were children together, and have been friends always."

"Quite so!" exclaimed Krail, smiling. "That's a pretty good story to tell the world. But there's a point where mere friendship must break, you know."

"What do you mean?" asked the other, glancing at him in surprise.

"Well, the story you tell other people may be picturesque and romantic, but with me it's just a trifle weak. Lady Heyburn doesn't give her pearls to be pawned, out of mere friendship, you know."

Flockart was silent. He knew too well that the man walking at his side was as clever an intriguer and as bold an adventurer as had ever moved up and down Europe "working the game" in search of pigeons to pluck. His shabbiness was assumed. He had alighted at Bordighera station from the *rapide* from Paris, spent the night at a third-rate hotel in order not to be recognised at the Angst or any of the smarter houses, and had met him by appointment to explain the present situation. His remarks, however, were the reverse of reassuring. What did he suspect?

"I don't quite follow you, Krail," Flockart said.

"I meant to imply that if friendship only links you with Lady Heyburn, the chain may quite easily snap," he remarked.

He looked at his friend, much puzzled. He could see no point in that observation.

Krail read what was passing in the other's mind, and added, "I know, *mon cher ami*, that affection from her ladyship is entirely out of the question. The gossips are liars. And -"

"Sir Henry himself is quite aware of that. I have already spoken quite plainly and openly to him, and suggested my departure from Glencardine on account of ill-natured remarks by her ladyship's enemies. But he would not hear of my leaving, and pressed me to remain."

Krail looked at him in blank surprise. "Well," he said, "if you've been bold enough to do this in face of the gossip, then you're a much cleverer man than ever I took you to be."

For answer, Flockart took some letters from his breast-pocket, selected one written in a foreign hand, and gave it to Krail to read. It was from the hermit of Glencardine, written at his dictation by Monsieur Goslin, and was couched in the warmest and most confidential terms.

"Look here, James," exclaimed the shabby man, handing back the letter, "I'm going to be perfectly frank with you. Tell me if I speak the truth or if I lie. It is neither affection nor friendship which links your life with that woman's. Am I right?"

Flockart did not answer for some moments. His eyes were cast upon the ground. "Yes, Krail," he admitted at last when the question had been put to him a second time - "yes, Krail. You speak the truth. It is neither affection nor friendship."

CHAPTER XXV

SHOWS GABRIELLE IN EXILE

Midway between historic Fotheringhay and ancient Apethorpe, the ancestral seat of the Earls of Westmorland, lay the long, straggling, and rather poverty-stricken village of Woodnewton. Like many other Northamptonshire villages, it consisted of one long street of cottages, many of them with dormer windows peeping from beneath the brown thatch, the better houses of stone, with old mullioned windows, but all of them more or less in stages of decay. With the depreciation in agriculture, Woodnewton, once quite a prosperous little place, was now terribly shabby and depressing.

As he entered the village, the first object that met the eye of the stranger was a barn with the roof half fallen away, and next it a ruined house with its moss-grown thatch full of holes. The paving was ill-kept, and even the several inns bore an appearance of struggles with poverty.

Half-way up the long, straight, dispiriting street stood a cottage larger and neater-looking than the rest. Its ugly exterior was half-hidden by ivy, which had been cut away from the diamond-paned windows; while, unlike its neighbours, its roof was tiled and its brown door newly painted and highly varnished.

Old Miss Heyburn lived there, and had lived there for the past half-century. The prim, grey-haired, and somewhat eccentric old lady was a well-known figure to all on that country-side. Twice each Sunday, with her large-type Prayer-book in her hand, and her steel-rimmed spectacles on her thin nose, she walked to church, while she was one of the principal supporters of the village clothing-club and such-like institutions inaugurated by the worthy rector.

Essentially an ascetic person, she was looked upon with fear by all the villagers. Her manner was brusque, her speech sharp, and her criticism of neglectful mothers caustic and much to the point. Prim, always in black bonnet and jet-trimmed cape of years gone by, both in summer and winter, she took no heed of the vagaries of fashion, even when they reached Woodnewton so tardily.

The common report was that when a girl she had been "crossed in love," for her single maidservant she always trained to a sober and loveless life like her own, and as soon as a girl cast an eye upon a likely swain she was ignominiously dismissed.

That the sharp-tongued spinster possessed means was undoubted. It was known that she was sister of Sir Henry Heyburn of Caistor, in Lincolnshire; and, on account of her social standing, she on rare occasions was bidden to the omnium gatherings at some of the mansions in the neighbourhood. She seldom accepted; but when she did it was only to satisfy her curiosity and to criticise.

The household of two, the old lady and her exemplary maid, was assuredly a dull one. Meals were taken with punctual regularity amid a cleanliness that was almost painful. The tiny drawing-room, with its row of window-plants, including a pot of strong-smelling musk, was hardly ever entered. Not a speck of dust was allowed anywhere, for Miss Emily's eye was sharp, and woe betide the maid if a mere suspicion of dirt were discovered! Everything was kept locked up. One maid who resigned hurriedly, refusing to be criticised, afterwards declared that her mistress kept the paraffin under lock and key.

And into this uncomfortably prim and proper household little Gabrielle had suddenly been introduced. Her heart over-burdened by grief, and full of regret at being compelled to part from the father she so fondly loved, she had accepted the inevitable, fully realising the dull greyness of the life that lay before her. Surely her exile there was a cruel and crushing one! The house seemed so tiny and so suffocating after the splendid halls and huge rooms at Glencardine, while her aunt's constant sarcasm about her father - whom she had not seen for eight years - was particularly galling.

The woman treated the girl as a wayward child sent there for punishment and correction. She showed her neither kindness nor consideration; for, truth to tell, it annoyed her to think that her brother should have imposed the girl upon her. She hated to be bothered with the girl; but, existing upon Sir Henry's charity, as she really did, though none knew it, she could do no otherwise than accept his daughter as her guest.

Days, weeks, months had passed, each day dragging on as its predecessor, a wretched, hopeless, despairing existence to a girl so full of life and vitality as Gabrielle. Though she had written several times to her father, he had sent her no reply. To her mother at San Remo she had also written, and from her had received one letter, cold and unresponsive. From Walter Murie nothing - not a single word.

The well-thumbed books in the village library she had read, as well as those in the possession of her aunt. She had tried needlework, problems of patience, and the translation of a few chapters of an Italian novel into English in order to occupy her time. But those hours when she was alone in her little upstairs room with the sloping roof passed, alas! So very slowly.

Upon her, ever oppressive, were thoughts of that bitter past. At one staggering blow she had lost all that had made her young life worth living - her father's esteem and her lover's love. She was innocent, entirely innocent, of the terrible allegations against her, and yet she was so utterly defenceless!

Often she sat at her little window for hours watching the lethargy of village life in the street below, that rural life in which the rector and the schoolmaster were the principal figures. The dullness of it all was maddening. Her aunt's mid-Victorian primness, her snappishness towards the trembling maid, and the thousand and one rules of her daily life irritated her and jarred upon her nerves.

So, in order to kill time, and at the same time to study the antiquities of the neighbourhood - her father having taught her so much deep antiquarian knowledge - it had been her habit for three months past to take long walks for many miles across the country, accompanied by the black collie Rover belonging to a young farmer who lived at the end of the village. The animal had one day attached itself to her while she was taking a walk on the Apethorpe road; and now, by her feeding him daily and making a pet of him, the girl and the dog had become inseparable. By long walks and short train-journeys she had, in three months, been able to inspect most of the antiquities of Northamptonshire. Much of the history of the county was intensely interesting: the connection of old Fotheringhay with the ill-fated Mary Queen of Scots, the beauties of Peterborough Cathedral, the splendid old Tudor house of Deene (the home of the Earls of Cardigan), the legends of King John concerning King's Cliffe, the gaunt splendour of ruined Kirby, and the old-world charm of Apethorpe. All these, and many others, had great attraction for her. She read them up in books she ordered from London, and then visited the old places with all the enthusiasm of a spectacled antiquary.

Every day, no matter what the weather, she might be seen, in her thick boots, burberry, and tam o'shanter, trudging along the roads or across the fields accompanied by the faithful collie. The winter had been a comparatively mild one, with excessive rain. But no downpour troubled her. She liked the rain to beat into her face, for the dismal, monotonous cheerlessness of the brown fields, bare trees, and muddy roads was in keeping with the tragedy of her own young life.

She knew that her aunt Emily disliked her. The covert sneers, the caustic criticisms, and the go-to-meeting attitude of the old lady irritated the girl beyond measure. She was not wanted in that painfully prim cottage, and had been made to understand it from the first day.

Hence it was that she spent all the time she possibly could out of doors. Alone she had traversed the whole county, seeking permission to glance at the interior of any old house or building that promised archaeological interest, and by that means making some curious friendships.

Many people regarded the pretty young girl who made a study of old churches and old houses as somewhat eccentric. Local antiquaries, however, stared at her in wonder when they found that she was possessed of knowledge far more profound than theirs, and that she could decipher old documents and read Latin inscriptions with ease.

She made few friends, preferring solitude and reflection to visiting and gossiping. Hers was, indeed, a pathetic little figure, and the countryfolk used to stare at her in surprise and sigh as she passed through the various little hamlets and villages so regularly, the black collie bounding before her.

Quickly she had become known as "Miss Heyburn's niece," and the report having spread that she was "a bit eccentric, poor thing," people soon ceased to wonder, and began to regard that pale, sad face with sympathy. The whole country-side was wondering why such a pretty young lady had gone to live in the deadly dullness of Woodnewton, and what was the cause of that great sorrow written upon her countenance.

Her daily burden of bitter reflection was, indeed, hard to bear. Her one thought, as she walked those miles of lonely rural byways, so bare and cheerless, was of Walter - her Walter - the man who, she knew, would have willingly given his very life for hers. She had met her just punishment, and was now endeavouring to bear it bravely. She had renounced his love for ever.

One afternoon, dark and rainy, in the gloom of early March, she was sitting at the old-fashioned and rather tuneless piano in the damp, unused "best room," which was devoid of fire for economic reasons. Her aunt was seated in the window busily crocheting, while she, with her white fingers running across the keys, raised her sweet contralto voice in that old-world Florentine song that for centuries has been sung by the populace in the streets of the city by the Arno:

> In questa notte in sogno l'ho veduto
> Era vestito tutto di braccato,
> Le piume sul berretto di velluto
> Ed una spada d'oro aveva allato.

> E poi m'ha detto con un bel sorriso;
> Io no, non posso star da te diviso,
> Da te diviso non ci posso stare
> E torno per mai pin non ti lasciare.

Miss Heyburn sighed, and looked up from her work. "Can't you sing something in English, Gabrielle? It would be much better," she remarked in a snappy tone.

The girl's mouth hardened slightly at the corners, and she closed the piano without replying.

"I don't mean you to stop," exclaimed the ascetic old lady. "I only think that girls, instead of learning foreign songs, should be able to sing English ones properly. Won't you sing another?"

"No," replied the girl, rising. "The rain has ceased, so I shall go for my walk;" and she left the room to put on her hat and mackintosh, passing along before the window a few minutes later in the direction of King's Cliffe.

It was always the same. If she indulged herself in singing one

William Le Queux

or other of those ancient love-songs of the hot-blooded Tuscan peasants her aunt always scolded. Nothing she did was right, for the simple reason that she was an unwelcome visitor.

She was alone. Rover was conducting sheep to Stamford market, as was his duty every week; therefore in the fading daylight she went along, immersed in her own sad thoughts. Her walk at that hour was entirely aimless. She had only gone forth because of the irritation she felt at her aunt's constant complaints. So entirely engrossed was she by her own despair that she had not noticed the figure of a man who, catching sight of her at the end of Woodnewton village, had held back until she had gone a considerable distance, and had then sauntered leisurely in the direction she had taken.

The man kept her in view, but did not approach her. The high, red mail-cart passed, and the driver touched his hat respectfully to her. The man who collected the evening mail from all the villages between Deene and Peterborough met her almost every evening, and had long ago inquired and learnt who she was.

For nearly two miles she walked onward, until, close by the junction of the road which comes down the hill from Nassington, the man who had been following hastened up and overtook her.

She heard herself addressed by name, and, turning quickly, found herself face to face with James Flockart.

CHAPTER XXVI

THE VELVET PAW

The new-comer stood before Gabrielle, hat in hand, smiling pleasantly and uttering a greeting of surprise.

Her response was cold, for was not all her present unhappiness due to him?

"I've come here to speak to you, Gabrielle - to speak to you in confidence."

"Whatever you have to say may surely be said in the hearing of a third person?" was her dignified answer. His sudden appearance had startled her, but only for a moment. She was cool again next instant, and on her guard against her enemy.

"I hardly think," he said, with a meaning smile, "that you would really like me to speak before a third party."

"I really care nothing," was her answer. "And I cannot see why you seek me here. When one is hopeless, as I am, one becomes callous of what the future may bring."

"Hopeless! Yes," he said in a changed voice, "I know that; living in this dismal hole, Gabrielle, you must be hopeless. I know that your exile here, away from all your friends and those you love, must be soul-killing. Don't think that I have not reflected upon it a hundred times."

William Le Queux

"Ah, then you have at last experienced remorse!" she cried bitterly, looking straight into the man's face. "You have estranged me from my father, and tried to ruin him! You lied to him - lied in order to save yourself!"

The man laughed. "My dear child," he exclaimed, "you really misjudge me entirely. I am here for two reasons: to ask your forgiveness for making that allegation which was imperative; and, secondly, to assure you that, if you will allow me, I will yet be your friend."

"Friend!" she echoed in a hollow voice. "You - my friend!"

"Yes. I know that you mistrust me," he replied; "but I want to prove that my intentions towards you are those of real friendship."

"And you, who ever since my girlhood days have been my worst enemy, ask me now to trust you!" she exclaimed with indignation. "No; go back to Lady Heyburn and tell her that I refuse to accept the olive-branch which you and she hold out to me."

"My dear girl, you don't follow me," he exclaimed impatiently. "This has nothing whatever to do with Lady Heyburn. I have come to you from purely personal motives. My sole desire is to effect your return to Glencardine."

"For your own ends, Mr. Flockart, without a doubt!" she said bitterly.

"Ah! there you are quite mistaken. Though you assert that I am your father's enemy, I am, I tell you, his friend. He is ever thinking of you with regret. You were his right hand. Would it not be far better if he invited you to return?"

She sighed at the thought of the blind man whom she regarded with such entire devotion, but answered, "No, I shall never return to Glencardine."

"Why?" he asked. "Was it anything more than natural that, believing you had been prying into his affairs, your father, in a moment of anger, condemned you to this life of appalling monotony?"

"No, not more natural than that you, the culprit, should have made me the scapegoat for the second time," was her defiant reply.

"Have I not already told you that the reason I'm here is to crave your forgiveness? I admit that my actions have been the reverse of honourable; but - well, there were circumstances which compelled me to act as I did."

"You got an impression of my father's safe-key, had a duplicate made in Glasgow, as I have found out, and one night opened the safe and copied certain private documents having regard to a proposed loan to the Greek Government. The night I discovered you was the second occasion when you went to the library and opened the safe. Do you deny that?"

"What you allege, Gabrielle, is perfectly correct," he replied. "I know that I was a blackguard to shield myself behind you - to tell the lie I did that night. But how could I avoid it?"

"Suppose I had, in retaliation, spoken the truth?" she asked, looking the man straight in the face.

"Ah! I knew that you would not do that."

"You believe that I dare not - dare not for my own sake, eh?"

He nodded in the affirmative.

"Then you are much mistaken, Mr. Flockart," she said in a hard voice. "You don't understand that a woman may become desperate."

"I can understand how desperate you have become, living in

this 'Sleepy Hollow.' A week of it would, I admit, drive me to distraction."

"Then if you understand my present position you will know that I am fearless of you, or of anybody else. My life has ended. I have neither happiness, comfort, peace of mind, nor love. All is of the past. To you - you, James Flockart - I am indebted for all this! You have held me powerless. I was a happy girl once, but you and your dastardly friends crossed my path like an evil shadow, and I have existed in an inferno of remorse ever since. I -"

"Remorse! How absurdly you talk!"

"It will not be absurd when I speak the truth and tell the world what I know. It will be rather a serious matter for you, Mr. Flockart."

"You threaten me, then?" he asked, his eyes flashing for a second.

"I think it is as well for us to understand one another at once," she said frankly.

They had halted upon a small bridge close to the entrance to Apethorpe village.

"Then I'm to understand that you refuse my proffered assistance?" he asked.

"I require no assistance from my enemies," was her defiant and dignified reply. "I suppose Lady Heyburn is at the villa at San Remo as usual, and that it was she who sent you to me, because she recognises that you've both gone a little too far. You have. When the opportunity arises, then I shall speak, regardless of the consequences. Therefore, Mr. Flockart, I wish you good-evening;" and she turned away.

"No, Gabrielle," he cried, resolutely barring her path. "You must hear me. You don't grasp the point of my argument."

"With me none of your arguments are of any avail," was her response in a bitter tone. "I, alas! have reason to know you too well. For you - by your clever intrigue - I committed a crime; but God knows I am innocent of what was intended. Now that you have estranged me from my father and my lover, I shall confess - confess all - before I make an end of my life."

He saw from her pale, drawn face that she was desperate. He grew afraid.

"But, my dear girl, think - of what you are saying! You don't mean it; you can't mean it. Your father has relented, and will welcome you back, if only you will consent to return."

"I have no wish to be regarded as the prodigal daughter," was her proud response.

"Not for Walter Murie's sake?" asked the crafty man. "I have seen him. I was at the club with him last night, and we had a chat about you. He loves you very dearly. Ah! you do not know how he is suffering."

She was silent, and he recognised in an instant that his words had touched the sympathetic chord in her heart.

"He is not suffering any greater grief than I am," she said in a low, mechanical voice, her brow heavily clouded.

"Of course I can quite understand that," he remarked sympathetically. "Walter is a good fellow, and - well, it is indeed sad that matters should be as they are. He is entirely devoted to you, Gabrielle."

"Not more so than I am to him," declared the girl quite frankly.

"Then why did you write breaking off your engagement?"

"He told you that?" she exclaimed in surprise.

The truth was that Murie had told Flockart nothing. He had not even seen him. It was only a wild guess on Flockart's part.

"Tell me," she urged anxiously, "what did he say concerning myself?"

Flockart hesitated. His mind was instantly active in the concoction of a story.

"Oh, well - he expressed the most profound regret for all that had occurred at Glencardine, and is, of course, utterly puzzled. It appears that just before Christmas he went home to Connachan and visited your father several times. From him, I suppose, he heard how you had been discovered."

"You told him nothing?"

"I told him nothing," declared Flockart - which was a fact.

"Did he express a wish to see me?" she inquired.

"Of course he did. Is he not over head and ears in love with you? He believes you have treated him cruelly."

"I - I know I have, Mr. Flockart," she admitted. "But I acted as any girl of honour would have done. I was compelled to take upon myself a great disgrace, and on doing so I released him from his promise to me."

"Most honourable!" the man declared with a pretence of admiration, yet underlying it all was a craftiness that surely was unsurpassed. That visit of his to Northamptonshire was made with some ulterior motive, yet what it was the girl was unable to discover. She would surely have been cleverer than most people had she been able to discern the hidden, sinister motives of James Flockart. The truth was that he had not seen Murie, and the story of his anxiety he had only concocted on the spur of the moment.

"Walter asked me to give you a message," he went on. "He asked me to urge you to return to Glencardine, and to withdraw that letter you wrote him before your departure."

"To return to Glencardine!" she repeated, staring into his face. "Walter wishes me to do that! Why?"

"Because he loves you. Because he will intercede with your father on your behalf."

"My father will hear nothing in my favour until -" and she paused.

"Until what?"

"Until I tell him the whole truth."

"That you will never do," remarked Flockart quickly.

"Ah! there you're mistaken," she responded. "In all probability I shall."

"Then, before you do so, pray weigh carefully the dire results," he urged in a changed tone.

"Oh, I've already done that long ago," she said. "I know that I am in your hands, utterly and irretrievably, Mr. Flockart, and the only way I can regain my freedom is by boldly telling the truth."

"You must never do that! By Heaven, you shall not!" he cried, looking fiercely into her clear eyes.

"I know! I'm quite well aware of your attitude towards me. The claws cannot be entirely concealed in the cat's paw, you know;" and she laughed bitterly into his face.

The corners of the man's mouth hardened. He was about to speak and show himself in his true colours; but by dint of great self-control he managed to smile and exclaim, "Then you will take no heed of these wishes of the man who loves you so dearly, of the man who is still your best and most devoted friend? You prefer to remain here, and wear out your young life with vain regrets and shattered affections. Come, Gabrielle, do be sensible."

The girl did not speak for several moments. "Does Walter really wish me to return?" she asked, looking straight at him, as though trying to discern whether he was really speaking the truth.

"Yes. He expressed to me a strong wish that you should either return to Glencardine or go and live at Park Street."

"He wishes to see me?"

"Of course. It would perhaps be better if you met him first, either down here or in London. Why should you two not be happy?" he went on. "I know it is my fault you are consigned to this dismal life, and that you and Walter are parted; but, believe me, Gabrielle, I am at this moment endeavouring to bring you together again, and to reinstate you in Sir Henry's good graces. He is longing for you to return. When I saw him last at Glencardine he told me that Monsieur Goslin was not so clever at typing or in grasping his meaning as you are, and he is only awaiting your return."

"That may be so," answered the girl in a slow, distinct voice; "but perhaps you'll tell me, Mr. Flockart, the reason you evinced such an unwonted curiosity in my father's affairs?"

"My dear girl," laughed the man, "surely that isn't a fair question. I had certain reasons of my own."

"Yes; assisted by Lady Heyburn, you thought that you could make money by obtaining knowledge of my father's secrets.

Oh yes, I know - I know more than you have ever imagined," declared the girl boldly. "You hope to get rid of Monsieur Goslin from Glencardine and reinstate me - for your own ends. I see it all."

The man bit his lip. With chagrin he recognised that he had blundered, and that she, shrewd and clever, had taken advantage of his error. He was, however, too clever to exhibit his annoyance.

"You are quite wrong in your surmise, Gabrielle," he said quickly. "Walter Murie loves you, and loves you well. Therefore, with regret at my compulsory denunciation of yourself, I am now endeavouring to assist you."

"Thank you," she responded coldly, again turning away abruptly. "I require no assistance from a man such as yourself - a man who entrapped me, and who denounced me in order to save himself."

"You will regret these words," he declared, as she walked away in the direction of Woodnewton.

She turned upon him in fierce anger, retorting, "And perhaps you, on your part, will regret your endeavour to entrap me a second time. I have promised to speak the truth, and I shall keep my promise. I am not afraid to sacrifice my own life to save my father's honour!"

The man stood staring after her. These words of hers held him motionless. What if she flung her good name to the winds and actually carried out her threat? What if she really spoke the truth? Ay, what then?

CHAPTER XXVII

BETRAYS THE BOND

The girl hurried on, her heart filled with wonder, her eyes brimming with tears of indignation. The one thought occupying her whole mind was whether Walter really wished to see her again. Had Flockart spoken the truth? The serious face of the man she loved so well rose before her blurred vision. She had been his - his very own - until she had sent off that fateful letter.

In five minutes Flockart had again overtaken her. His attitude was appealing. He urged her to at least see her lover again even if she refused to write or return to her father.

"Why do you come here to taunt me like this?" she cried, turning upon him angrily. "Once, because you were my mother's friend, I believed in you. But you deceived me, and in consequence you hold me in your power. Were it not for that I could have spoken to my father - have told him the truth and cleared myself. He now believes that I have betrayed his business secrets, while at the same time he considers you to be his friend!"

"I am his friend, Gabrielle," the man declared.

"Why tell me such a lie?" she asked reproachfully. "Do you think I too am blind?"

"Certainly not. I give you credit for being quite as clever and as intelligent as you are dainty and charming. I -"

"Thank you!" she cried in indignation. "I require no compliments from you."

"Lady Heyburn has expressed a wish to see you," he said. "She is still in San Remo, and asked me to invite you to go down there for a few weeks. Your aunt has written her, I think, complaining that you are not very comfortable at Woodnewton."

"I have not complained. Why should Aunt Emily complain of me? You seem to be the bearer of messages from the whole of my family, Mr. Flockart."

"I am here entirely in your own interests, my dear child," he declared with that patronising air which so irritated her.

"Not entirely, I think," she said, smiling bitterly.

"I tell you, I much regret all that has happened, and -"

"You regret!" she cried fiercely. "Do you regret the end of that woman - you know whom I mean?"

Beneath her straight glance he quivered. She had referred to a subject which he fain would have buried for ever. This dainty neat-waisted girl knew a terrible secret. Was it not only too true, as Lady Heyburn had vaguely suggested a dozen times, that her mouth ought to be effectually sealed?

He had sealed it once, as he thought. Her fear to explain to her father the incident of the opening of the safe had given him confidence that no word of the truth regarding the past would ever pass her lips. Yet he saw that his own machinations were now likely to prove his undoing. The web which, with her ladyship's assistance, he had woven about her was now stretched to breaking-point. If it did yield, then the result must be ruin - and worse. Therefore, he was straining every effort to again reinstate her in her father's good graces and restore in her mind something akin to confidence. But all his arguments, as he walked on at her side in the gathering gloom, proved useless. She was in no mood to listen to the man who had been her evil genius ever since her school-days. As he was speaking she was wondering if she dared go to Walter Murie and tell him everything. What would her lover think of her? What indeed? He would only cast her aside as worthless. No. Far better that he should remain in ignorance and retain only sad memories of their brief happiness.

"I am going to Glencardine to-night," Flockart went on. "I shall join the mail at Peterborough. What shall I tell your father?"

"Tell him the truth," was her reply. "That, I know, you will not do. So why need we waste further words?"

"Do you actually refuse, then, to leave this dismal hole?" he demanded impatiently.

"Yes, until I speak, and tell my father the plain and ghastly story."

"Rubbish!" he ejaculated. "You'll never do that - unless you wish to stand beside me in a criminal dock."

"Well, rather that than be your cat's-paw longer, Mr. Flockart!" she cried, her face flushing with indignation.

"Oh, oh!" he laughed, still quite imperturbed. "Come, come! This is scarcely a wise reply, my dear little girl!"

"I wish you to leave me. You have insulted my intelligence enough this evening, surely - you, who only a moment ago declared yourself my friend!"

Slowly he selected a cigarette from his gold case, and, halting, it it. "Well, if you meet my well-meant efforts on your behalf with open antagonism like this I can't make any further suggestion."

"No, please don't. Go up to Glencardine and do your worst for me. I am now fully able to take care of myself," she exclaimed in defiance. "You can also write to Lady Heyburn, and tell her that I am still, and that I always will remain, my blind father's friend."

"But why don't you listen to reason, Gabrielle?" he implored her. "I don't now seek to lessen or deny the wrongs I have done you in the past, nor do I attempt to conceal from you my own position. My only object is to bring you and Walter together again. Her ladyship knows the whole circumstances, and deeply regrets them."

"Her regret will be the more poignant some day, I assure you."

"Then you really intend to act vindictively?"

"I shall act just as I think proper," she exclaimed, halting a moment and facing him. "Please understand that though I have been forced in the past to act as you have indicated, because I feared you - because I had my reputation and my father's honour at stake - I hold you in terror no longer, Mr. Flockart."

"Well, I'm glad you've told me that," he said, laughing as though he treated her declaration with humour. "It's just as well, perhaps, that we should now thoroughly understand each other. Yet if I were you I wouldn't do anything rash. By telling the truth you'd be the only sufferer, you know."

"The only sufferer! Why?"

"Well, you don't imagine I should be such a fool as to admit that what you said was true, do you?"

William Le Queux

She looked at him in surprise. It had never occurred to her that he, with his innate unscrupulousness and cunning, might deny her allegations, and might even be able to prove them false.

"The truth could not be denied," she said simply. "Recollect the cutting from the Edinburgh paper."

"Truth is denied every day in courts of law," he retorted. "No. Before you act foolishly, remember that, put to the test, your word would stand alone against mine and those of other people.

"Why, the very story you would tell would be so utterly amazing and startling that the world would declare you had invented it. Reflect upon it for a moment, and you'll find, my dear girl, that silence is golden in this, as in any other circumstance in life."

She raised her eyes to his, and met his gaze firmly. "So you defy me to speak?" she cried. "You think that I will still remain in this accursed bondage of yours?"

"I utter no threats, my dear child," replied Flockart. "I have never in my life threatened you. I merely venture to point out certain difficulties which you might have in substantiating any allegation which you might make against me. For that reason, if for none other, is it not better for us to be friends?"

"I am not the friend of my father's enemy!" she declared.

"You are quite heroic," he declared with a covert sneer. "If you really are bent upon providing the halfpenny newspapers with a fresh sensation, pray let me know in plenty of time, won't you?"

"I've had sufficient of your taunts," cried the girl, bursting into a flood of hot tears. "Leave me. I - I'll say no further word to you."

"Except to forgive me," He added.

"Why should I?" she asked through her tears.

"Because, for your own sake - for the sake of your future - it will surely be best," he pointed out. "You, no doubt, in ignorance of legal procedure, believed that what you alleged would be accepted in a court of justice. But reflect fully before you again threaten me. Dry your eyes, or your aunt may suspect something wrong."

She did not reply. What he said impressed her, and he did not fail to recognise that fact. He smiled within himself when he saw that he had triumphed. Yet he had not gained his point.

She had dashed away her tears with the little wisp of lace, annoyed with herself at betraying her indignation in that womanly way. She knew him, alas! too well. She mistrusted him, for she was well aware of how cleverly he had once conspired with Lady Heyburn, and with what ingenuity she herself had been drawn into the disgraceful and amazing affair.

True it was that her story, if told in a criminal court, would prove so extraordinary that it would not be believed; true also that he would, of course, deny it, and that his denial would be borne out by the woman who, though her father's wife, was his worst enemy.

The man placed his hand on her shoulder, saying, "May we not be friends, Gabrielle?"

She shook him off roughly, responding in the negative.

"But we are not enemies - I mean we will not be enemies as we have been, shall we?" he urged.

To this she made no reply. She only quickened her pace, for the twilight was fast deepening, and she wished to be back again at her aunt's house.

Why had that man followed her? Why, indeed, had he troubled to come there? She could not discern his motive.

They walked together in silence. He was watching her face, reading it like a book.

Then, when they neared the first thatched cottage at the entrance to the village, he halted, asking, "May we not now become friends, Gabrielle? Will you not listen, and take my advice? Or will you still remain buried here?"

"I have nothing further to say, Mr. Flockart, than what I have already said," was her defiant response. "I shall act as I think best."

"And you will dare to speak, and place yourself in a ridiculous position, you mean?"

"I shall use my own judgment in defending my father from his enemies," was her cold response as, with a slight shrug of her shoulders, she turned and left him, hurrying forward in the darkening twilight along the village street to her aunt's home.

He, on his part, turned upon his heel with a muttered remark and set out again to walk towards Nassington Station, whence, after nearly an hour's wait in the village inn, he took train to Peterborough.

The girl had once again defied him.

CHAPTER XXVIII

THE WHISPERS AGAIN

Was it really true what Flockart had told her? Did Walter actually wish to see her again? At one moment she believed in her lover's strong, passionate devotion to her, for had she not seen it displayed in a hundred different ways? But the next she recollected how that man Flockart had taken advantage of her youth and inexperience in the past, how he had often lied so circumstantially that she had believed his words to be the truth. Once, indeed, he had openly declared to her that one of his maxims was never to tell the truth unless obliged. After dinner, a simple meal served in the poky little dining-room, she made an excuse to go to her room, and there sat for a long time, deeply reflecting. Should she write to Walter? Would it be judicious to explain Flockart's visit, and how he had urged their reconciliation? If she wrote, would it lower her dignity in her lover's eyes? That was the great problem which now troubled her. She sat staring before her undecided. She recalled all that Flockart had told her. He was the emissary of Lady Heyburn without a doubt. The girl had told him openly of her decision to speak the truth and expose him, but he had only laughed at her. Alas! she knew his true character, unscrupulous and pitiless. But she placed him aside.

Recollection of Walter - the man who had held her so often in his arms and pressed his hot lips to hers, the man who was her father's firm friend and whose uprightness and honesty of purpose she had ever admired - crowded upon her. Should she

William Le Queux

write to him? Rigid and staring, she sat in her chair, her little white hands clenched, as she tried to summon courage. It had been she who had written declaring that their secret engagement must be broken, she who had condemned herself. Therefore, had she not a right to satisfy that longing she had had through months, the longing to write to him once again. The thought decided her; and, going to the table whereon the lamp was burning, she sat down, and after some reflection, penned a letter as follows: -

"MY SWEETHEART, MY DARLING, MY OWN, MY SOUL - MINE - ONLY MINE, - I am wondering how and where you are! True, I wrote you a cruel letter; but it was imperative, and under the force of circumstance. I am full of regrets, and I only wish with all my heart that I might kiss you once again, and press you in my arms as I used to do.

"But how are you? I have had you before my eyes to-night, and I feel quite sure that at this very moment you are thinking of me. You must know that I love you dearly. You gave me your heart, and it shall not belong to any other. I have tried to be brave and courageous; but, alas! I have failed. I love you, my darling, and I must see you soon - very soon.

"Mr. Flockart came to see me to-day and says that you expressed to him a desire to meet me again. Gratify that desire when you will, and you will find your Gabrielle just the same - longing ever to see you, living with only the memories of your dear face.

"Can you doubt of my great, great love for you? You never wrote in reply to my letter, though I have waited for months. I know my letter was a cruel one, and to you quite unwarranted; but I had a reason for writing it, and the reason was because I felt that I ought not to deceive you any longer.

"You see, darling, I am frank and open. Yes, I have deceived you. I am terribly ashamed and downhearted. I have tried to conceal my grief, even from you; but it is impossible. I love you as much as I ever loved you, and I swear to you that I have never once wavered.

"Grim circumstance forced me to write to you as I did. Forgive me, I beg of you. If it is true what Mr. Flockart says, then send me a telegram, and come here to see me. If it be false, then I shall know by your silence.

"I love you, my own, my well-beloved! *Au revoir*, my dearest heart. I look at your photograph which to-night smiles at me. Yes, you love me!

"With many fond and sweet kisses like those I gave you in the well-remembered days of our happiness.

"My love - My king!"

She read the letter carefully through, placed it in an envelope, and, marking it private, addressed it to Walter's chambers in the Temple, whence she knew it must be forwarded if he were away. Then, putting on her tam o' shanter, she went out to the village grocer's, where she posted it, so that it left by the early morning mail. When would his welcome telegram arrive? She calculated that he would get the letter by mid-day, and by one o'clock she could receive his reply - his reassurance of love.

So she went to her bed, with its white dimity hangings, more calm and composed than for months before. For a long time she lay awake, thinking of him, listening hour by hour to the chiming bells of the old Norman church. They marked the passing of the night. Then she dropped off to sleep, to be awakened by the sun streaming into the room.

That same morning, away up in the Highlands at Glencardine, Sir Henry had groped his way across the library to his accustomed chair, and Hill had placed before him one of the shallow drawers of the cabinet of seal-impressions.

There were fully half a dozen which had been sent to him by

the curator of the museum at Norwich, sulphur-casts of seals recently acquired by that institution.

The blind man had put aside that morning to examine them, and settled himself to his task with the keen and pleasurable anticipation of the expert.

They were very fine specimens. The blind man, sitting alone, selected one, and, fingering it very carefully for a long time, at last made out its design and the inscription upon it.

"The seal of Abbot Simon de Luton, of the early thirteenth century," he said slowly to himself. "The wolf guards the head of St. Edmund as it does in the seal of the Benedictine Abbey of Bury St. Edmunds, while the Virgin with the Child is over the canopy. And the verse is indeed curious for its quaintness:"

+ VIRGO . DEUM . FERT . DUX . CAPUD . AUFERT . QUOD . LUPUS . HIC . FERT +

Then he again retraced the letters with his sensitive fingers to reassure himself that he had made no mistake.

The next he drew towards him proved to be the seal of the Vice-Warden of the Grey Friars of Cambridge, a pointed one used about the year 1244, which to himself he declared, in heraldic language, to bear the device of "a cross raguly debruised by a spear, and a crown of thorns in bend dexter, and a sponge on a staff in bend sinister, between two threefold *flagella* in base" - surely a formidable array of the instruments used in the Passion.

Deeply interested, and speaking to himself aloud, as was his habit when alone, he examined them one after the other. Among the collection were the seals of Berengar de Brolis, Plebanus of Pacina (in Syracuse), and those of the Commune of Beauvais (1228); Mathilde (or Mahaut), daughter of Henri Duke of Brabant (1265); the town of Oudenbourg in West Flanders, and of the Vicar-Provincial of the Carmelite Order at

Palermo (1350); Jacobus de Gnapet, Bishop of Rennes (1480); and of Bondi Marquis of Sasolini of Bologna (1323).

He had almost concluded when Goslin, the grey-bearded Frenchman, having breakfasted alone in the dining-room, entered. "Ah, *mon cher* Sir Henry!" he exclaimed, "at work so early! The study of seals must be very fascinating to you, though I confess that, for myself, I could never see in them very much to interest one."

"No. To the ordinary person, my dear Goslin, it appears no doubt, a most dryasdust study, but to a man afflicted like myself it is the only study that he can pursue, for with his finger tips he can learn the devices and decipher the inscriptions," the blind Baronet declared. "Take, for instance, only this little collection of a dozen or so impressions which they have so kindly sent to me from Norwich. Each one of them tells me something. Its device, its general character, its heraldry, its inscription, are all highly instructive. For the collector there are opportunities for the study of the historical allusions, the emblematology and imagery, the hagiology, the biographical and topographical episodes, and the other peculiarities and idiosyncrasies in all the seals he possesses."

Goslin, like most other people, had been many times bored by the old man's technical discourses upon his hobby. But he never showed it. He, just the same as other people, made pretence of being interested. "Yes," he remarked, "they must be most instructive to the student. I recollect seeing a great quantity in the Bargello at Florence."

"Ah, a very fine collection - part of the Medici collection, and contains some of the finest Italian and Spanish specimens," remarked the blind connoisseur. "Birch of the British Museum is quite right in declaring that the seal, portable and abounding in detail, not difficult of acquisition nor hard to read if we set about deciphering the story it has to tell, takes us back as we look upon it to the very time of its making, and sets us, as it were, face to face with the actual owners of the relic."

The Frenchman sighed. He saw he was in for a long disser-
tation; and, moving uneasily towards the window, changed the
topic of conversation by saying, "I had a long letter from Paris
this morning. Krail is back again, it appears."

"Ah, that man!" cried the other impatiently. "When will his
extraordinary energies be suppressed? They are watching him
carefully, I suppose."

"Of course," replied the Frenchman. "He left Paris about a
month ago, but unfortunately the men watching him did not
follow. He took train for Berlin, and has been absent until
now."

"We ought to know where he's been, Goslin," declared the
elder man. "What fool was it who, keeping him under survei-
llance, allowed him to slip from Paris?"

"The Russian Tchernine."

"I thought him a clever fellow, but it seems that he's a bungler
after all."

"But while we keep Krail at arm's length, as we are doing, what
have we to fear?" asked Goslin.

"Yes, but how long can we keep him at arm's length?" queried
Sir Henry. "You know the kind of man - one of the most
extraordinarily inventive in Europe. No secret is safe from him.
Do you know, Goslin," he added, in a changed voice, "I live
nowadays somehow in constant apprehension."

"You've never possessed the same self-confidence since you
found Mademoiselle Gabrielle with the safe open," he
remarked.

"No. Murie, or some other man she knows, must have induced
her to do that, and take copies of those documents. Fortunately, I suspected an attempt, and baited the trap accordingly."

"What caused you to suspect?"

"Because more than once both Murie and the girl seemed to be seized by an unusual desire to pry into my business."

"You don't think that our friend Flockart had anything to do with the affair?" the Frenchman suggested.

"No, no. Not in the least. I know Flockart too well," declared the old man. "Once I looked upon him as my enemy, but I have now come to the conclusion that he is a friend - a very good friend."

The Frenchman pulled a rather wry face, and remained silent.

"I know," Sir Henry went on, "I know quite well that his constant association with my wife has caused a good deal of gossip; but I have dismissed it all with the contempt that such attempted scandal deserves. It has been put about by a pack of women who are jealous of my wife's good looks and her *chic* in dress."

"Are not Flockart and mademoiselle also good friends?" inquired Goslin.

"No. I happen to know that they are not, and that very fact in itself shows me that Gabrielle, in trying to get at the secret of my business, was not aided by Flockart, for it was he who exposed her."

"Yes," remarked the Frenchman, "so you've told me before. Have you heard from mademoiselle lately?"

"Only twice since she has left here," was the old man's bitter reply, "and that was twice too frequently. I've done with her, Goslin - done with her entirely. Never in all my life did I receive such a crushing blow as when I found that she, in whom I reposed the utmost confidence, had played her own father false, and might have ruined him!"

"Yes," remarked the other sympathetically, "it was a great blow to you, I know. But will you not forgive mademoiselle?"

"Forgive her!" he cried fiercely, "forgive her! Never!"

The grey-bearded Frenchman, who had always been a great favourite with Gabrielle, sighed slightly, and gave his shoulders a shrug of regret.

"Why do you ask that?" inquired Sir Henry, "when she herself admitted that she had been at the safe?"

"Because -" and the other hesitated. "Well, for several reasons. The story of your quarrel with mademoiselle has leaked out."

"The Whispers - eh, Goslin?" laughed the old man in defiance. "Let the people believe what they will. My daughter shall never return to Glencardine - never!"

As he had been speaking the door had opened, and James Flockart stood upon the threshold. He had overheard the blind man's words, and as he came forward he smiled, more in satisfaction than in greeting.

CHAPTER XXIX

CONTAINS A FURTHER MYSTERY

"My dear Edgar, when I met you in the Devonshire Club last night I could scarcely believe my own eyes. Fancy you turning up again!"

"Yes, strange, isn't it, how two men may drift apart for years, and then suddenly meet in a club, as we have done, Murie?"

"Being with those fellows who were anxious to go along and see the show at the Empire last night, I had no opportunity of having a chat with you, my dear old chap. That's why I asked you to look in."

The two men were seated in Walter's dingy chambers on the second floor in Fig-Tree Court, Temple. The room was an old and rather frowsy one, with shabby leather furniture from which the stuffing protruded, panelled walls, a carpet almost threadbare, and a formidable array of calf-bound volumes in the cases lining one wall. The place was heavy with tobacco-smoke as the pair, reclining in easy-chairs, were in the full enjoyment of very excellent cigars.

Walter's visitor was a tall, dark man, some six or seven years his senior, a rather spare, lantern-jawed young fellow, whose dark-grey clothes were of unmistakable foreign cut; and whose moustache was carefully trained to an upward trend. No second glance was required to decide that Edgar Hamilton was

William Le Queux

a person who, having lived a long time on the Continent, had acquired the cosmopolitan manner both in gesture and in dress.

"Well," exclaimed Murie at last, blowing a cloud of smoke from his lips, "since we parted at Oxford I've been called to the Bar, as you see. As for practice - well, I haven't any. The gov'nor wants me to go in for politics, so I'm trying to please him by getting my hand in. I make an odd speech or two sometimes in out-of-the-world villages, and I hope, one day, to find myself the adopted candidate for some borough or other. Last year I was sent round the world by my fond parents in order to obtain a broader view of life. Is it not Tacitus who says, '*Sua cuique vita obscura est*'?"

"Yes, my dear fellow," replied Hamilton, stretching himself lazily in his chair. "And surely we can say with Martial, '*Non est vivere, sed valere vita*' - I am well, therefore I am alive! Mine has been a rather curious career up to the present. I only once heard of you after Oxford - through Arthur Price, who was, you'll remember, at Balliol. He wrote that he'd spoken one night to you when at supper at the Savoy. You had a bevy of beauties with you, he said."

Both men laughed. In the old days, Edgar Hamilton had been essentially a ladies' man; but, since they had parted one evening on the station-platform at Oxford, Hamilton had gone up to town and completely out of the life of Walter Murie. They had not met until the previous evening, when Walter, having dined at the Devonshire - that comfortable old-world club in St. James's Street which was the famous Crockford's gaming-house in the days of the dandies - he had met his old friend in the strangers' smoking-room, the guest of a City stockbroker who was entertaining a party. A hurried greeting of surprise, and an invitation to call in at the Temple resulted in that meeting on that grey afternoon.

Six years had gone since they had parted; and, judging from Edgar's exterior, he had been pretty prosperous.

Walter was laughing and commenting upon it when his friend, removing his cigar from his lips, said, "My dear fellow, my success has been entirely due to one incident which is quite romantic. In fact, if anybody wrote it in a book people would declare it to be fiction."

"That's interesting! Tell me all about it. My own life has been humdrum enough in all conscience. As a budding politician, I have to browse upon blue-books and chew statistics."

"And mine has been one of travel, adventure, and considerable excitement," declared Hamilton. "Six months after I left Oxford I found myself out in Transcaucasia as a newspaper correspondent. As you know, I often wrote articles for some of the more precious papers when at college. Well, one of them sent me out to travel through the disturbed Kurdish districts. I had a tough time from the start. I was out with a Cossack party in Thai Aras valley, east of Erivan, for six months, and wrote lots of articles which created a good deal of sensation here in England. You may have seen them, but they were anonymous. The life of excitement, sometimes fighting and at others in ambush in the mountains, suited me admirably, for I'm a born adventurer, I believe. One day, however, a strange thing happened. I was riding along alone through one of the mountain passes towards the Caspian when I discovered three wild, fierce-looking Kurds maltreating a girl, believing her to be a Russian. I called upon them to release her, for she was little more than a child; and, as they did not, I shot two of the men. The third shot and plugged me rather badly in the leg; but I had the satisfaction that my shots attracted my Cossack companions, who, coming quickly on the spot, killed all three of the girl's assailants, and released her."

"By Jove!" laughed Murie. "Was she pretty?"

"Not extraordinarily - a fair-haired girl of about fifteen, dressed in European clothes. I fainted from loss of blood, and don't remember anything else until I found myself in a tent, with two Cossacks patching up my wound. When I came to, she rushed forward, and thanked me profusely for saving her. To my surprise, she spoke in French, and on inquiry I found that she was the daughter of a certain Baron Conrad de Hetzendorf, an Austrian, who possessed a house in Budapest and a chateau at Semlin, in South Hungary. She told us a curious story. Her father had some business in Transcaucasia, and she had induced him to take her with him on his journey. Only certain districts of the country were disturbed; and apparently, with their guide and escort, they had unwittingly entered the Aras region - one of the most lawless of them all - in ignorance of what was in progress. She and her father, accompanied by a guide and four Cossacks, had been riding along when they met a party of Kurds, who had attacked them. Both father and daughter had been seized, whereupon she had lost consciousness from fright, and when she came to again found that the four Cossacks had been killed, her father had been taken off, and she was alone in the brutal hands of those three wild-looking tribesmen. As soon as she had told us this, the officer of the Cossacks to which I had attached myself called the men together, and in a quarter of an hour the whole body went forth to chase the Kurds and rescue the Baron. One big Cossack, in his long coat and astrakhan cap, was left to look after me, while Nicosia - that was the girl's name - was also left to assist him. After three days they returned, bringing with them the Baron, whose delight at finding his daughter safe and unharmed was unbounded. They had fought the Kurds and defeated them, killing nearly twenty. Ah, my dear Murie, you haven't any notion of the lawless state of that country just then! And I fear it is pretty much the same now."

"Well, go on," urged his friend. "What about the girl? I suppose you fell in love with her, and all that, eh?"

"No, you're mistaken there, old chap," was his reply. "When she explained to her father what had happened, the Baron thanked me very warmly, and invited me to visit him in Budapest when my leg grew strong again. He was a man of about fifty, who, I found, spoke English very well. Nicosia also spoke English, for she had explained to me that her mother, now dead, had been a Londoner. The Baron's business in Transcaucasia was, he told me vaguely, in connection with the survey of a new railway which the Russian Government was projecting eastward from Erivan. For two days he remained with us; but during those days my wound was extremely painful owing to lack of surgical appliances, so we spoke of very little else besides the horrible atrocities committed by the Kurds. He pressed me to visit him; and then, with an escort of our Cossacks, he and his daughter left for Tiflis; whence he took train back to Hungary.

"For six months I remained, still leading that roving, adventurous life. My leg was well again, but my journalistic commission was at an end, and one day I found myself in Odessa, very short of funds. I recollected the Baron's invitation to Budapest, therefore I took train there, and found his residence to be one of those great white houses on the Franz Josef Quay. He received me with marked enthusiasm, and compelled me to be his guest. During the first week I was there I told him, in confidence, my position, whereupon he offered me a very lucrative post as his secretary, a post which I have retained until this moment."

"And the girl?" Walter asked, much interested.

"Oh, she finished her education in Dresden and in Paris, and now lives mostly with her aunt in Vienna," was Hamilton's response. "Quite recently she's become engaged to young Count de Solwegen, the son of one of the wealthiest men in Austria."

"I thought you'd probably become the happy lover."

"Lover!" cried his friend. "How could a poor devil like myself ever aspire to the hand of the daughter of the Baron de Hetzendorf? The name doesn't convey much to you, I suppose?"

"No, I don't take much interest in unknown foreigners, I confess," replied Walter, with a smile.

"Ah, you're not a cosmopolitan nor a financier, or you would know the thousand-and-one strings which are pulled by Conrad de Hetzendorf, or the curious stories afloat concerning him."

"Curious stories!" echoed Murie. "Tell me some. I'm always interested in anything mysterious."

Hamilton was silent for a few moments.

"Well, old chap, to tell you the truth, even though I've got such a comfortable and lucrative post, I'm, even after these years, considerably mystified."

"How?"

"By the real nature of the Baron's business."

"Oh, he's a mysterious person, is he?"

"Very. Though I'm his confidential secretary, and deal with his affairs in his absence, yet in some matters he is remarkably close, as though he fears me."

"You live always in Budapest, I suppose?"

"No. In summer we are at the country house, a big place overlooking the Danube outside Semlin, and commanding a wide view of the great Hungarian plain."

"The Baron transacts his business there, eh?"

"From there or from Budapest. His business is solely with an office in the Boulevard des Capucines in Paris, and a registered telegraphic address also in Paris."

"Well, there's nothing very mysterious in that, surely. Some business matters must, of necessity, be conducted with secrecy."

"I know all that, my dear fellow, but -" and he hesitated, as though fearing to take his friend into his confidence.

"But what?"

"Well - but there, no! You'd laugh at me if I told you the real reason of my uneasiness."

"I certainly won't, my dear Hamilton," Murie assured him. "We are friends to-day, dear old chap, just as we were at college. Surely it is not the place of a man to poke fun at his friend?"

The argument was apparently convincing. The Baron's secretary smoked on in thoughtful silence, his eyes fixed upon the wall in front of him.

"Well," he said at last, "if you promise to view the matter in all seriousness, I'll tell you. Briefly, it's this. Of course, you've never been to Semlin - or Zimony, as they call it in the Magyar tongue. To understand aright, I must describe the place. In the extreme south of Hungary, where the river Save joins the Danube, the town of Semlin guards the frontier. Upon a steep hill, five kilometres from the town, stands the Baron's residence, a long, rather inartistic white building, which, however, is very luxuriously furnished. Comparatively modern, it stands near the ruins of a great old castle of Hetzendorf, which commands a wide sweep of the Danube. Now, amid those ruins strange noises are sometimes heard, and it is said that upon all who hear them falls some terrible calamity. I'm not superstitious, but I've heard them - on three occasions! And somehow - well, somehow - I cannot get rid of an uncanny feeling that some catastrophe is to befall me! I can't go back to Semlin. I'm unnerved, and dare not return there."

"Noises!" cried Walter Murie. "What are they like?" he asked quickly, starting from his chair, and staring at his friend.

"They seem to emanate from nowhere, and are like deep but

distant whispers. So plain they were that I could have sworn that some one was speaking, and in English, too!"

"Does the baron know?"

"Yes, I told him, and he appeared greatly alarmed. Indeed, he gave me leave of absence to come home to England."

"Well," exclaimed Murie, "what you tell me, old chap, is most extraordinary! Why, there is almost an exactly similar legend connected with Glencardine!"

"Glencardine!" cried his friend. "Glencardine Castle, in Scotland! I've heard of that. Do you know the place?"

"The estate marches with my father's, therefore I know it well. How extraordinary that there should be almost exactly the same legend concerning a Hungarian castle!"

"Who is the owner of Glencardine?"

"Sir Henry Heyburn, a friend of mine."

"Heyburn!" echoed Hamilton. "Heyburn the blind man?" he gasped, grasping the arm of his chair and staring back at his companion. "And he is your friend? You know his daughter, then?"

"Yes, I know Gabrielle," was Walter's reply, as there flashed across him the recollection of that passionate letter to which he had not replied. "Why?"

"Is she also your friend?"

"She certainly is."

Hamilton was silent. He saw that he was treading dangerous ground. The legend of Glencardine was the same as that of the old Magyar stronghold of Hetzendorf. Gabrielle Heyburn was

Murie's friend. Therefore he resolved to say no more.

Gabrielle Heyburn!

CHAPTER XXX

REVEALS SOMETHING TO HAMILTON

Edgar Hamilton sat with his eyes fixed upon the dingy,
inartistic, smoke-begrimed windows of the chambers opposite.
The man before him was acquainted with Gabrielle Heyburn!
For over a year he had not been in London. He recollected the
last occasion - recollected it, alas! only too well. His thin
countenance wore a puzzled, anxious expression, the
expression of a man face to face with a great difficulty.

"Tell me, Walter," he said at last, "what kind of place is
Glencardine Castle? What kind of man is Sir Henry
Heyburn?"

"Glencardine is one of the most beautiful estates in Scotland.
It lies between Perth and Stirling. The ruins of the ancient
castle, where the great Marquis of Glencardine, who was such
a figure in Scottish history, was born, stands perched up above
a deep, delightful glen; and some little distance off stands the
modern house, built in great part from the ruins of the
stronghold."

"And there are noises heard there the same as at Hetzendorf,
you say?"

"Well, the countryfolk believe that, on certain nights, there can
be heard in the castle courtyard distinct whispering - the
counsel of the devil himself to certain conspirators who took

the life of the notorious Cardinal Setoun."

"Has any one actually heard them?"

"They say so - or, at any rate, several persons after declaring that they had heard them have died quite suddenly."

Hamilton pursed his lips. "Well," he exclaimed, "that's really most remarkable! Practically, the same legend is current in South Hungary regarding Hetzendorf. Strange - very strange!"

"Very," remarked the heir to the great estate of Connachan. "But, after all, cannot one very often trace the same legend through the folklore of various countries? I remember I once attended a lecture upon that very interesting subject."

"Oh, of course. Many ancient legends have sprung from the same germ, so that often we have practically the same fairy-story all over Europe. But this, it seems to me, is no fairy story."

"Well," laughed Murie, "the history of Glencardine Castle and the historic family is so full of stirring episodes that I really don't wonder that the ruins are believed to be the abode of something supernatural. My father possesses some of the family papers, while Sir Henry, when he bought Glencardine, also acquired a quantity. Only a year ago he told me that he had had an application from a well-known historical writer for access to them, as he was about to write a book upon the family."

"Then you know Sir Henry well?"

"Very well indeed. I'm often his guest, and frequently shoot over the place."

"I've heard that Lady Heyburn is a very pretty woman," remarked the other, glancing at his friend with a peculiar look.

"Some declare her to be beautiful; but to myself, I confess, she's not very attractive."

"There are stories about her, eh?" Hamilton said.

"As there are about every good-looking woman. Beauty cannot escape unjust criticism or the scars of lying tongues."

"People pity Sir Henry, I've heard."

"They, of course, sympathise with him, poor old gentleman, because he's blind. His is, indeed, a terrible affliction. Only fancy the change from a brilliant Parliamentary career to idleness, darkness, and knitting."

"I suppose he's very wealthy?"

"He must be. The price he paid for Glencardine was a very heavy one; and, besides that, he has two other places, as well as a house in Park Street and a villa at San Remo."

"Cotton, or steel, or soap, or some other domestic necessity, I suppose?"

Murie shrugged his shoulders. "Nobody knows," he answered. "The source of Sir Henry's vast wealth is a profound mystery."

His friend smiled, but said nothing. Walter Murie had risen to obtain matches, therefore he did not notice the curious expression upon his friend's face, a look which betrayed that he knew more than he intended to tell.

"Those noises heard in the castle puzzle me," he remarked after a few moments.

"At Glencardine they are known as the Whispers," Murie remarked.

"By Jove! I'd like to hear them."

"I don't think there'd be much chance of that, old chap," laughed the other. "They're only heard by those doomed to an early death."

"I may be. Who knows?" he asked gloomily.

"Well, if I were you I wouldn't anticipate catastrophe."

"No," said his friend in a more serious tone, "I've already heard those at Hetzendorf, and - well, I confess they've aroused in my mind some very uncanny apprehensions."

"But did you really hear them? Are you sure they were not imagination? In the night sounds always become both magnified and distorted."

"Yes, I'm certain of what I heard. I was careful to convince myself that it was not imagination, but actual reality."

Walter Murie smiled dubiously. "Sir Henry scouts the idea of the Whispers being heard at Glencardine," he said.

"And, strangely enough, so does the Baron. He's a most matter-of-fact man."

"How curious that the cases are almost parallel, and yet so far apart! The Baron has a daughter, and so has Sir Henry."

"Gabrielle is at Glencardine, I suppose?" asked Hamilton.

"No, she's living with a maiden aunt at an out-of-the-world village in Northamptonshire called Woodnewton."

"Oh, I thought she always lived at Glencardine, and acted as her father's right hand."

"She did until a few months ago, when -" and he paused. "Well," he went on, "I don't know exactly what occurred, except that she left suddenly, and has not since returned."

"Her mother, perhaps. No girl of spirit gets on well with her stepmother."

"Possibly that," Walter said. He knew the truth, but had no desire to tell even his old friend of the allegation against the girl whom he loved.

Hamilton noted the name of the village, and sat wondering at what the young barrister had just told him. It had aroused suspicions within him - strange suspicions.

They sat together for another half-hour, and before they parted arranged to lunch together at the Savoy in two days' time.

Turning out of the Temple, Edgar Hamilton walked along the Strand to the Metropole, in Northumberland Avenue, where he was staying. His mind was full of what his friend had said - full of that curious legend of Glencardine which coincided so strangely with that of far-off Hetzendorf. The jostling crowd in the busy London thoroughfare he did not see. He was away again on the hill outside the old-fashioned Hungarian town, with the broad Danube shining in the white moonbeams. He saw the grim walls that had for centuries withstood the brunt of battle with the Turks, and from them came the whispering voice - the voice said to be that of the Evil One. The Tziganes - that brown-faced race of gipsy wanderers, the women with their bright-coloured skirts and head-dresses, and the men with the wonderful old silver filigree buttons upon their coats - had related to him many weird stories regarding Hetzendorf and the meaning of those whispers. Yet none of their stories was so curious as that which Murie had just told him. Similar sounds were actually heard in the old castle up in the Highlands! His thoughts were wholly absorbed in that one extraordinary fact.

He went to the smoking-room of the hotel, and, obtaining a railway-guide, searched it in vain. Then, ordering from a waiter a map of England, he eagerly searched Northampton-shire and discovered the whereabouts of Woodnewton. Therefore, that night he left London for Oundle, and put up at the old-fashioned "Talbot."

At ten o'clock on the following morning, after making a detour, he alighted from a dogcart before the little inn called the Westmorland Arms at Apethorpe, just outside the lodge-gates of Apethorpe Hall, and making excuse to the groom that he was going for a walk, he set off at a brisk pace over the little bridge and up the hill to Woodnewton.

The morning was dark and gloomy, with threatening rain, and the distance was somewhat greater than he had calculated from the map. At last, however, he came to the entrance to the long village street, with its church and its rows of low thatched cottages.

A tiny inn, called the "White Lion," stood before him, therefore he entered, and calling for some ale, commenced to chat with the old lady who kept the place.

After the usual conventionalities about the weather, he said, "I suppose you don't have very many strangers in Woodnewton, eh?"

"Not many, sir," was her reply. "We see a few people from Oundle and Northampton in the summer - holiday folk. But that's all."

Then, by dint of skilful questioning, he elucidated the fact that old Miss Heyburn lived in the tiled house further up the village, and that her niece, who lived with her, had passed along with her dog about a quarter of an hour before, and taken the footpath towards Southwick.

Ascertaining this, he was all anxiety to follow her; but, knowing how sharp are village eyes upon a stranger, he was compelled to conceal his eagerness, light another cigarette, and continue his chat.

At last, however, he wished the woman good-day, and,

strolling half-way up the village, turned into a narrow lane which led across a farmyard to a footpath which ran across the fields, following a brook. Eager to overtake the girl, he sped along as quickly as possible.

"Gabrielle Heyburn!" he ejaculated, speaking to himself. Her name was all that escaped his lips. A dozen times that morning he had repeated it, uttering it in a tone almost of wonder - almost of awe.

Across several ploughed fields he went, leaving the brook, and, skirting a high hedge to the side of a small wood, he followed the well-trodden path for nearly half-an-hour, when, of a sudden, he emerged from a narrow lane between two hedgerows into a large pasture.

Before him, he saw standing together, on the brink of the river Nene, two figures - a man and a woman.

The girl was dressed in blue serge, and wore a white woollen tam-o'-shanter, while the man had on a dark grey overcoat with a brown felt hat, and nearby, with his eye upon some sheep grazing some distance away, stood a big collie.

Hamilton started, and drew back.

The pair were standing together in earnest conversation, the man facing him, the girl with her back turned.

"What does this mean?" gasped Hamilton aloud. "What can this secret meeting mean? Why - yes, I'm certainly not mistaken - it's Krail – Felix Krail, by all that's amazing!"

CHAPTER XXXI

DESCRIBES A CURIOUS CIRCUMSTANCE

To Hamilton it was evident that the man Krail, now smartly dressed in country tweeds, was telling the girl something which surprised her. He was speaking quickly, making involuntary gestures which betrayed his foreign birth, while she stood pale, surprised, and yet defiant. The Baron's secretary was not near enough to overhear their words. Indeed, he remained there in concealment in order to watch.

Why had Gabrielle met Felix Krail - of all men? She was beautiful. Yes, there could be no two opinions upon that point, Edgar decided. And yet how strange it all was, how very remarkable, how romantic!

The man was evidently endeavouring to impress upon the girl some plain truths to which, at first, she refused to listen. She shrugged her shoulders impatiently and swung her walking-stick before her in an attempt to remain unconcerned. But from where Hamilton was standing he could plainly detect her agitation. Whatever Krail had told her had caused her much nervous anxiety. What could it be?

Across the meadows, beyond the river, could be seen the lantern-tower of old Fotheringhay church, with the mound behind where once stood the castle where ill-fated Mary met her doom.

William Le Queux

And as the Baron's secretary watched, he saw that the foreigner's attitude was gradually changing from persuasive to threatening. He was speaking quickly, probably in French, making wild gestures with his hands, while she had drawn back with an expression of alarm. She was now, it seemed, frightened at the man, and to Edgar Hamilton this increased the interest tenfold.

Through his mind there flashed the recollection of a previous occasion when he had seen the man now before him. He was in different garb, and acting a very different part. But his face was still the same - a countenance which it was impossible to forget. He was watching the changing expression upon the girl's face. Would that he could read the secret hidden behind those wonderful eyes! He had, quite unexpectedly, discovered a mysterious circumstance. Why should Krail meet her by accident at that lonely spot?

The pair moved very slowly together along the path which, having left the way to Southwick, ran along the very edge of the broad, winding river towards Fotheringhay. Until they had crossed the wide pasture-land and followed the bend of the stream Hamilton dare not emerge from his place of concealment. They might glance back and discover him. If so, then to watch Krail's movements further would be futile.

He saw that, by the exercise of caution, he might perhaps learn something of deeper interest than he imagined. So he watched until they disappeared, and then sped along the path they had taken until he came to a clump of bushes which afforded further cover. From where he stood, however, he could see nothing. He could hear voices - a man's voice raised in distinct threats, and a woman's quick, defiant response.

He walked round the bushes quickly, trying to get sight of the pair, but the river bent sharply at that point in such a manner that he could not get a glimpse of them.

Again he heard Krail speaking rapidly in French, and still again the girl's response. Then, next instant, there was a shrill scream and a loud splash.

Next moment, he had darted from his hiding-place to find the girl struggling in the water, while at the same time he caught sight of Krail disappearing quickly around the path. Had he glanced back he could not have seen the girl in the stream.

At that point the bank was steep, and the stillness of the river and absence of rushes told that it was deep.

The girl was throwing up her hand, shrieking for help; therefore, without a second's hesitation, Hamilton, who was a good swimmer, threw off his coat, and, diving in, was soon at her side.

By this time Krail had hurried on, and could obtain no glimpse of what was in progress owing to the sharp bend of the river.

After considerable splashing - Hamilton urging her to remain calm - he succeeded in bringing her to land, where they both struggled up the bank dripping wet and more or less exhausted. Some moments elapsed before either spoke; until, indeed, Hamilton, looking straight into the girl's face and bursting out laughing, exclaimed, "Well, I think I have the pleasure of being acquainted with you, but I must say that we both look like drowned rats!"

"I look horrid!" she declared, staring at him half-dazed, putting her hands to her dripping hair. "I know I must. But I have to thank you for pulling me out. Only fancy, Mr. Hamilton - you!"

"Oh, no thanks are required! What we must do is to get to some place and get our clothes dried," he said. "Do you know this neighbourhood?"

"Oh, yes. Straight over there, about a quarter of a mile away, is

Wyatt's farm. Mrs. Wyatt will look after us, I'm sure." And as she rose to her feet, regarding her companion shyly, her skirts clung around her and the water squelched from her shoes.

"Very well," he answered cheerily. "Let's go and see what can be done towards getting some dry kit. I'm glad you're not too frightened. A good many girls would have fainted, and all that kind of thing."

"I certainly should have gone under if you hadn't so fortunately come along!" she exclaimed. "I really don't know how to thank you sufficiently. You've actually saved my life, you know! If it were not for you I'd have been dead by this time, for I can't swim a stroke."

"By Jove!" he laughed, treating the whole affair as a huge joke, "how romantic it sounds! Fancy meeting you again after all this time, and saving your life! I suppose the papers will be full of it if they get to know - gallant rescue, and all that kind of twaddle."

"Well, personally, I hope the papers won't get hold of this piece of intelligence," she said seriously, as they walked together, rather pitiable objects, across the wide grass-fields.

He glanced at her pale face, her hair hanging dank and wet about it, and saw that, even under these disadvantageous conditions, she had grown more beautiful than before. Of late he had heard of her - heard a good deal of her - but had never dreamed that they would meet again in that manner.

"How did it happen?" he asked in pretence of ignorance of her companion's presence.

She raised her fine eyes to his for a moment, and wavered beneath his inquiring gaze.

"I - I - well, I really don't know," was her rather lame answer. "The bank was very slippery, and - well, I suppose I walked too near."

Her reply struck him as curious. Why did she attempt to shield the man who, by his sudden flight, was self-convicted of an attempt upon her life?

Felix Krail was not a complete stranger to her. Why had their meeting been a clandestine one? This, and a thousand similar queries ran through his mind as they walked across the field in the direction of a long, low, thatched farmhouse which stood in the distance.

"I'm a complete stranger in these parts," Hamilton informed her. "I live nowadays mostly abroad, away above the Danube, and am only home for a holiday."

"And I'm afraid you've completely spoilt your clothes," she laughed, looking at his wet, muddy trousers and boots.

"Well, if I have, yours also are no further good."

"Oh, my blouse will wash, and I shall send my skirt to the cleaners, and it will come back like new," she answered. "Women's outdoor clothing never suffers by a wetting. We'll get Mrs. Wyatt to dry them, and then I'll get home again to my aunt in Woodnewton. Do you know the place?"

"I fancy I passed through it this morning. One of those long, lean villages, with a church at the end."

"That's it - the dullest little place in all England, I believe."

He was struck by her charm of manner. Though bedraggled and dishevelled, she was nevertheless delightful, and treated her sudden immersion with careless unconcern.

Why had Krail attempted to get rid of her in that manner? What motive had he?

They reached the farmhouse, where Mrs. Wyatt, a stout, ruddy-faced woman, detecting their approach, met them upon the threshold. "Lawks, Miss Heyburn! why, what's happened?" she asked in alarm.

"I fell into the river, and this gentleman fished me out. That's all," laughed the girl. "We want to dry our things, if we may."

In a few minutes, in bedrooms upstairs, they had exchanged their wet clothes for dry ones. Then Edgar in the farmer's Sunday suit of black, and Gabrielle in one of Mrs. Wyatt's stuff dresses, in the big folds of which her slim little figure was lost, met again in the spacious farmhouse-kitchen below.

They laughed heartily at the ridiculous figure which each presented, and drank the glasses of hot milk which the farmer's wife pressed upon them.

Old Miss Heyburn had been Mrs. Wyatt's mistress years ago, when she was in service, therefore she was most solicitous after the girl's welfare, and truth to tell looked askance at the good-looking stranger who had accompanied her.

Gabrielle, too, was puzzled to know why Mr. Hamilton should be there. That he now lived abroad "beside the Danube" was all the information he had vouchsafed regarding himself, yet from certain remarks he had dropped she was suspicious. She recollected only too vividly the occasion when they had met last, and what had occurred.

They sat together on the bench outside the house, enjoying the full sunshine, while the farmer's wife chattered on. A big fire had been made in the kitchen, and their clothes were rapidly drying.

Hamilton, by careful questions, endeavoured to obtain from the girl some information concerning her dealings with the man Krail. But she was too wary. It was evident that she had some distinct object in concealing the fact that he had deliberately flung her into the water after that heated altercation.

Felix Krail! The very name caused him to clench his hands. Fortunately, he knew the truth, therefore that dastardly attempt upon the girl's life should not go unpunished. As he sat there chatting with her, admiring her refinement and innate daintiness, he made a vow within himself to seek out that cowardly fugitive and meet him face to face.

Felix Krail! What could be his object in ridding the world of the daughter of Sir Henry Heyburn! What would the man gain thereby? He knew Krail too well to imagine that he ever did anything without a motive of gain. So well did he play his cards always that the police could never lay hands upon him. Yet his "friends," as he termed them, were among the most dangerous men in all Europe - men who were unscrupulous, and would hesitate at nothing in order to accomplish the *coup* which they had devised.

What was the *coup* in this particular instance? Ay, that was the question.

William Le Queux

CHAPTER XXXII

OUTSIDE THE WINDOW

Late on the following afternoon Gabrielle was seated at the old-fashioned piano in her aunt's tiny drawing-room, her fingers running idly over the keys, her thoughts wandering back to the exciting adventure of the previous morning. Her aunt was out visiting some old people in connection with the village clothing club, therefore she sat gloomily amusing herself at the piano, and thinking - ever thinking.

She had been playing almost mechanically Berger's "Amoureuse" valse and some dreamy music from *The Merry Widow*, when she suddenly stopped and sat back with her eyes fixed out of the window upon the cottages opposite.

Why was Mr. Hamilton in that neighbourhood? He had given her no further information concerning himself. He seemed to be disinclined to talk about his recent movements. He had sprung from nowhere just at the critical moment when she was in such deadly peril. Then, after their clothes had been dried, they had walked together as far as the little bridge at the entrance to Fotheringhay.

There he had stopped, bent gallantly over her hand, congratulated her upon her escape, and as their ways lay in opposite directions - she back to Woodnewton and he on to Oundle - they had parted. "I hope, Miss Heyburn, that we may meet again one day," he had laughed cheerily as he raised his hat, "Good-bye." Then he had turned away, and had been lost to view round the bend of the road.

She was safe. That man whom she had known long ago under such strange circumstances, whom she would probably never see again, had been her rescuer. Of this curious and romantic fact she was now thinking.

But where was Walter? Why had he not replied to her letter? Ah! that was the one thought which oppressed her always, sleeping and waking, day and night. Why had he not written? Would he never write again?

She had at first consoled herself with the thought that he was probably on the Continent, and that her letter had not been forwarded. But as the days went on, and no reply came, the truth became more and more apparent that her lover - the man whom she adored and worshipped - had put her aside, had accepted her at her own estimate as worthless.

A thousand times she had regretted the step she had taken in writing that cruel letter before she left Glencardine. But it was all too late. She had tried to retract; but, alas! it was now impossible.

Tears welled in her splendid eyes at thought of the man whom she had loved so well. The world had, indeed, been cruel to her. Her enemies had profited by her inexperience, and she had fallen an unhappy victim of an unscrupulous blackguard. Yes, it was only too true. She did not try to conceal the ugly truth from herself. Yet she had been compelled to keep Walter in ignorance of the truth, for he loved her.

A hardness showed at the corners of her sweet lips, and the tears rolled slowly down her cheeks. Then, bestirring herself with an effort, her white fingers ran over the keys again, and in her sweet, musical voice she sang "L'Heure d'Aimer," that pretty *valse chantee* so popular in Paris: -

Voici l'heure d'aimer, l'heure des tendresses;
Dis-moi les mots tres doux qui vont me griser,
Ah! prends-moi dans tes bras, fais-moi des caresses;
Je veux mourir pour revivre sous ton baiser.
Emporte-moi dans un reve amoureux,
Bien loin sur la terre inconnue,
Pour que longtemps, meme en rouvrant les yeux,
Ce reve continue.

Croyons, aimons, vivons un jour;
C'est si bon, mais si court!
Bonheur de vivre ici-bas diminue
Dans un moment d'amour.

The Hour of Love! How full of burning love and sentiment! She stopped, reflecting on the meaning of those words.

She was not like the average miss who, parrot-like, knows only a few French or Italian songs. Italian she loved even better than French, and could read Dante and Petrarch in the original, while she possessed an intimate knowledge of the poetry of Italy from the mediaeval writers down to Carducci and D'Annunzio.

With a sigh, she glanced around the small room, with its old-fashioned furniture, its antimacassars of the early Victorian era, its wax flowers under their glass dome, and its gipsy-table covered with a hand-embroidered cloth. It was all so very dispiriting. The primness of the whatnot decorated with pieces of treasured china, the big gilt-framed overmantel, and the old punch-bowl filled with pot-pourri, all spoke mutely of the thin-nosed old spinster to whom the veriest speck of dust was an abomination.

Sighing still again, the girl turned once more to the old-fashioned instrument, with its faded crimson silk behind the walnut fretwork, and, playing the plaintive melody, sang an ancient serenade:

Di questo cor tu m'hai ferito il core
A cento colpi, piu non val mentire.
Pensa che non sopporto piu il dolore,
E se segu cosi, vado a morire.
Ti tengo nella mente a tutte l'ore,
Se lavoro, se velio, o sto a dormre ...
E mentre dormo ancora un sonno grato,
Mi trovo tutto lacrime bagnato!

While she sang, there was a rap at the front-door, and, just as she concluded, the prim maid entered with a letter upon a salver.

In an instant her heart gave a bound. She recognised the handwriting. It was Walter's.

The moment the girl had left the room she tore open the envelope, and, holding her breath, read what was written within.

The words were:

"DEAREST HEART, - Your letter came to me after several wanderings. It has caused me to think and to wonder if, after all, I may be mistaken - if, after all, I have misjudged you, darling. I gave you my heart, it is true. But you spurned it - under compulsion, you say! Why under compulsion? Who is it who compels you to act against your will and against your better nature? I know that you love me as well and as truly as I love you yourself. I long to see you with just as great a longing. You are mine - mine, my own - and being mine, you must tell me the truth.

"I forgive you, forgive you everything. But I cannot under-stand what Flockart means by saying that I have spoken of you. I have not seen the man, nor do I wish to see him. Gabrielle, do not trust him. He is your enemy, as he is mine. He has lied to you. As grim circumstance has forced you to treat me cruelly, let us hope that smiling fortune will be ours at last. The world is very small. I have just met my old friend Edgar Hamilton, who was at college with me, and who, I find, is secretary to some wealthy foreigner, a certain Baron de Hetzendorf. I have not seen him for years, and yet he turns up here, merry and prosperous, after struggling for a long time with adverse circumstances.

"But, Gabrielle, your letter has puzzled and alarmed me. The more I think of it, the more mystifying it all becomes. I must see you, and you must tell me the truth - the whole truth. We love each other, dear heart, and no one shall force you to lie again to me as you did in that letter you wrote from Glencardine. You wish to see me, darling. You shall - and you shall tell me the truth. My dear love, *au revoir* - until we meet, which I hope may be almost as soon as you receive this letter. - My love, my sweetheart, I am your own WALTER."

She sat staring at the letter. He demanded an explanation. He intended to come there and demand it! And the explanation was one which she dared not give. Rather that she took her own life than tell him the ghastly circumstances.

He had met an old chum named Hamilton. Was this the Mr. Hamilton who had snatched her from that deadly peril? The name of Hetzendorf sounded to be Austrian or German. How strange if Mr. Hamilton her rescuer were the same man who had been years ago her lover's college friend!

She passed her white hand across her brow, trying to collect her senses.

She had longed - ah, with such an intense longing! - for a response to that letter of hers, and here at last it had come. But what a response! He intended her to make confession. He demanded to know the actual truth. What could she do? How should she act?

Holding the letter in her hand, she glanced around the little room in utter despair.

He loved her. His words of reassurance brought her great comfort. But he wished to know the truth. He suspected something. By her own action in writing those letters she had aroused suspicion against herself. She regretted, yet what was the use of regret? Her own passionate words had revealed to him something which he had not suspected. And he was coming down there, to Woodnewton, to demand the truth! He might even then be on his way!

If he asked her point-blank, what could she reply? She dare not tell him the truth. There were now but two roads open - either death by her own hand or to lie to him.

Could she tell him an untruth? No. She loved him, therefore she could not resort to false declarations and deceit. Better - far better - would it be that she took her own life. Better, she thought, if Mr. Hamilton had not plunged into the river after her. If her life had ended, Walter Murie would at least have been spared the bitter knowledge of a disgraceful truth. Her face grew pale and her mouth hardened at the thought.

She loved him with all the fierce passion of her young heart. He was her hero, her idol. Before her tear-dimmed eyes his dear, serious face rose, a sweet memory of what had been. Tender remembrances of his fond kisses still lingered with her. She recollected how around her waist his strong arm would steal, and how slowly and yet irresistibly he would draw her in his arms in silent ecstasy.

Alas! that was all past and over. They loved each other, but she was now face to face with what she had so long dreaded - face to face with the inevitable. She must either confess the truth, and by so doing turn his love to hatred, or else remain silent and face the end.

She reread the letter still seated at the piano, her elbows resting inertly upon the keys. Then she lifted her pale face again to the window, gazing out blankly upon the village street, so dull, so silent, so uninteresting. The thought of Mr. Hamilton - the man who held a secret of hers, and who only a few hours before had rescued her from the peril in which Felix Krail had placed her - again recurred to her. Was it not remarkable that he, Walter's old friend, should come down into that neighbourhood? There was some motive in his visit! What could it be? He had spoken of Hungary, a country which had always possessed for her a strange fascination. Was it not quite likely that, being Walter's friend, Hamilton on his return to London would relate the exciting incident of the river? Had he seen Krail? And, if so, did he know him?

Those two points caused her the greatest apprehension. Suppose he had recognised Krail! Suppose he had overheard that man's demands, and her defiant refusal, he would surely tell Walter!

She bit her lip, and her white fingers clenched themselves in desperation.

Why should all this misfortune fall upon her, to wreck her young life? Other girls were gay, careless, and happy. They visited and motored and flirted and danced, and went to theatres in town and to suppers afterwards at the Carlton or Savoy, and had what they termed "a ripping good time." But to her poor little self all pleasure was debarred. Only the grim shadows of life were hers.

Her mind had become filled with despair. Why had this great calamity befallen her? Why had she, by her own action in writing to her lover, placed herself in that terrible position from which there was no escape - save by death?

The recollection of the Whispers - those fatal Whispers of Glencardine - flashed through her distressed mind. Was it actually true, as the countryfolk declared, that death overtook all those who overheard the counsels of the Evil One? It really seemed as though there actually was more in the weird belief than she had acknowledged. Her father had scouted the idea, yet old Stewart, who had personally known instances, had declared that evil and disaster fell inevitably upon any one who chanced to hear those voices of the night.

The recollection of that moonlight hour among the ruins, and the distinct voices whispering, caused a shudder to run through her. She had heard them with her own ears, and ever since that moment nothing but catastrophe upon catastrophe had fallen upon her.

Yes, she had heard the Whispers, and she could not escape their evil influence any more than those other unfortunate persons to whom death had come so unexpectedly and swiftly.

A shadow passed the window, causing her to start. The figure was that of a man. She rose from the piano with a cry, and stood erect, motionless, statuesque.

CHAPTER XXXIII

IS ABOUT THE MAISON LENARD

The big, rather severely but well-furnished room overlooked the busy Boulevard des Capucines in Paris. In front lay the great white facade of the Grand Hotel; below was all the bustle, life, and movement of Paris on a bright sunny afternoon. Within the room, at a large mahogany table, sat four grave-faced men, while a fifth stood at one of the long windows, his back turned to his companions.

The short, broad-shouldered man looking forth into the street, in expectancy, was Monsieur Goslin. He had been speaking, and his words had evidently caused some surprise, even alarm, among his companions, for they now exchanged glances in silence.

Three of the men were well-dressed and prosperous-looking; while the fourth, a shrivelled old fellow, in faded clothes which seemed several sizes too large for him, looked needy and ill-fed as he nervously chafed his thin bony hands.

Next moment they all began chatting in French, though from their countenances it was plain that they were of various nationalities - one being German, the other Italian, and the third, a sallow-faced man, had the appearance of a Levantine.

Goslin alone remained silent and watchful. From where he stood he could see the people entering and leaving the Grand

Hotel. He glanced impatiently at his watch, and then paced the room, his hand thoughtfully stroking his grey beard. Only half an hour before he had alighted at the Gare du Nord, coming direct from far-off Glencardine, and had driven there in an auto-cab to keep an appointment made by telegram. As he paced the big room, with its dark-green walls, its Turkey carpet, and sombre furniture, his companions regarded him in wonder. They instinctively knew that he had some news of importance to impart. There was one absentee. Until his arrival Goslin refused to say anything.

The youngest of the four assembled at the table was the Italian, a rather thin, keen-faced, dark-moustached man of refined appearance. "*Madonna mia!*" he cried, raising his face to the Frenchman, "why, what has happened? This is unusual. Besides, why should we wait? I've only just arrived from Turin, and haven't had time to go to the hotel. Let us get on. *Avanti!*"

"Not until he is present," answered Goslin, speaking earnestly in French. "I have a statement to make from Sir Henry. But I am not permitted to make it until all are here." Then, glancing at his watch, he added, "His train was due at Est Station at 4.58. He ought to be here at any moment."

The shabby old man, by birth a Pole, still sat chafing his chilly fingers. None who saw Antoine Volkonski, as he shuffled along the street, ever dreamed that he was head of the great financial house of Volkonski Freres of Petersburg, whose huge loans to the Russian Government during the war with Japan created a sensation throughout Europe, and surely no casual observer looking at that little assembly would ever entertain suspicion that, between them, they could practically dictate to the money-market of Europe.

The Italian seated next to him was the Commendatore Rudolphe Cusani, head of the wealthy banking firm of Montemartini of Rome, which ranked next to the Bank of Italy. Of the remaining two, one was a Greek from Smyrna, and the other, a rather well-dressed man with longish grey hair,

Josef Frohnmeyer of Hamburg, a name also to conjure with in the financial world.

The impatient Italian was urging Goslin to explain why the meeting had been so hastily summoned when, without warning, the door opened and a tall, distinguished man, with carefully trained grey moustache, and wearing a heavy travelling ulster, entered.

"Ah, my dear Baron!" cried the Italian, jumping from his chair and taking the new-comer's hand, "we were waiting for you." And he drew a chair next to his.

The man addressed tossed his soft felt travelling hat aside, saying, "The 'wire' reached me at a country house outside Vienna, where I was visiting. But I came instantly." And he seated himself, while the chair at the head of the table was taken by the stout Frenchman.

"Messieurs," Goslin commenced, and - speaking in French - began apologising at being compelled to call them together so soon after their last meeting. "The matter, however, is of such urgency," he went on, "that this conference is absolutely necessary. I am here in Sir Henry's place, with a statement from him - an alarming statement. Our enemies have unfortunately triumphed."

"What do you mean?" cried the Italian, starting to his feet.

"Simply this. Poor Sir Henry has been the victim of treachery. - Those papers which you, my dear Volkonski, brought to me in secret at Glencardine a month ago have been stolen!"

"Stolen!" gasped the shabby old man, his grey eyes starting from his head; "stolen! *Dieu!* Think what that means to us - to me - to my house! They will be sold to the Ministry of Finance in Petersburg, and I shall be ruined - ruined!"

"Not only you will be ruined!" remarked the man from

Hamburg, "but our control of the market will be at an end."

"And together we lose over three million roubles," said Goslin in as quiet a voice as he could assume.

The six men - those men who dealt in millions, men whose names, every one of them, were as household words on the various Bourses of Europe and in banking circles, men who lent money to reigning Sovereigns and to States, whose interests were world-wide and whose influences were greater than those of Kings and Ministers - looked at each other in blank despair.

"We have to face this fact, as Sir Henry points out to you, that at Petersburg the Department of Finance has no love for us. We put on the screw a little too heavily when we sold them secretly those three Argentine cruisers. We made a mistake in not being content with smaller profit."

"Yes, if it had been a genuinely honest deal on their side," remarked the Italian. "But it was not. In Russia the crowd made quite as great a profit as we did."

"And all three ships were sent to the bottom of the sea four months afterwards," added Frohnmeyer with a grim laugh.

"That isn't the question," Goslin said. "What we have now to face is the peril of exposure. No one can, of course, allege that we have ever resorted to any sharper practices than those of other financial groups; but the fact of our alliance and our impregnable strength will, when it is known, arouse the fiercest antagonism in certain circles."

"No one suspects the secret of our alliance," the Italian ejaculated. "It must be kept - kept at all hazards."

Each man seated there knew that exposure of the tactics by which they were ruling the Bourse would mean the sudden end of their great prosperity.

"But this is not the first occasion that documents have been stolen from Sir Henry at Glencardine," remarked the Baron Conrad de Hetzendorf. "I remember the last time I went there to see him he explained how he had discovered his daughter with the safe open, and some of the papers actually in her hands."

"Unfortunately that is so," Goslin answered. "There is every evidence that we owe our present peril to her initiative. She and her father are on bad terms, and it seems more than probable that though she is no longer at Glencardine she has somehow contrived to get hold of the documents in question - at the instigation of her lover, we believe."

"How do you know that the documents are stolen?" the Baron asked.

"Because three days ago Sir Henry received an anonymous letter bearing the postmark of 'London, E.C.,' enclosing correct copies of the papers which our friend Volkonski brought from Petersburg, and asking what sum he was prepared to pay to obtain repossession of the originals. On receipt of the letter," continued Goslin, "I rushed to the safe, to find the papers gone. The door had been unlocked and relocked by an unknown hand."

"And how does suspicion attach to the girl's lover?" asked the man from Hamburg.

"Well, he was alone in the library for half an hour about five days before. He called to see Sir Henry while he and I were out walking together in the park. It is believed that the girl has a key to the safe, which she handed to her lover in order that he might secure the papers and sell them in Russia."

"But young Murie is the son of a wealthy man, I've heard," observed the Baron.

"Certainly. But at present his allowance is small," was

Goslin's reply.

"Well, what's to be done?" inquired the Italian.

"Done?" echoed Goslin. "Nothing can be done."

"Why?" they all asked almost in one breath.

"Because Sir Henry has replied, refusing to treat for the return of the papers."

"Was that not injudicious? Why did he not allow us to discuss the affair first?" argued the Levantine.

"Because an immediate answer by telegraph to a post-office in Hampshire was demanded," Goslin replied. "Remember that to Sir Henry's remarkable foresight all our prosperity has been due. Surely we may trust in his judicious treatment of the thief!"

"That's all very well," protested Volkonski; "but my fortune is at stake. If the Ministry obtains those letters they will crush and ruin me."

"Sir Henry is no novice," remarked the Baron. "He fights an enemy with his own weapons. Remember that Greek deal of which the girl gained knowledge. He actually prepared bogus contracts and correspondence for the thief to steal. They were stolen, and, passing through a dozen hands, were at last offered in Athens. The Ministry there laughed at the thieves for their pains. Let us hope the same result will be now obtained."

"I fear not," Goslin said quietly. "The documents stolen on the former occasion were worthless. The ones now in the hands of our enemies are genuine."

"But," said the Baron, "you, Goslin, went to live at Glencardine on purpose to protect our poor blind friend from his enemies!"

"I know," said the man addressed. "I did my best - and failed. The footman Hill, knowing young Murie as a frequent guest at Glencardine, the other day showed him into the library and left him there alone. It was then, no doubt, that he opened the safe with a false key and secured the documents."

"Then why not apply for a warrant for his arrest?" suggested the Commendatore Cusani. "Surely your English laws do not allow thieves to go unpunished? In Italy we should quickly lay hands on them."

"But we have no evidence."

"You have no suspicion that any other man may have committed the theft - that fellow Flockart, for instance? I don't like him," added the Baron. "He is altogether too friendly with everybody at Glencardine."

"I have already made full inquiries. Flockart was in Rome. He only returned to London the day before yesterday. No. Everything points to the girl taking revenge upon her father, who, I am compelled to admit, has treated her with rather undue harshness. Personally, I consider mademoiselle very charming and intelligent."

They all admitted that her correspondence and replies to reports were marvels of clear, concise instruction. Every man among them knew well her neat round handwriting, yet only Goslin had ever seen her.

The Frenchman was asked to describe both the girl and her lover. This he did, declaring that Gabrielle and Walter were a very handsome pair.

"Whatever may be said," remarked old Volkonski, "the girl was a most excellent assistant to Sir Henry. But it is, of course, the old story - a young girl's head turned by a handsome lover. Yet surely the youth is not so poor that he became a thief of necessity. To me it seems rather as though he stole the documents at her instigation."

"That is exactly Sir Henry's belief," Goslin remarked with a sigh. "The poor old fellow is beside himself with grief and fear."

"No wonder!" remarked the Italian. "None of us would care to be betrayed by our own daughters."

"But cannot a trap be laid to secure the thief before he approaches the people in Russia?" suggested the crafty Levantine.

"Yes, yes!" cried Volkonski, his hands still clenched. "The Ministry would give a hundred thousand roubles for them, because by their aid they could crush me - crush you all. Remember, there are names there - names of some of the most prominent officials in the Empire. Think of the power of the Ministry if they held that list in their hands!"

"No," said the Baron in a clear, distinct voice, his grey eyes fixed thoughtfully upon the wall opposite. "Rather think of our positions, of the exultation of our enemies if this great combine of ours were exposed and broken! Myself, I consider it folly that we have met here openly to-day. This is the first time we have all met, save in secret, and how do we know but some spy may be on the *boulevard* outside noting who has entered here?"

"*Mille diavoli!*" gasped Cusani, striking the table with his fist and sinking back into his chair. "I recollect I passed outside here a man I know - a man who knows me. He was standing on the kerb. He saw me. His name is Krail - Felix Krail!"

"Is he still there?" cried the men, as with one accord they left their chairs and dashed eagerly across to the window.

"Krail!" cried the Russian in alarm. "Where is he?"

"See!" the Italian pointed out, "see the man in black yonder, standing there near the *kiosque*, smoking a cigarette. He is still watching. He has seen us meet here!"

"Ah!" said the Baron in a hoarse voice, "I said so. To meet openly like this was far too great a risk. Nobody knew anything of Lenard et Morellet of the Boulevard des Capucines except that they were unimportant financiers. To-morrow the world will know who they really are. Messieurs, we are the victims of a very clever ruse. We have been so tricked that we have been actually summoned here and our identity disclosed!"

The five monarchs of finance stood staring at each other in absolute silence.

CHAPTER XXXIV

SURPRISES MR. FLOCKART

"Well, you and your friend Felix have placed me in a very pleasant position, haven't you?" asked Lady Heyburn of Flockart, who had just entered the green-and-white morning-room at Park Street. "I hope now that you're satisfied with your blunder!"

The man addressed, in a well-cut suit of grey, a fancy vest, and patent-leather boots, still carrying his hat and stick in his hand, turned to her in surprise.

"What do you mean?" he asked. "I arrived from Paris at five this morning, and I've brought you good news."

"Nonsense!" cried the woman, starting from her chair in anger. "You can't deceive me any longer."

"Krail has discovered the whole game. The syndicate held a meeting at the office in Paris. He and I watched the arrivals. We now know who they are, and exactly what they are doing. By Jove! we never dreamed that your husband, blind though he is, is head of such a smart and influential group. Why, they're the first in Europe."

"What does that matter? Krail wants money, so do we; but even with all your wonderful schemes we get none!"

William Le Queux

"Wait, my dear Winnie, remain patient, and we shall obtain plenty."

It was indeed strange for a woman within that smart town-house, and with her electric brougham at the door, to complain of poverty. The house had been a centre of political activity in the days before Sir Henry met with that terrible affliction. The room in which the pair stood had been the scene of many a private and momentous conference, and in the big drawing-room upstairs many a Cabinet Minister had bent over the hand of the fair Lady Heyburn.

Into the newly decorated room, with its original Adams ceiling, its dead-white panelling and antique overmantel, shone the morning sun, weak and yellow as it always is in London in the spring-time.

Lady Heyburn, dressed in a smart walking-gown of grey, pushed her fluffy fair hair from her brow, while upon her face was an expression which told of combined fear and anger.

Her visitor was surprised. After that watchful afternoon in the Boulevard des Capucines, he had sat in a corner of the Cafe Terminus listening to Krail, who rubbed his hands with delight and declared that he now held the most powerful group in Europe in the hollow of his hand.

For the past six years or so gigantic *coups* had been secured by that unassuming and apparently third-rate financial house of Lenard et Morellet. From a struggling firm they had within a year grown into one whose wealth seemed inexhaustible, and whose balances at the Credit Lyonnais, the Societe Generale, and the Comptoir d'Escompte were possibly the largest of any of the customers of those great corporations. The financial world of Europe had wondered. It was a mystery who was behind Lenard et Morellet, the pair of steady-going, highly respectable business men who lived in unostentatious comfort, the former at Enghien, just outside Paris, and the latter out in the country at Melum. The mystery was so well and so carefully preserved that not even the bankers themselves could obtain knowledge of the truth.

Krail had, however, after nearly two years of clever watching and ingenious subterfuge, succeeded, by placing the group in a "hole" in calling them together. That they met, and often, was undoubted. But where they met, and how, was still a complete mystery.

As Flockart had sat that previous afternoon listening to Krail's unscrupulous and self-confident proposals, he had remained in silent wonder at the man's audacious attitude. Nothing deterred him, nothing daunted him.

Flockart had returned that night from Paris, gone to his chambers in Half-Moon Street, breakfasted, dressed, and had now called upon her ladyship in order to impart to her the good news. Yet, instead of welcoming him, she only treated him with resentment and scorn. He knew the quick flash of those eyes, he had seen it before on other occasions. This was not the first time they had quarrelled, yet he, keen-witted and cunning, had always held her powerless to elude him, had always compelled her to give him the sums he so constantly demanded. That morning, however, she was distinctly resentful, distinctly defiant.

For an instant he turned from her, biting his lip in annoyance. When facing her again, he smiled, asking, "Tell me, Winnie, what does all this mean?"

"Mean!" echoed the Baronet's wife. "Mean! How can you ask me that question? Look at me - a ruined woman! And you -"

"Speak out!" he cried. "What has happened?"

"You surely know what has happened. You have treated me like the cur you are - and that is speaking plainly. You've sacrificed me in order to save yourself."

"From what?"

"From exposure. To me, ruin is not a matter of days, but of hours."

"You're speaking in enigmas. I don't understand you," he cried impatiently. "Krail and I have at last been successful. We know now the true source of your husband's huge income, and in order to prevent exposure he must pay - and pay us well too."

"Yes," she laughed hysterically. "You tell me all this after you've blundered."

"Blundered! How?" he asked, surprised at her demeanour.

"What's the use of beating about the bush?" asked her lady-ship. "The girl is back at Glencardine. She knows everything, thanks to your foolish self-confidence."

"Back at Glencardine!" gasped Flockart. "But she dare not speak. By heaven! if she does - then - then -"

"And what, pray, can you do?" inquired the woman harshly. "It is I who have to suffer, I who am crushed, humiliated, ruined, while you and your precious friend shield yourselves behind your cloaks of honesty. You are Sir Henry's friend. He believes you as such - you!" And she laughed the hollow laugh of a woman who was staring death in the face. She was haggard and drawn, and her hands trembled with nervousness which she strove in vain to repress. Lady Heyburn was desperate.

"He still believes in me, eh?" asked the man, thinking deeply, for his clever brain was already active to devise some means of escape from what appeared to be a distinctly awkward dilemma. He had never calculated the chances of Gabrielle's return to her father's side. He had believed that impossible.

"I understand that my husband will hear no word against you," replied the tall, fair-haired woman. "But when I speak he will listen, depend upon it."

"You dare!" he cried, turning upon her in threatening attitude. "You dare utter a single word against me, and, by Heaven! I'll tell what I know. The country shall ring with a scandal - the shame of your attitude towards the girl, and a crime for which you will be arraigned, with me, before an assize-court. Remember!"

The woman shrank from him. Her face had blanched. She saw that he was equally as determined as she was desperate. James Flockart always kept his threats. He was by no means a man to trifle with.

For a moment she was thoughtful, then she laughed defiantly in his face. "Speak! Say what you will. But if you do, you suffer with me."

"You say that exposure is imminent," he remarked. "How did the girl manage to return to Glencardine?"

"With Walter's aid. He went down to Woodnewton. What passed between them I have no idea. I only returned the day before yesterday from the South. All I know is that the girl is back with her father, and that he knows much more than he ought to know."

"Murie could not have assisted her," Flockart declared decisively. "The old man suspects him of taking those Russian papers from the safe."

"How do you know he hasn't cleared himself of the suspicion? He may have done. The old man dotes upon the girl."

"I know all that."

"And she may have turned upon you, and told the truth about the safe incident. That's more than likely."

"She dare not utter a word."

"You're far too self-confident. It is your failing."

"And when, pray, has it failed? Tell me."

"Never, until the present moment. Your bluff is perfect, yet there are moments when it cannot aid you, depend upon it. She told me one night long ago, in my own room, when she had disobeyed, defied, and annoyed me, that she would never rest until Sir Henry knew the truth, and that she would place before him proofs of the other affair. She has long intended to do this; and now, thanks to your attitude of passive inertness, she has accomplished her intentions."

"What!" he gasped in distinct alarm, "has she told her father the truth?"

"A telegram I received from Sir Henry late last night makes it only too plain that he knows something," responded the unhappy woman, staring straight before her. "It is your fault - your fault!" she went on, turning suddenly upon her companion again. "I warned you of the danger long ago."

Flockart stood motionless. The announcement which the woman had made staggered him.

Felix Krail had come to him in Paris, and after some hesitation, and with some reluctance, had described how he had followed the girl along the Nene bank and thrown her into the deepest part of the river, knowing that she would be hampered by her skirts and that she could not swim. "She will not trouble us further. Never fear!" he had said. "It will be thought a case of suicide through love. Her mental depression is the common talk of the neighbourhood."

And yet the girl was safe and now home again at Glencardine! He reflected upon the ugly facts of "the other affair" to which her ladyship sometimes referred, and his face went ashen pale.

Just at the moment when success had come to them after all their ingenuity and all their endeavours - just at a moment when they could demand and obtain what terms they liked from Sir Henry to preserve the secret of the financial combine - came this catastrophe.

"Felix was a fool to have left his work only half-done," he remarked aloud, as though speaking to himself.

"What work?" asked the hollow-eyed woman eagerly. But he did not satisfy her. To explain would only increase her alarm and render her even more desperate than she was.

"Did I not tell you often that, from her, we had all to fear?" cried the woman frantically. "But you would not listen. And now I am - I'm face to face with the inevitable. Disaster is before me. No power can avert it. The girl will have a bitter and terrible revenge."

"No," he cried quickly, with fierce determination. "No, I'll save you, Winnie. The girl shall not speak. I'll go up to Glencardine to-night and face it out. You will come with me."

"I!" gasped the shrinking woman. "Ah, no. I - I couldn't. I dare not face him. You know too well I dare not!"

CHAPTER XXXV

DISCLOSES A SECRET

The grey mists were still hanging upon the hills of Glencardine, although it was already midday, for it had rained all night, and everywhere was damp and chilly.

Gabrielle, in her short tweed skirt, golf-cape, and motor-cap, had strolled, with Walter Murie at her side, from the house along the winding path to the old castle. From the contented expression upon her pale, refined countenance, it was plain that happiness, to a great extent, had been restored to her.

When he had gone to Woodnewton it was to fetch her back to Glencardine. He had asked for an explanation, it was true; but when she had refused one he had not pressed it. That he was puzzled, sorely puzzled, was apparent.

At first, Sir Henry had point-blank refused to receive his daughter. But on hearing her appealing voice he had to some extent relented; and, though strained relations still existed between them, yet happiness had come to her in the knowledge that Walter's affection was still as strong as ever.

Young Murie had, of course, heard from his mother the story told by Lady Heyburn concerning the offence of her step-daughter. But he would not believe a single word against her.

They had been strolling slowly, and she had been speaking

expressing her heartfelt thanks for his action in taking her from that life of awful monotony at Woodnewton. Then he, on his part, had pressed her soft hand and repeated his promise of lifelong love.

They had entered the old grass-grown courtyard of the castle, when suddenly she exclaimed, "How I wish, Walter, that we might elucidate the secret of the Whispers!"

"It certainly would be intensely interesting if we could," he said, "The most curious thing is that my old friend Edgar Hamilton, who is secretary to the well-known Baron Conrad de Hetzendorf, tells me that a similar legend is current in connection with the old chateau in Hungary. He had heard the Whispers himself."

"Most remarkable!" she exclaimed, gazing blankly around at the ponderous walls about her.

"My idea always has been that beneath where we are standing there must be a chamber, for most mediaeval castles had a subterranean dungeon beneath the courtyard."

"Ah, if we could only find entrance to it!" cried the girl enthusiastically. "Shall we try?"

"Have you not often tried, and failed?" he asked laughingly.

"Yes, but let's search again," she urged. "My strong belief is that entrance is not to be obtained from this side, but from the glen down below."

"Yes, no doubt in the ages long ago the hill was much steeper than it now is, and there were no trees or undergrowth. On that side it was impregnable. The river, however, in receding, silted up much earth and boulders at the bend, and has made the ascent possible."

Together they went to a breach in the ponderous walls and

peered down into the ancient river-bed, now but a rippling burn.

"Very well," replied Murie, "let us descend and explore."

So they retraced their steps until, when about half-way to the house, they left the path and went down to the bottom of the beautiful glen until they were immediately beneath the old castle.

The spot was remote and seldom visited. Few ever came there, for it was approached by no path on that side of the burn, so that the keepers always passed along the opposite bank. They had no necessity to penetrate there. Besides, it was too near the house.

Through the bracken and undergrowth, passing by big trees that in the ages had sprung up from seedlings dropped by the birds or sown by the winds, they slowly ascended to the frowning walls far above - the walls that had withstood so many sieges and the ravages of so many centuries.

Half a dozen times the girl's skirt became entangled in the briars, and once she tore her cape upon some thorns. But, enjoying the adventure, she went on, Walter going first and clearing a way for her as best he could.

"Nobody has ever been up here before, I'm quite certain," Gabrielle cried, halting, breathless, for a moment. "Old Stewart, who says he knows every inch of the estate, has never climbed here, I'm sure."

"I don't expect he has," declared her lover.

At last they found themselves beneath the foundations of one of the flanking-towers of the castle walls, whereupon he sugg-ested that if they followed the wall right along and examined it closely they might discover some entrance.

"I somehow fear there will not be any door on the exposed side," he added.

The base of the walls was all along hidden by thick undergrowth, therefore the examination proved extremely difficult. Nevertheless, keenly interested in their exploration, the pair kept on struggling and climbing until the perspiration rolled off both their faces.

Suddenly, Walter uttered a cry of surprise. "Why, look here! This seems like a track. People *have* been up here after all!"

And his companion saw that from the burn below, up through the bushes, ran a narrow winding path, which showed little sign of frequent use.

Walter went on before her, quickly following the path until it turned at right-angles and ended before a low door of rough wood which filled a small breach in the wall - a breach made, in all probability, at the last siege in the early seventeenth century.

"This must lead somewhere!" cried Walter excitedly; and, lifting the roughly constructed wooden latch, he pushed the door open, disclosing a cavernous darkness.

A dank, earthy smell greeted their nostrils. It was certainly an uncanny place.

"By Jove!" cried Walter, "I wonder where this leads to?" And, taking out his vestas, he struck one, and, holding it before him, went forward, passing through the breach in the broken wall into a stone passage which led to the left for a few yards and gave entrance to exactly what Gabrielle had expected - a small, windowless stone chamber probably used in olden days as a dungeon.

Here they found, to their surprise, several old chairs, a rough table formed of two deal planks upon trestles, and a couple of half-burned candles in candlesticks which Gabrielle recognised as belonging to the house. These were lit, and by their aid the place was thoroughly examined.

Upon the floor was a heap of black tinder where some papers had been burnt weeks or perhaps months ago. There were cigar-ends lying about, showing that whoever had been there had taken his ease.

In a niche was a small tin box containing matches and fresh candles, while in a corner lay an old newspaper, limp and damp, bearing a date six months before. On the floor, too, were a number of pieces of paper - a letter torn to fragments.

They tried to piece it together, laying it upon the table carefully, but were unsuccessful in discovering its import, save that it was in Russian, from somebody in Odessa, and addressed to Sir Henry.

Carrying the candles in their hands, they went into the narrow passage to explore the subterranean regions of the old place. But neither way could they proceed far, for the passage had fallen in at both ends and was blocked by rubbish. The only exit or entrance was by that narrow breach in the walls so cunningly concealed by the undergrowth and closed by the rudely made door of planks nailed together. Above, in the stone roof of the chamber, there was a wide crack running obliquely, and through which any sound could be heard in the courtyard above.

They remained in the narrow, low-roofed little cell for a full half-hour, making careful examination of everything, and discussing the probability of the Whispers heard in the court-yard above emanating from that hidden chamber.

For what purpose was the place used, and by whom? In all probability it was the very chamber in which Cardinal Setoun had been treacherously done to death.

Though they made a most minute investigation they discovered nothing further. Up to a certain point their explorations had been crowned by success, yet the discovery rather tended to increase the mystery than diminish it.

That the Whispers were supernatural Gabrielle had all along refused to believe. The question was, to what use that secret chamber was put?

At last, more puzzled than ever, the pair, having extinguished the candles, emerged again into the light of day, closing and latching the little door after them.

Then, following the narrow secret path, they found that it wound through the bushes, and emerged by a circuitous way some distance along the glen, its entrance being carefully concealed by a big lichen-covered boulder which hid it from any one straying there by accident. So near was it to the house, and so well concealed, that no keeper had ever discovered it.

"Well," declared Gabrielle, "we've certainly made a most interesting discovery this morning. But I wonder if it really does solve the mystery of the Whispers?"

"Scarcely," Walter admitted. "We have yet to discover to whom the secret of the existence of that chamber is known. No doubt the Whispers are heard above through the crack in the roof. Therefore, at present, we had better keep our knowledge strictly to ourselves."

And to this the girl, of course, agreed.

They found Sir Henry seated alone in the sunshine in one of the big bay-windows of the drawing-room, a pathetic figure, with his blank, bespectacled countenance turned towards the light, and his fingers busily knitting to employ the time which, alas! hung so heavily upon his hands.

Truth to tell, with Flockart's influence upon him, he was not

William Le Queux

quite convinced of the sincerity of either Gabrielle or Walter Murie. Therefore, when they entered, and his daughter spoke to him; his greeting was not altogether cordial.

"Why, dear dad, how is it you're sitting here all alone? I would have gone for a walk with you had I known."

"I'm expecting Goslin," was the old man's snappy reply. "He left Paris yesterday, and should certainly have been here by this time. I can't make out why he hasn't sent me a 'wire' explaining the delay."

"He may have lost his connection in London," Murie suggested.

"Perhaps so," remarked the Baronet with a sigh, his fingers moving mechanically.

Murie could see that he was unnerved and unlike himself. He, of course, was unaware of the great interests depending upon the theft of those papers from his safe. But the old man was anxious to hear from Goslin what had occurred at the urgent meeting of the secret syndicate in Paris.

Gabrielle was chatting gaily with her father in an endeavour to cheer him up, when suddenly the door opened, and Flockart, still in his travelling ulster, entered, exclaiming, "Good-morning, Sir Henry."

"Why, my dear Flockart, this is really quite unexpected. I - I thought you were abroad," cried the Baronet, his face brightening as he stretched out his hand for his visitor to grasp.

"So I have been. I only got back to town yesterday morning, and left Euston last night."

"Well," said Sir Henry, "I'm very glad you are here again. I've missed you very much - very much indeed. I hope you'll make another long stay with us at Glencardine."

The man addressed raised his eyes to Gabrielle's.

She looked him straight in the face, defiant and unflinching. The day of her self-sacrifice to protect her helpless father's honour and welfare had come. She had suffered much in silence - suffered as no other girl would suffer; but she had tried to conceal the bitter truth. Her spirit had been broken. She was obsessed by one fear, one idea.

For a moment the girl held her breath. Walter saw the sudden change in her countenance, and wondered.

Then, with a calmness that was surprising, she turned to her father, and in a clear, distinct voice said, "Dad, now that Mr. Flockart has returned, I wish to tell you the truth concerning him - to warn you that he is not your friend, but your very worst enemy!"

"What is that you say?" cried the man accused, glaring at her. "Repeat those words, and I will tell the whole truth about yourself - here, before your lover!"

The blind man frowned. He hated scenes. "Come, come," he urged, "please do not quarrel. Gabrielle, I think, dear, your words are scarcely fair to our friend."

"Father," she said firmly, her face pale as death, "I repeat them. That man standing there is as much your enemy as he is mine!"

Flockart laughed satirically. "Then I will tell my story, and let your father judge whether you are a worthy daughter," he said.

CHAPTER XXXVI

IN WHICH GABRIELLE TELLS A STRANGE STORY

Gabrielle fell back in fear. Her handsome countenance was blanched to the lips. This man intended to speak - to tell the terrible truth - and before her lover too! She clenched her hands and summoned all her courage.

Flockart laughed at her - laughed in triumph. "I think, Gabrielle," he said, "that you should put an end to this deceit towards your poor blind father."

"What do you mean?" cried Walter in a fury, advancing towards Flockart. "What has this question - whatever it is - to do with you? Is it your place to stand between father and daughter?"

"Yes," answered the other in cool defiance, "it is. I am Sir Henry's friend."

"His friend! His enemy!"

"You are not my father's friend, Mr. Flockart," declared the girl, noticing the look of pain upon the afflicted old gentleman's face. "You have all along conspired against him for years, and you are actually conspiring with Lady Heyburn at this moment."

"You lie!" he cried. "You say this in order to shield yourself.

You know that your mother and I are aware of your crime, and have always shielded you."

"Crime!" gasped Walter Murie, utterly amazed. "What is this man saying, dearest?"

But the girl stood, blanched and rigid, her jaw set, unable to utter a word.

"Let me tell you briefly," Flockart went on. "Lady Heyburn and myself have been this girl's best friends; but now I must speak openly, in defence of the allegation she is making against me."

"Yes, speak!" urged Sir Henry. "Speak and tell me the truth."

"It is a painful truth, Sir Henry; would that I were not compelled to make such a charge. Your daughter deliberately killed a young girl named Edna Bryant. She poisoned her on account of jealousy."

"Impossible!" cried Sir Henry, starting up. "I - I can't believe it, Flockart. What are you saying? My daughter a murderess!"

"Yes, I repeat my words. And not only that, but Lady Heyburn and myself have kept her secret until - until now it is imperative that the truth should be told to you."

"Let me speak, dad - let me tell you -"

"No," cried the old man, "I will hear Flockart." And, turning to his wife's friend, he said hoarsely, "Go on. Tell me the truth."

"The tragedy took place at a picnic, just before Gabrielle left her school at Amiens. She placed poison in the girl's wine. Ah, it was a terrible revenge!"

"I am innocent!" cried the girl in despair.

"Remember the letter which you wrote to your mother concerning her. You told Lady Heyburn that you hated her. Do you deny writing that letter? Because, if you do, it is still in existence."

"I deny nothing which I have done," she answered. "You have told my father this in order to shield yourself. You have endeavoured, as the coward you are, to prejudice me in his eyes, just as you compelled me to lie to him when you opened his safe and copied certain of his papers!"

"You opened the safe!" he protested. "Why, I found you there myself!"

"Enough!" she exclaimed quite coolly. "I know the dread charge against me. I know too well the impossibility of clearing myself, especially in the face of that letter I wrote to Lady Heyburn; but it was you and she who entrapped me, and who held me in fear because of my inexperience."

"Tell us the truth, the whole truth, darling," urged Murie, standing at her side and taking her hand confidently in his.

"The truth!" she said, in a strange voice as though speaking to herself. "Yes, let me tell you! I know that it will sound extraordinary, yet I swear to you, by the love you bear for me, Walter, that the words I am about to utter are the actual truth."

"I believe you," declared her lover reassuringly.

"Which is more than anyone else will," interposed Flockart with a sneer, but perfectly confident. It was the hour of his triumph. She had defied him, and he therefore intended to ruin her once and for all.

The girl was standing pale and erect, one hand grasping the back of a chair, the other held in her lover's clasp, while her father had risen, his expressionless face turned towards them, his hand groping until it touched a small table upon which stood an old punch-bowl full of sweet-smelling pot-pourri.

"Listen, dad," she said, heedless of Flockart's remark. "Hear me before you condemn me. I know that the charge made against me by this man is a terrible one. God alone knows what I have suffered these last two years, how I have prayed for deliverance from the hands of this man and his friends. It happened a few months before I left Amiens. Lady Heyburn, you'll recollect, rented a pretty flat in the Rue Leonce-Reynaud in Paris. She obtained permission for me to leave school and visit her for a few weeks."

"I recollect perfectly," remarked her father in a low voice.

"Well, there came many times to visit us an American girl named Bryant, who was studying art, and who lived somewhere off the Boulevard Michel, as well as a Frenchman named Felix Krail and an Englishman called Hamilton."

"Hamilton!" echoed Murie. "Was his name Edgar Hamilton - my friend?"

"Yes, the same," was her quiet reply. Then she turned to Murie, and said, "We all went about a great deal together, for it was summer-time, and we made many pleasant excursions in the district. Edna Bryant was a merry, cheerful girl, and I soon grew to be very friendly with her, until one day Lady Heyburn, when alone with me, repeated in strict confidence that the girl was secretly devoted to you, Walter."

"To me!" he cried. "True, I knew a Miss Bryant long ago, but for the past three years or so have entirely lost sight of her."

"Lady Heyburn told me that you were very fond of the girl, and this, I confess, aroused my intense jealousy. I believed that the girl I had trusted so implicitly was unprincipled and fickle, and that she was trying to secure the man whom I had loved ever since a child. I had to return to school, and from there I wrote to Lady Heyburn, who had gone to Dieppe, a letter saying hard things of the girl, and declaring that I would take secret revenge - that I would kill her rather than allow Walter to be taken from me. A month afterwards I again returned to Paris. That man standing there" - she indicated Flockart - "was living at the Hotel Continental, and was a frequent visitor. He told me that it was well known in London that Walter admired Miss Bryant, a declaration that I admit drove me half-mad with jealousy."

"It was a lie!" declared Walter. "I never made love to the girl. I admired her, that's all."

"Well," laughed Flockart, "go on. Tell us your version of the affair."

"I am telling you the truth," she cried, boldly facing him. One day Lady Heyburn, having arranged a cycling picnic, invited Mr. Hamilton, Mr. Kratil, Mr. Flockart, Miss Bryant, and myself, and we had a beautiful run to Chantilly, a distance of about forty kilometres, where we first made a tour of the old chateau, and afterwards entered the cool shady Foret de Pontarme. While the others went away to explore the paths in the splendid wood I was left to spread the luncheon upon the ground, setting before each place a half-bottle of red wine which I found in the baskets. Then, when all was ready, I called to them, but there was no response. They were all out of hearing. I left the spot, and searched for a full twenty minutes or so before I discovered them. First I found Mr. Krail and Mr. Flockart strolling together smoking, while the others were on ahead. They had lost their way among the trees. I led them back to the spot where luncheon was prepared; and, all of us being hungry, we quickly sat down, chatting and laughing merrily. Of a sudden Miss Bryant stared straight before her, dropped her glass, and threw up her arms. 'Heavens! Why - ah, my throat!' she shrieked. 'I - I'm poisoned!'

"In an instant all was confusion. The poor girl could not breathe. She tore at her throat, while her face became convulsed. We obtained water for her, but it was useless, for within five minutes she was stretched rigid upon the grass, unconscious, and a few moments later she was still - quite dead! Ah, shall I ever forget the scene! The effect produced upon us was appalling. All was so sudden, so tragic, so horrible!

"Lady Heyburn was the first to speak. 'Gabrielle,' she said, 'what have you done? You have carried out the secret revenge which in your letter you threatened!' I saw myself trapped. Those people had some motive in killing the girl and placing this crime upon myself! I could not speak, for I was too utterly dumfounded."

"The fiends!" ejaculated Walter fiercely.

"Then followed a hurried consultation, in which Krail showed himself most solicitous on my behalf," the pale-faced girl went on. "Aided by Flockart, I think, he scraped away a hole in a pit full of dead leaves, and there the body must have been concealed just as it was. To me they all took a solemn vow to keep what they declared to be my secret. The bottle containing the wine from which the poor American girl had drunk was broken and hidden, the plates and food swiftly packed up, and we at once fled from the scene of the tragedy. With Krail wheeling the girl's empty cycle, we reached the high road, where we all mounted and rode back in silence to Paris. Ah, shall I ever rid myself of the memory of that fatal afternoon?" she cried as she paused for breath.

"Fearing that he might be noticed taking along the empty cycle, Krail threw it into the river near Valmondois," she went on. "Arrived back at the Rue Leonce-Reynaud, I protested that nothing had been introduced into the wine. But they declared that, owing to my youth and the terrible scandal it would cause if I were arrested, they would never allow the matter to pass their lips, Mr. Hamilton, indeed, making the extraordinary declaration that such a crime had extenuating circumstances when love was at stake. I then saw that I had fallen the victim of some clever conspiracy; but so utterly overcome was I by the awful scene that I could make but faint protest.

"Ah! think of my horrible position - accused of a crime of which I was entirely innocent! The days slipped on, and I was sent back to Amiens, and in due course came home here to dear old Glencardine. From that day I have lived in constant fear, until on the night of the ball at Connachan - you remember the evening, dad? - on that night Mr. Flockart returned in secret, beckoned me out upon the lawn, and showed me something which held me petrified in fear. It was a cutting from an Edinburgh paper that evening reporting that two of the forest-guards at Pontarme had discovered the body of the missing Miss Bryant, and that the French police were making active inquiries."

"He threatened you?" asked Walter.

"He told me to remain quiet, and that he and Lady Heyburn would do their best to shield me. For that reason, dad," she went on, turning to the blind man, "for that reason I feared to denounce him when I discovered him with your safe open, for that reason I was compelled to take all the blame and all your anger upon myself."

The old man's brow knit. "Where is my wife?" he asked. "I must speak to her before we go further. This is a very serious matter."

"Lady Heyburn is still at Park Street," Flockart replied.

"I will hear no more," declared the blind Baronet, holding up his hand, "not another word until my wife is present."

CHAPTER XXXVII

INCREASES THE INTEREST

"But, dad," cried Gabrielle, "I am telling you the truth! Cannot you believe me, your daughter, before this man who is your enemy?"

"Because of my affliction I am, it seems, deceived by every one," was his hard response.

To where they stood had come the sound of wheels upon the gravelled drive outside, and a moment later Hill entered, announcing, "A gentleman to see you very urgently, Sir Henry. He is from Baron de Hetzendorf."

"From the Baron!" gasped the blind man. "I'll see him later."

"Why, it may be Hamilton!" cried Murie; who, looking through the door, saw his old friend in the corridor, and quickly called him in.

As he faced Flockart he drew himself up. The attitude of them all made it apparent to him that something unusual was in progress.

"You've arrived at a very opportune moment, Hamilton," Murie said. "You have met Miss Heyburn before, and also Flockart, I believe, at Lady Heyburn's, in Paris."

"Yes, but -"

"Sir Henry," Walter said in a quiet tone, "this gentleman sent by the Baron is his secretary, the same Mr. Edgar Hamilton of whom Gabrielle has just been speaking."

"Ah, then, perhaps he can furnish us with further facts regarding this most extraordinary statement of my daughter's," the blind man exclaimed.

"Gabrielle has just told her father the truth regarding a certain tragic occurrence in the Forest of Pontarme. Explain to us all you know, Edgar."

"What I know," said Hamilton, "is very quickly told. Has Miss Heyburn mentioned the man Krail?"

"Yes, I have told them about him," the girl answered.

"You have, however, perhaps omitted to mention one or two small facts in connection with the affair," he said. "Do you not remember how, on that eventful afternoon in the forest, when searching for us, you first encountered Krail walking with this man Flockart at some distance from the others?"

"Yes, I recollect."

"And do you remember that when we returned to sit down to luncheon Flockart insisted that I should take the seat which was afterwards occupied by the unfortunate Miss Bryant? Do you recollect how I spread a rug for her at that spot and preferred myself to stand? The reason of their invitation to me to sit there I did not discover until afterwards. That wine had been prepared for *me*, not for her."

"For you!" the girl gasped, amazed.

"Yes. The plot was undoubtedly this -"

"There was no plot," protested Flockart, interrupting. "This girl killed Edna Bryant through intense jealousy."

"I repeat that there was a foul and ingenious plot to kill me, and to entrap Miss Heyburn," Hamilton said. "It was, of course, clear that Miss Heyburn was jealous of the girl, for she had written to her mother making threats against Miss Bryant's life. Therefore, the plot was that I should drink the fatal wine, and that Miss Gabrielle should be declared to be the murderess, she having intended the wine to be partaken of by the girl she hated with such deadly hatred. The marked cordiality of Krail and Flockart that I should take that seat aroused within me some misgivings, although I had never dreamed of this dastardly and cowardly plot against me - not until I saw the result of their foul handiwork."

"It's a lie! You are trying to implicate Krail and myself! The girl is the only guilty person. She placed the wine there!"

"She did not!" declared Hamilton boldly. "She was not there when the bottle was changed by Krail, but I was!"

"If what you say is true, then you deliberately stood by and allowed the girl to drink."

"I watched Krail go to the spot where luncheon was laid out, but could not see what he did. If I had done so I should have saved the girl's life. You were a few yards off, awaiting him; therefore you knew his intentions, and you are as guilty of that girl's tragic death as he."

"What!" cried Flockart, his eyes glaring angrily, "do you declare, then, that I am a murderer?"

"You yourself are the best judge of your own guilt," answered Hamilton meaningly.

"I deny that Krail or myself had any hand in the affair."

"You will have an opportunity of making that denial in a criminal court ere long," remarked the Baron's secretary with a grim smile.

"What," gasped Lady Heyburn's friend, his cheeks paling in an instant, "have you been so indiscreet as to inform the police?"

"I have - a week ago. I made a statement to M. Hamard of the Surete in Paris, and they have already made a discovery which you will find of interest and somewhat difficult to disprove."

"And pray what is that?"

Hamilton smiled again, saying, "No, my dear sir, the police will tell you themselves all in due course. Remember, you and your precious friend plotted to kill me."

"But why, Mr. Hamilton?" inquired the blind man. "What was their motive?"

"A very strong one," was the reply. "I had recognised in Krail a man who had defrauded the Baron de Hetzendorf of fifty thousand kroners, and for whom the police were in active search, both for that and for several other serious charges of a similar character. Krail knew this, and he and his friend - this gentleman here - had very ingeniously resolved to get rid of me by making it appear that Miss Gabrielle had poisoned me by accident."

"A lie!" declared Flockart fiercely, though his efforts to remain imperturbed were now palpable.

"You will be given due opportunity of disproving my allegations," Hamilton said. "You, coward that you are, placed the guilt upon an innocent, inexperienced girl. Why? Because, with Lady Heyburn's connivance, you with your cunning accomplice Krail were endeavouring to discover Sir Henry's business secrets in order, first, to operate upon the valuable financial knowledge you would thus gain, and so make a big *coup*; and, secondly, when you had done this, it was your intention to expose the methods of Sir Henry and his friends. Ah! don't imagine that you and Krail have not been very well watched of late," laughed Hamilton.

"Do you allege, then, that Lady Heyburn is privy to all this?" asked the blind man in distress.

"It is not for me to judge, sir," was Hamilton's reply.

"I know! I know how I have been befooled!" cried the poor helpless man, "befooled because I am blind!"

"Not by me, Sir Henry," protested Flockart.

"By you and by every one else," he cried angrily. "But I know the truth at last - the truth how my poor little daughter has been used as an instrument by you in your nefarious operations."

"But -"

"Hear me, I say!" went on the old man. "I ask my daughter to forgive me for misjudging her. I now know the truth. You obtained by some means a false key to my safe, and you copied certain documents which I had placed there in order to entrap any who might seek to learn my secrets. You fell into that trap, and though I confess I thought that Gabrielle was the culprit, on Murie's behalf, I only lately found out that you and your accomplice Krail were in Greece endeavouring to profit by knowledge obtained from here, my private house."

"Krail has been living in Auchterarder of late, it appears," Hamilton remarked, "and it is evidently he who, gaining access to the house one night recently, used his friend's false key, and obtained those confidential Russian documents from your safe."

"No doubt," declared Sir Henry. Then, again addressing

Flockart, he asked, "Where are those documents which you and your scoundrelly accomplice have stolen, and for the return of which you are trying to make me pay?"

"I don't know anything about them," answered Flockart sullenly, his face livid.

"He'll know more about them when he is taken off by the two detectives from Edinburgh who hold the extradition warrant," Hamilton remarked with a grim smile.

The fellow started at those words. His demeanour was that of a guilty man. "What do you mean?" he gasped, white as death. "You - you intend to give me into custody? If you do, I warn you that Lady Heyburn will suffer also."

"She, like Miss Gabrielle, has only been your tool," Hamilton declared. "It was she who, under compulsion, has furnished you with means for years, and whose association with you has caused something little short of a scandal. Times without number she has tried to get rid of you and your evil influence in this household, but you have always defied her. Now," he said firmly, looking the other straight in the face, "you have upon you those stolen documents which you have, by using an assumed name and a false address, offered to sell back to their owner, Sir Henry. You have threatened that if they are not purchased at the exorbitant price you demand you will sell them to the Russian Ministry of Finance. That is the way you treat your friend and benefactor, the man who is blind and helpless! Come, give them back to Sir Henry, and at once."

"You must ask Krail," stammered the man, now so cornered that all further excuse or denial had become impossible.

"That's unnecessary. I happen to know that those papers are in your pocket at this moment, a fact which shows how watchful an eye we've been keeping upon you of late. You have brought them here so that your friend Krail may come to terms with Sir Henry for their repossession. He arrived from London with you, and is at the 'Strathavon Arms' in the village, where he stayed before, and is well known."

"Flockart," demanded the blind man very seriously, "you have papers in your possession which are mine. Return them to me."

A dead silence fell. All eyes save those of Sir Henry were turned upon the man who until that moment had stood so defiant and so full of sarcasm. But in an instant, at mention of Krail's presence in Auchterarder, his demeanour had suddenly changed. He was full of alarm.

"Give them to me and leave my house," Sir Henry said, holding up his thin white hand.

"I - I will - on one condition: if I may be allowed to go."

"We shall not prevent you leaving," was the Baronet's calm reply.

The man fumbled nervously in the inner pocket of his coat, and at last brought out a sealed and rather bulgy foolscap envelope.

"Open it, Gabrielle, and see what is within," her father said.

She obeyed, and in a few moments explained the various documents it contained.

"Then let the man go," her father said.

"But, Sir Henry," cried Hamilton, "I object to this! Krail is down in the village forming a plot to make you pay for the return of those papers. He arrived from London by the same train as this man. If we allow him to leave he will inform his accomplice, and both will escape."

Murie had his back to the door, the long window on the

opposite side of the room being closed.

"It was a promise of Sir Henry's," declared the unhappy adventurer.

"Which will be observed when Krail has been brought face to face with Sir Henry," answered Murie, at the same time calling Hill and one of the gardeners who chanced to be working on the lawn outside.

Then, with a firmness which showed that they were determined, Hamilton and Murie conducted Flockart to a small upstairs room, where Hill and the gardener, with the assistance of Stewart, who happened to have come into the kitchen, mounted guard over him.

His position, once the honoured guest at Glencardine, was the most ignominious conceivable. But Sir Henry sat in gratification that at least he had got back those documents and saved the reputation of his friend Volkonski, as well as that of his co-partners.

CHAPTER XXXVIII

"THAT MAN'S VOICE!"

Stokes the chauffeur had driven Murie and Hamilton in the car down to the village, where the last-named, after a conversation with the police inspector, went to the "Strathavon Arms," together with two constables who happened to be off duty, in plain clothes.

They found Krail sitting in the bar, calmly smoking, awaiting a message from his accomplice.

Upon Hamilton's recognition he was, after a brief argument, arrested on the charge of theft from Glencardine, placed in the car between the two stalwart Scotch policemen, and conveyed in triumph to the castle, much, of course, against his will. He demanded to be taken straight to the police station; but as Sir Henry had ordered him to be brought to Glencardine, and as Sir Henry was a magistrate, the inspector was bound to obey his orders.

The man's cruel, colourless eyes seemed to contract closer as he sat in the car with his enemy Hamilton facing him. He had never dreamed that they would ever meet again; but, now they had, he saw that the game was up. There was no hope of escape. He was being taken to meet Sir Henry Heyburn, the very last man in all the world he wished to face. His sallow countenance was drawn, his lips were thin and bloodless, and upon his cheeks were two red spots which showed that he was now in a deadly terror.

Gabrielle, who had been weeping at the knees of her father, heard the whirr of the car coming up the drive; and, springing to the window, witnessed the arrival of the party.

A moment later, Krail, between the two constables, and with the local inspector standing respectfully at the rear, stood in the big, long library into which the blind man was led by his daughter.

When all had assembled, Sir Henry, in a clear, distinct voice, said, "I have had you arrested and brought here in order to charge you with stealing certain documents from my safe yonder, which you opened by means of a duplicate key. Your accomplice Flockart has given evidence against you; therefore, to deny it is quite needless."

"Whatever he has said to you is lies," the foreigner replied, his accent being the more pronounced in his excitement. "I know nothing about it."

"If you deny that," exclaimed Hamilton quickly, "you will perhaps also deny that it was you who secretly poisoned Miss Bryant in the Pontarme Forest, even though I myself saw you at the spot; and, further, that a witness has been found who actually saw you substitute the wine-bottles. You intended to kill me!"

"What ridiculous nonsense you are talking!" cried the accused, who was dressed with his habitual shabby gentility. "The girl yonder, mademoiselle, killed Miss Bryant."

"Then why did you make that deliberate attempt upon my life at Fotheringhay?" demanded the girl boldly. "Had it not been for Mr. Hamilton, who must have seen us together and guessed that you intended foul play, I should certainly have been drowned."

"He believed that you knew his secret, and he intended, both on his own behalf and on Flockart's also, to close your lips," Murie said. "With you out of the way, their attitude towards your father would have been easier; but with you still a living witness there was always danger to them. He thought your death would be believed to be suicide, for he knew your despondent state of mind."

Sir Henry stood near the window, his face sphinx-like, as though turned to stone.

"She fell in," was his lame excuse.

"No, you threw me in!" declared the girl. "But I have feared you until now, and I therefore dared not to give information against you. Ah, God alone knows how I have suffered!"

"You dare now, eh?" he snarled, turning quickly upon her.

"It really does not matter what you deny or what you admit," Hamilton remarked. "The French authorities have applied for your extradition to France, and this evening you will be on your way to the extradition court at Bow Street, charged with a graver offence than the burglary at this house. The Surete of Paris make several interesting allegations against you - or against Felix Gerlach, which is your real name."

"Gerlach!" cried the blind man in a loud voice, groping forward. "Ah," he shrieked, "then I was not mistaken when - when I thought I recognised the voice! That man's voice! *Yes, it is his - his!*"

In an instant Krail had sprung forward towards the blind and defenceless man, but his captors were fortunately too quick and prevented him. Then, at the inspector's orders, a pair of steel bracelets were quickly placed upon his wrists.

"Gerlach! Felix Gerlach!" repeated the blind Baronet as though to himself, as he heard the snap of the lock upon the prisoner's wrists.

The fellow burst out into a peal of harsh, discordant laughter. He was endeavouring to retain a defiant attitude even then.

"You apparently know this man, dad?" Gabrielle exclaimed in surprise.

"Know him!" echoed her father hoarsely. "Know Felix Gerlach! Yes, I have bitter cause to remember the man who stands there before you accused of the crime of murder."

Then he paused, and drew a long breath.

"I unmasked him once, as a thief and a swindler, and he swore to be avenged," said the Baronet in a bitter voice. "It was long ago. He came to me in London and offered me a concession which he said he had obtained from the Ottoman Government for the construction of a railroad from Smyrna to the Bosphorus. The documents appeared to be all right and in order, and after some negotiations he sold the concession to me and received ten thousand pounds in cash of the purchase-money in advance. A week afterwards I discovered that, though the concession had been granted by the Minister of Public Works at the Sublime Porte, it had been sold to the Eckmann Group in Vienna, and that the papers I held were merely copies with forged signatures and stamps. I applied to the police, this man was arrested in Hamburg, and brought back to London, where he was tried, and, a previous conviction having been proved against him, sent to penal servitude for seven years. In the dock at the Old Bailey he swore to be avenged upon me and upon my family."

"And he seems to have kept his word," Walter remarked.

"When he came out of prison he found me in the zenith of my political career," Sir Henry went on. "On that well-remembered night of my speech at the Albert Hall I can only surmise that he went there, heard me, and probably became fiercely resentful that he had found a man cleverer than himself. The fact remains that he must have gone in a cab in front of my carriage to Park Street, alighted before me, and secreted himself within the portico. It was midnight, and the street was deserted. My carriage stopped, I got out, and it then drove on to the mews. I was in the act of opening the door with my latch-key when, by an unknown hand, there was flung full into my eyes some corrosive fluid which burned terribly, and caused me excruciating pain. I heard a man's exultant voice cry, 'There! I promised you that, and you have it!' The voice I recognised as that of the blackguard standing before you. Since that moment," he added in a blank, hoarse voice, "I have been totally blind!"

"You got me seven years!" cried the foreigner with a harsh laugh, "so think yourself very lucky that I didn't kill you."

"You placed upon me an affliction, a perpetual darkness, that to a man like myself is almost akin to death," replied his accuser very gravely. "Secure from recognition, you wormed yourself into the confidence of my wife, for you were bent upon ruining her also; and you took as partner in your schemes that needy adventurer Flockart. I now see it all quite plainly. Hamilton had recognised you as Gerlach, and you therefore formed a plot to get rid of him and throw the crime upon my poor unfortunate daughter, even though she was scarcely more than a child. In all probability, Lady Heyburn, in telling the girl the story regarding Murie and Miss Bryant, believed it, and if so she would also suspect my daughter to be the actual criminal."

"This is all utterly astounding, dad!" cried Gabrielle. "If you knew who it was who deliberately blinded you, why didn't you prosecute him?"

"Because there was no witness of his dastardly act, my child. And I myself never saw him. Therefore I was compelled to remain in silence, and allow the world to believe my affliction due to natural causes," was his blank response.

The sallow-faced foreigner laughed again, laughed in the face of the man whose eyesight he had so deliberately taken. He could not speak. What had he to say?

"Well," remarked Hamilton, "we have at least the satisfaction of knowing that both this man and his accomplice will stand their trial for their heartless crime in France, and that they will meet their just punishment according to the laws of God and of man."

"And I," added Walter, in a voice broken by emotion, as he again took Gabrielle's hand tenderly, "have the supreme satisfaction of knowing that my darling is cleared of a foul, dastardly, and terrible charge."

CHAPTER XXXIX

CONTAINS THE CONCLUSION

After long consultation - Krail having been removed in custody back to the village - it was agreed that the only charges that could be substantiated against Flockart were those of complicity in the ingenious attempt upon Hamilton's life by which poor Miss Bryant had been sacrificed, and also in the theft of Sir Henry's papers.

But was it worth while?

At the Baronet's suggestion, he was allowed freedom to leave the upstairs room where he had been detained by the three stalwart servants; and, without waiting to speak to any one, he had made his way down the drive. He had, as was afterwards found, left Auchterarder Station for London an hour later.

The painful impression produced upon everybody by Sir Henry's statement of what had actually occurred on the night of the great meeting at the Albert Hall having somewhat subsided, Murie mentioned to the blind man the legend of the Whispers, and also the curious discovery which Gabrielle and he had made earlier in the morning.

"Ah," laughed the old gentleman a trifle uneasily, "and so you've discovered the truth at last, eh?"

"The truth - no!" Murie said. "That is just what we are so very

William Le Queux

anxious to hear from you, Sir Henry."

"Well," he said, "you may rest your minds perfectly content that there's nothing supernatural about them. It was to my own advantage to cause weird reports and uncanny legends to be spread in order to preserve my secret, the secret of the Whispers."

"But what is the secret, Sir Henry?" asked Hamilton eagerly. "We, curiously enough, have similar Whispers at Hetzendorf. I've heard them myself at the old chateau."

"And of course you have believed in the story which my good friend the Baron has caused to be spread, like myself: the legend that those who hear them die quickly and suddenly," said the old man, with a smile upon his grey face. "Like myself, he wished to keep away all inquisitive persons from the spot."

"But why?" asked Murie.

"Well, truth to tell, the reason is very simple," he answered. "As we are speaking here in the strictest privacy, I will tell you something which I beg that neither of you will repeat. If you do it might result in my ruin."

Murie, Hamilton, and Gabrielle all gave their promise.

"Then it is this," he said. "I am head of a group of the leading financial houses in Europe, who, remaining secret, are carrying on business in the guise of an unimportant house in Paris. The members of the syndicate are all of them men of enormous financial strength, including Baron de Hetzendorf, to whom our friend Hamilton here acts as confidential secretary. The strictest secrecy is necessary for the success of our great undertakings, which I may add are perfectly honest and legitimate. Yet never, unless absolutely imperative, do we entrust documents or letters to the post. Like the house of Rothschild, we have our confidential messengers, and hold frequent meetings, no 'deal' being undertaken without we are all of us in full accord. Monsieur Goslin acts as confidential messenger, and brings me the views of my partners in Paris, Petersburg, and Vienna. To this careful concealment of our plans, or of the fact that we are ever in touch with one another, is due the huge successes we have made from time to time - successes which have staggered the Bourses of the Continent and caused amazement in Wall Street. But being unfortunately afflicted as I am, I naturally cannot travel to meet the others, and, besides, we are compelled always to take fresh and most elaborate precautions in order to conceal the fact that we are in connection with each other. If that one fact ever leaked out it would at once stultify our endeavours and weaken our position. Hence, at intervals, two or even three of my partners travel here, and I meet them at night in the little chamber which you, Walter, discovered to-day, and which until the present has never been found, owing to the weird fables I have invented regarding the Whispers. To Hetzendorf, too, once or twice a year, perhaps, the members pay a secret visit in order to consult the Baron, who, as you perhaps may know, unfortunately enjoys very precarious health."

"Then meetings of Frohnmeyer, Volkonski, and the rest were held here in secret sometimes?" echoed Hamilton in surprise.

"On certain occasions, when it is absolutely necessary that I should meet them," answered Sir Henry. "They stay at the Station Hotel in Perth, coming over to Auchterarder by the last train at night and leaving by the first train in the morning from Crieff Junction. They never approach the house, for fear that servants or one or other of the guests may recognise them, but go separately along the glen and up the path to the ruins. When we thus meet, our voices can be heard through the crack in the roof of the chamber in the courtyard above. On such occasions I take good care that Stewart and his men are sent on a false alarm of poachers to another part of the estate, while I can find my way there myself with my stick," he laughed. "The Baron, I believe, acts on the same principle at his chateau in Hungary."

"Well," declared Hamilton, "so well has the Baron kept the secret that I have never had any suspicion until this moment. By Jove! the invention of the Whispers was certainly a clever mode of preserving the secret, for nobody cares deliberately to court disaster and death, especially among a superstitious populace like the villagers here and the Hungarian peasantry."

Both Gabrielle and her lover expressed their astonishment, the latter remarking how cleverly the weird legend of the Whispers invented by Sir Henry had been made to fit historical fact.

*   *   *   *   *

When the eight o'clock train from Stirling stopped at Auchterarder Station that evening, a tall, well-dressed man alighted, and inquired his way to the police-station. The porter knew by his accent that he was a Londoner, but did not dream that he was "a gentleman from Scotland Yard."

Half an hour later, after a chat with the rural inspector, the pair went along to the cell behind the small village police-station in order that the stranger should read over to the prisoner the warrant he had brought with him from London - the application of the French police for the arrest and extradition of Felix Gerlach, *alias* Krail, *alias* Benoist, for the wilful murder of Edna Mary Bryant in the Forest of Pontarme, near Chantilly.

The inspector had related to the London detective the dramatic scene up at Glencardine that day, and the officer of the Criminal Investigation Department walked along to the cell much interested to see what manner of man was this, who was even more bold and ingenious in his criminal methods than many with whom his profession brought him daily into contact. He had hoped that he himself would have the credit of making the arrest, but found that the man wanted had already been apprehended on the charge of burglary at Glencardine.

The inspector unlocked the door and threw it open, but next instant the startling truth became plain.

Felix Krail lay dead upon the flagstones. He had taken his life by poison - probably the same poison he had placed in the wine at the fatal picnic - rather than face his accuser and bear his just punishment.

*   *   *   *   *

Many months have now passed. A good deal has occurred since that never-to-be-forgotten day, but it is all quickly related.

James Flockart, unmasked as he has been, never dared to return. The last heard of him was six months ago, in Honduras, where for the first time in his life he had been compelled to work for his living, and had, three weeks after landing, succumbed to fever.

At Sir Henry's urgent request, his wife came back to Glencardine a week after the tragic end of Gerlach, and was compelled to make full confession how, under the man's sinister influence, both she and Flockart had been forced to act. To her husband she proved beyond all doubt that she had been in complete ignorance of the truth concerning the affair in the Pontarme Forest until long afterwards. She had at first believed Gabrielle guilty of the deed, but when she learned the truth and saw how deeply she had been implicated it was impossible for her then to withdraw.

With a whole-hearted generosity seldom found in men, Sir Henry, after long reflection and a desperate struggle with himself, forgave her, and now has the satisfaction of knowing that she prefers quiet, healthful Glencardine to the social gaieties of Park Street, Paris, or San Remo, while she and Gabrielle have lately become devoted to each other.

The secret syndicate, with Sir Henry Heyburn at its head, still

William Le Queux

operates, for no word of its existence has leaked out to either financial circles or to the public, while the Whispers of Glencardine are still believed in and dreaded by the whole countryside across the Ochils.

Edgar Hamilton, though compelled to return to the Baron, whose right hand he is, often travels to Glencardine with confidential messages, and documents for signature, and is, of course, an ever-welcome guest.

The unpretentious house of Lenard et Morellet of Paris now and then effects deals so enormous that financial circles are staggered, and the world stands amazed. The true facts of who is actually behind that apparently unimportant firm are, however, still rigorously and ingeniously concealed.

Who would ever dream that that quiet, grey-faced man with the sightless eyes, living far away up in Scotland, passing his hours of darkness with his old bronze seals or his knitting, was the brain which directed their marvellously successful operations!

The Laird of Connachan died quite suddenly about seven months ago, and Walter Murie succeeded to the noble estate. Gabrielle - sweet, almost child-like in her simple tastes and delightful charm, and more devoted to Walter than ever - is now little Lady Murie, having been married in Edinburgh a month ago.

At the moment that I pen these final lines the pair are spending a blissful honeymoon at the great old chateau of Hetzendorf, high up above the broad-flowing Danube, the Baron having kindly vacated the place and put it at their disposal for the summer. Happy in each other's love and mutual trust, they spend the long blissful days in company, wandering often hand in hand, for when Walter looks into those wonderful eyes of hers he sees mirrored there a perfect and abiding affection such as is indeed given few men to possess.

Together they have in secret explored the ruins of the ancient stronghold, and, by directions given them by the Baron, have found there a stone chamber by no means dissimilar to that at Glencardine.

Meanwhile, Sir Henry Heyburn, impatient for his beloved daughter to be again near him and to assist him, passes his weary hours with his favourite hobby; his wife, full of sympathy, bearing him company. From her, however, he still withholds one secret, and one only - the Secret of the House of Whispers.

William Le Queux